PLEASE CHECK FOR CD

SCHOLASTIC

100
SCIENCE
LESSONS

NEW EDITION

TERMS AND CONDITIONS

IMPORTANT - PERMITTED USE AND WARNINGS - READ CAREFULLY BEFORE USING

SCOTTISH PRIMARY 5

YEAR
4

Minimum specification:
- PC with a CD-ROM drive and 512 Mb RAM (recommended)
- Windows 98SE or above/Mac OSX.1 or above
- Recommended minimum processor speed: 1 GHz

For all technical support queries, please phone
Scholastic Customer Services on 0845 603 9091.

WS 2252792 3

0
507
ONE

J 2008

Kendra McMahon

Author
Kendra McMahon

Series Editor
Peter Riley

Editors
Nicola Morgan
Tracy Kewley
Kate Pedlar

Project Editor
Fabia Lewis

Illustrators
Debbie Clark
Robin Lawrie
Theresa Tibbetts/Beehive Illustration

Series Designers
Catherine Perera and Joy Monkhouse

Designer
Catherine Perera

CD-ROM developed in association with
Vivid Interactive

ACKNOWLEDGEMENTS

With thanks to Louise Petheram for the use of all lessons in Chapters 6 and Chapter 8 of this book taken from *100 Science Lessons – Year 5* by David Glover, Ian Mitchell, Louise Petheram and Peter Riley, © 2001, David Glover, Ian Mitchell, Louise Petheram and Peter Riley (2001, Scholastic Ltd), revised by Louise Petheram for this edition.

All Flash activities developed by Vivid Interactive

Material from the National Curriculum © Crown copyright. Reproduced under the terms of the Click Use Licence.

Extracts from the QCA Scheme of Work © Qualifications and Curriculum Authority.

Extracts from the Primary School Curriculum for Ireland, www.ncca.ie, National Council for Curriculum and Assessment.

Post-It is a registered trademark of 3M.

LEGO® is a brand name and the property of the LEGO Group © 2007 The LEGO Group.

Every effort has been made to trace copyright holders for the works reproduced in this book, and the publishers apologise for any inadvertent omissions.

Published by Scholastic Ltd
Villiers House
Clarendon Avenue
Leamington Spa
Warwickshire CV32 5PR

www.scholastic.co.uk

Designed using Adobe InDesign.

Printed by Bell and Bain Ltd, Glasgow

2 3 4 5 6 7 8 9   7 8 9 0 1 2 3 4 5 6

Revised text © 2007 Kendra McMahon
© 2007 Scholastic Ltd

British Library Cataloguing-in-Publication Data
A catalogue record for this book is available from the British Library.

ISBN 978-0439-94506-6

507
OWE

This new edition of *100 Science Lessons* follows the QCA Science Scheme of Work and also meets many of the demands of the curricula for England, Wales, Scotland, Northern Ireland and Eire. The book is divided into eight units – one unit to match each unit of the QCA scheme for Year 4, and two enrichment units.

The planning grid at the start of each unit shows the objectives and outcomes of each lesson, and gives a quick overview of the lesson content (starter, main activity, group activities and plenary). The QCA objectives for Year 4 provide the basis for the lesson objectives used throughout the book.

After the planning grid is a short section on Scientific Enquiry. It is based on a QCA activity and provides a context for children to develop certain enquiry skills and for you to assess them. The section ends by showing where the activity can be embedded within one of the lessons.

Each unit is divided into a number of key lessons, which closely support the QCA scheme and all units end with an assessment lesson which is based on those key lessons. In addition to the key lessons, a unit may also contain one or more enrichment lessons to provide greater depth or a broader perspective. They may follow on from a key lesson or form a whole section, near the end of the unit, before the assessment lesson. The lesson objectives are based on the statements of the national curricula for England, Wales, Scotland, Northern Ireland and Eire, which are provided, in grid format, on the CD-ROM.

Lesson plans

There are detailed and short lesson plans for the key and enrichment lessons. About 60 per cent of the lesson plans in this book are detailed lesson plans. The short lesson plans are closely related to them and cover similar topics and concepts. They contain the essential features of the detailed lesson plans, allowing you to plan for progression and assessment. The detailed lesson plans have the following structure:

OBJECTIVES

The objectives are stated in a way that helps to focus on each lesson plan. At least one objective is related to content knowledge and there may be one or more relating to Scientific Enquiry. When you have read through the lesson you may wish to add your own objectives. You can find out how these objectives relate to those of the various national curricula by looking at the relevant grids on the CD-ROM. You can also edit the planning grids to fit with your own objectives (for more information see 'How to use the CD-ROM' on page 6).

RESOURCES AND PREPARATION

The Resources section provides a list of everything you will need to deliver the lesson, including any photocopiables presented in this book. The Preparation section describes anything that needs to be done in advance of the lesson, such as collecting environmental data.

As part of the preparation of all practical work, you should consult your school's policies on practical work and select activities for which you are confident to take responsibility. The ASE publication *Be Safe!* gives very useful guidance on health and safety issues in primary science.

BACKGROUND

This section may briefly refer to the science concepts which underpin the teaching of individual lessons. It may also highlight specific concepts which children tend to find difficult and gives some ideas on how to address these during the lesson. Suggestions may be given for classroom displays as well as useful tips for obtaining resources. Safety points and sensitive issues may also be addressed in this sections, where appropriate.

VOCABULARY

There is a vocabulary list of science words associated with the lesson which children should use in discussing and presenting their work. Time should be spent defining each word at an appropriate point in the lesson.

STARTER

This introductory section contains ideas to build up interest at the beginning of the lesson and set the scene.

MAIN TEACHING ACTIVITY

This section presents a direct, whole-class (or occasionally group) teaching session that will help you deliver the content knowledge outlined in the lesson objectives before group activities begin. It may include guidance on discussion, or on performing one or more demonstrations or class investigations to help the children understand the work ahead.

The relative proportions of the lesson given to the starter, main teaching activity and group activities vary. If you are reminding the children of their previous work and getting them onto their own investigations, the group work may dominate the lesson time; if you are introducing a new topic or concept, you might wish to spend all or most of the lesson engaged in whole-class teaching.

GROUP ACTIVITIES

The group activities are very flexible. Some may be best suited to individual work, while others may be suitable for work in pairs or larger groupings. There are usually two group activities provided for each lesson. You may wish to use one after the other; use both together (to reduce demand on resources and your attention); or, where one is a practical activity, use the other for children who successfully complete their practical work early. You may even wish to use activities as follow-up homework tasks.

Some of the group activities are supported by a photocopiable sheet. These sheets can be found in the book as well as on the CD-ROM. For some activities, there are also accompanying differentiated ideas, interactive activities and diagrams – all available on the CD-ROM (for more information, see 'How to use the CD-ROM' on page 6).

The group activities may include some writing. These activities are also aimed at strengthening the children's science literacy and supporting their English literacy skills. They may involve writing labels and captions, developing scientific vocabulary, writing about or recording investigations, presenting data, explaining what they have observed, or using appropriate secondary sources. The children's mathematical skills are also developed through number and data handling work in the context of science investigations.

ICT LINKS
Many lessons have this section in which suggestions for incorporating ICT are given. ICT links might include: using the internet and CD-ROMs for research; preparing graphs and tables using a computer; using the graphing tool, interactive activities and worksheets from the CD-ROM.

DIFFERENTIATION
Where appropriate, there are suggestions for differentiated work to support less able learners or extend more able learners in your class. Some of the photocopiable sheets are also differentiated into less able support, core ability, and more able extension to support you in this work. The book contains the worksheets for the core ability while the differentiated worksheets are found on the accompanying CD-ROM.

ASSESSMENT
This section includes advice on how to assess the children's learning against the lesson objectives. This may include suggestions for questioning or observation opportunities, to help you build up a picture of the children's developing ideas and guide your future planning. A separate summative assessment lesson is provided at the end of each unit of work. One may also be provided for a group of enrichment lessons if they form a section towards the end of a unit.

PLENARY
Suggestions are given for drawing together the various strands of the lesson in this section. The lesson objectives and outcomes may be reviewed and key learning points may be highlighted. The scene may also be set for another lesson.

HOMEWORK
On occasions, tasks may be suggested for the children to do at home. These may involve using photocopiables or the setting of a research project, perhaps involving the use the books on display (as suggested in the background section) to broaden the knowledge of the topic being studied.

OUTCOMES
These are statements related to the objectives; they describe what the children should have achieved by the end of the lesson.

LINKS
These are included where appropriate. They may refer to subjects closely related to science, such as technology or maths, or to content and skills from subjects such as art, history or geography.

ASSESSMENT LESSONS
The last lesson in every unit focuses on summative assessment. This assessment samples the content of the unit, focusing on its key theme(s); its results should be used in conjunction with other assessments you have made during the teaching of the unit. The lesson usually comprises of two assessment activities, which may take the form of photocopiable sheets to complete or practical activities with suggested assessment questions for you to use while you are observing the children. These activities may include a mark scheme, but this will not be related directly to curriculum attainment targets and level descriptors. These tasks are intended to provide you with a guide to assessing the children's performance.

PHOTOCOPIABLE SHEETS
These are an integral part of many of the lessons. They may provide resources such as quizzes, instructions for practical work, worksheets to complete whilst undertaking a task, information, guidance for written assignments and so on.

Photocopiable sheets printed in the book are suitable for most children. The CD-ROM includes differentiated versions of many photocopiables to support less confident learners and stretch more confident learners.

How to use the CD-ROM

SYSTEM REQUIREMENTS

Minimum specifications:
● PC with CD-ROM drive and at least 32 MB RAM
● Pentium 166 MHz processor
● Microsoft Windows 98, NT, 2000 or XP
● SVGA screen display with at least 64K colours at a screen resolution of 800 x 600 pixels.

GETTING STARTED

The accompanying CD-ROM includes a range of lesson and planning resources. The first screen requires the user to select the relevant country (England, Scotland, Wales, Northern Ireland, Eire). There are then several menus enabling the user to search the material according to various criteria, including lesson name, QCA unit, National Curriculum topic and resource type.

Searching by lesson name enables the user to see all resources associated with that particular lesson. The coloured tabs on the left-hand side of this screen indicate the differentiated worksheets; the tabs at the top of the page lead to different *types* of resource (diagram, interactive or photocopiable).

PHOTOCOPIABLES

The photocopiables that are printed in the book are also provided on the CD-ROM, as PDF files. In addition, differentiated versions of the photocopiables are provided where relevant:
● green indicates a support worksheet for less confident children;
● red indicates the core photocopiable, as printed in the book;
● blue indicates an extension worksheet for more confident children.

There are no differentiated photocopiables for assessment activities.

The PDF files can be annotated on screen using the panel tool provided (see below). The tools allow the user to add notes, highlight items and draw lines and boxes.

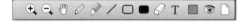

PDF files of photocopiables can be printed from the CD-ROM and there is also an option to print the full screen, including any drawings and annotations that have been added using the tools. (NB where PDF files are landscape, printer settings may need to be adjusted.)

INTERACTIVE ACTIVITIES

The CD-ROM includes twelve activities for children to complete using an interactive whiteboard or individual computers. Each activity is based on one of the photocopiables taken from across the units. Activities include: building a food chain, completing wordsearches, adding text to a decision tree and labelling a human skeleton.

GRAPHING TOOL

The graphing tool supports lessons where the children are asked to gather and record data. The tool enables children to enter data into a table, which can then be used to create a block graph, pie chart or line graph.

When inserting data into the table, the left-hand column should be used for labels for charts; the right-hand column is for numeric data only (see example below). The pop-up keypad can be used to enter numbers into the table.

DIAGRAMS

Where appropriate, diagrams printed in the book have been included as separate files on the CD-ROM. These include examples of tables and diagrams for children to refer to when undertaking experiments or building objects, such as the marble run in 'Pushes and pulls'. These can be displayed on an interactive whiteboard.

GENERAL RESOURCES

In addition to lesson resources, the CD-ROM also includes the planning grids for each unit, as printed in the book, and the relevant curriculum grid for England, Scotland, Wales, Northern Ireland and Eire. The curriculum grids indicate how elements of each country's National Curriculum are addressed by lessons in the book. The planning grids are supplied as editable Word files; the curriculum grids are supplied as Word and PDF files. Selection of a planning grid leads to a link, which opens the document in a separate window; this then needs to be saved to the computer or network before editing.

CHAPTER 1   Moving and growing

Lesson	Objectives	Main activity	Group activities	Plenary	Outcomes
Lesson 1 Our bodies	• To elicit children's existing ideas about the body.		Drawing what children think is inside our bodies into an outline of a body.	Discussion of children's ideas of the functions of different parts of the body	• Teacher has understanding of the children's existing ideas. • Children have more awareness of their own ideas and want to learn more.
Lesson 2 My skeleton	• To know that the skeleton is made from bones. • To understand that we have lots of joined bones to give a greater range of movement. • To make observations.	Comparing the movements of joints of dolls with our own joints.	Observing how different parts of our bodies move and noting this on a drawing of a skeleton. Mirroring each other's movements.	Identify ribs, skull and spine. Discussing why joints are needed.	• Can recognise that the skeleton is made up of lots of different bones. • Can recognise and name the skull, ribs and spine. • Can understand why the skeleton is made of lots of different bones. • Can make observations.
Lesson 3 A bag of bones	• To know that bones have some features that can be compared. • To make close observations recorded as drawings. • To raise questions.	Using a feely bag to enhance observation of bones.	Observational drawings of bones and raising questions about bones. Descriptive writing about the bones.	Considering the range of questions raised and how the answers might be found.	• Can compare the features of different bones. • Can make careful observational drawings. • Can raise scientific questions.
Lesson 4 Animal skeletons	• To know that some animals have skeletons of bones and some do not. • To use secondary sources to answer questions.	Researching answers to questions raised using secondary sources.		Oral feedback of information gathered, recorded and made into a display.	• Can use secondary sources to answer a question. • Can give examples of animals with skeletons of bones. • Understands that not all animals have skeletons made of bones.
Lesson 5 Planning a survey	• To know that the skeleton grows from birth to adulthood. • To plan a survey (on bone growth). • To consider what sources of information they will use to answer questions.	Discuss how children's arms grow as they get older.	Planning a survey of children's forearm length in different age groups. Practising measuring the length of forearms.	Finalise planning for the survey.	• Can state that the skeleton grows from birth to adulthood. • Has participated in the planning of the survey. • Can consider the information that needs to be collected to answer a question.
Lesson 6 Bone-growth survey	• To know that the skeleton grows from birth to adulthood. • To carry out a survey of bone growth. • To interpret the data from the survey.	Organisation of survey of forearm length. Survey own class.	Carry out the survey by visiting other classes and measuring children's forearms.	Collating the data in the form of a graph and discussion of patterns in it.	• Can carry out a survey in collaboration with others. • Can use the data from the survey to develop their ideas about bone growth.
Lesson 7 Science challenge	• To apply and develop survey-planning skills. • To decide on appropriate measurements to answer the question. • To carry out measurements with a good degree of accuracy. • To work collaboratively. • To be introduced to scattergrams as a way of looking for trends in data.	Producing a scattergram showing arm length to head size.	Plan and carry out a survey.	Discussion of the children's findings to try to identify any general trends.	• Can plan and carry out a survey with as much independence as possible. • Can identify scattergrams as a means of analysing survey data.
Lesson 8 Skeleton models	• To know that a skeleton supports the body. • To explore ideas by making models.	Making model joints with straws and pipe cleaners.		Discuss how the skeleton supports the soft body parts.	• Can recognise that a skeleton provides support. • Can use model making to explore ideas..

Lesson	Objectives	Main activity	Group activities	Plenary	Outcomes
Enrichment Lesson 9 Inside our bodies	• To know that the skeleton supports and protects organs in the human body. • To locate and name some of the organs of the body. • To use secondary sources of information to answer questions.	Positioning and naming the main organs of the body.	Answering questions about the body by using information books and presenting this information as a diagram.	Groups present their findings to the class.	• Can name and locate some of the organs of the body. • Can describe how the skeleton protects some of the internal organs.
Lesson 10 Muscles for moving	• To know that the actions of muscles help the body to move. • To observe their own bodies closely.	Demonstration and model of how muscles work in pairs.	Observing how muscles harden and soften as limbs move. Making models of how muscles work.	Discuss how muscles help us to move.	• Can explain that we need both skeleton and muscles to move. • Can explain that muscles pull on the bones to move our limbs. • Can observe themselves in a focused way.
Lesson 11 Exercising muscles	• To know that when muscles work hard they also affect the body in other ways • To relate their work in science to PE.	Observing changes in their bodies during a PE lesson.		Linking understanding of muscles to activity in PE.	• Can describe how their body feels after exercise. • Can relate their science work to PE.
Enrichment Lesson 12 How do minibeasts move?	• To develop observation skills and recording of observations. • To learn about the variety of ways that minibeasts move.	Collecting minibeasts and recording observations about how they move.		Share findings, compare different creatures' movements and watch video footage.	• Have a greater knowledge of diversity of life. • Can make and record detailed observations.
Lesson 13 Short legs – short strides?	• To decide what data to gather to answer a question. • To carry out a survey and present the results.	Deciding how to answer the question 'Do people with short legs take smaller strides than people with longer legs?'		Groups present their findings. The different approaches and conclusions are compared.	• Can make decisions about how to answer a question. • Can conduct a survey and present their findings to the class.
Lesson 14 Sinking in the sand	• To model a situation in order to investigate it. • To choose a suitable range of variables to test.	Deciding how to answer the question 'Do animals with big feet sink into sand as much as animals with small feet?' without needing animals in the classroom!		Share findings and discuss differences. Consider questions raised by the investigation.	• Can explain how the model was used to explore a real life question. • Can choose a range of variables in order to investigate a question.

Assessment	Objectives	Activity 1	Activity 2
Lesson 15	• To assess the children's knowledge and understanding of the skeletal system. • To assess the children's ability to interpret survey data.	Can the children explain that the skeleton has a role in protecting organs and in movement?	Can the children interpret the table of data provided?

SC1 SCIENTIFIC ENQUIRY

Longest arms - biggest heads?

LEARNING OBJECTIVES AND OUTCOMES
- Apply and develop survey planning skills.
- Decide on appropriate measurements to answer the question.
- To carry out measurements with a good degree of accuracy.
- To work collaboratively.
- To be introduced to scattergrams as a way of looking for trends in data.

ACTIVITY
The children work in groups as independently as possible to devise their own enquiry to answer the question: *Do the people with the longest arms have the biggest heads?* Their approaches and answers to the question are discussed and evaluated and then scattergrams are introduced as a useful way of looking for trends in data.

LESSON LINKS
This Sc1 activity forms an integral part of Lesson 7, Science challenge.

Lesson 1 ◖ Our bodies

Objective
- To elicit children's existing ideas about the body.

Vocabulary
body, human, ourselves

RESOURCES
Group activity: Thick felt-tipped pens, pencils, large sheets of paper such as wallpaper.

PREPARATION
Put the resources out ready for each group.

BACKGROUND
Children will hold their own ideas about what is inside their bodies. For example, some may be aware that we have bones, but imagine them as separate items without the joints. They may be aware of the existence of some internal organs, but may not know what they look like. A common example is to represent the heart as 'heart-shaped'. Children are likely to have little awareness of the digestive system as a whole and often represent it as a sack that food goes into. An awareness of the ideas held by different children can inform differentiation, and this activity will also give you an insight into the levels of understanding across the class so that planning can be adjusted accordingly.

STARTER
Explain that you are beginning a science topic on 'Ourselves' and that you want to find out what ideas the children already have about their bodies.

MAIN ACTIVITY
In this lesson, the focus is on finding out the children's existing ideas about their bodies, before introducing new ones.

GROUP ACTIVITY
The children work in groups of three or four. Ask one of the children in each group to lie on a large sheet of paper while the others draw around him or her. Then, ask the children to draw inside the outline what they think they would find inside their bodies.

Circulate, asking children questions about what they have drawn, for example: *What can you tell me about that part there? Do you think these are connected? What do you think this does?*

ASSESSMENT

When analysing the drawings the groups have produced, look out for ideas they hold that are not in line with scientific ideas. Note any children who will need particular support or extension.

PLENARY

Make a temporary display of the pictures and discuss the ideas shown on them with the class. Using the display, ask questions such as: *How does this part help us?*

OUTCOMES

- Teacher has understanding of the children's existing ideas.
- Children have more awareness of their own ideas and want to learn more.

Lesson 2 ▪ My skeleton

Objective
- To know that the skeleton is made from bones.
- To understand that we have lots of joined bones to give a greater range of movement.
- To make observations.

Vocabulary
bone, joint, rib, skeleton, skull, spine

RESOURCES 💿

Main activity: A collection of male and female jointed dolls (or ask the children to bring in their own); a model of the skeleton (card or realistic); large labels for the skull, ribs and spine; Blu-Tack® .
Group activities: 1 Copy of photocopiable page 24 (also 'My skeleton' (red), on the CD-ROM) for each child, pencils, secondary sources such as books and CD-ROMs showing pictures of the human skeleton, a full-length mirror. **2** Optional digital camera/video camera.
ICT link: 'My skeleton' interactive, from the CD-ROM.

PREPARATION

Share the dolls between each group, or ask the children to use their own. Have the resources for the Main activity to hand.

BACKGROUND

The human skeleton is made up of about 206 bones (some people have more bones in their hands and feet than others). Bones are living tissue – they are supplied with blood vessels and can grow and repair themselves. Children often think of bones as being 'dead', because that is their common experience of bones.

Another idea held by some children is that bones are not joined, but separate from each other. Some of the joins are fixed, other joints allow movement in certain directions.

STARTER

Begin with the children seated in groups, with one or more dolls per group. Explain that you want them to look at how the parts of the dolls move, compare them with how humans move and then talk to the class about it. Give them ten minutes to explore the movement of the dolls and themselves. They will need to stand up and move around.

MAIN ACTIVITY

Ask some children to explain and show how their dolls move and how they move. Ask them: *Do we move in the same way? In what ways are they different?* Discuss with the children how some of the dolls have rigid knees and elbows, whereas ours bend, and that we can move our shoulders and hips in a wide range of movements, but dolls often cannot.

Differentiation
Group activity 1
Some children may benefit from looking in a full-length mirror at their movements. To extend children, give them 'My skeleton' (blue), from the CD-ROM, and ask them to find out the names of some other bones and to label them on the sheet.

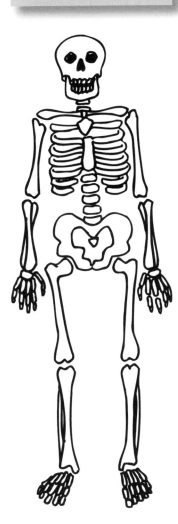

Ask the children: *What have we got inside our bodies that helps us to move?* (Bones and muscles.) Show the children the skeleton and explain that where the bones meet there are 'joints' – places where the bones join but can still move. We have more joints than the dolls and so more of our parts can move. Ask the children to look at their hands and identify different joints. Look back at the skeleton and pick out all the small bones that make up the hand. Ask: *Which directions can we move our fingers and thumbs in? Which directions can't we move them in?*

Show the children the ribs on the model. Ask them to feel their own torsos and see if they can feel their own ribs. Stick the label for the ribs on the model with Blu-Tack®. Do the same with the skull. Look at the spine on the model. Ask: *Is it all made of one bone?* (It is made of lots of small bones.) *Can you suggest a reason for that?* (So that the back can bend.) Label the spine on the model. Explain that each of the bones has a name, but that you want the children to concentrate on the names you have labelled.

GROUP ACTIVITIES
1. Give each child a copy of photocopiable page 24. Ask the children to label the skull, spine and ribs on the drawing of the skeleton. Then ask them to annotate different joints with a comment about how they move by exploring their own bodies. Have secondary sources available for the children to read.
2. Ask the children to work in pairs, taking it in turns to 'mirror' the movements of their partner. Challenge them to find a movement for every joint in their body. Ask: *Can you work out how many joints you are moving now?* If you have digital or video cameras available, ask the children to capture images of movement to share with the class in the plenary.

ICT LINK
Children can use the 'My skeleton' interactive, from the CD-ROM, to label parts of the skeleton on the computer.

ASSESSMENT
Can the children recognise and name the ribs, spine and skull? Can they explain why we are made of lots of small bones and not one large bone?

PLENARY
Ask the children to point to their own ribs, skull and spine. Ask some children to tell the others what they have noted about different joints. Those who have researched names for other bones can label the class skeleton or interactive whiteboard version for the others. Ask the class to explain why the skeleton is made of lots of small bones. Can they imagine what it would be like with one solid bone? If children have used digital photography invite them to share their images of joints and movements on the whiteboard.

OUTCOMES
● Can recognise that the skeleton is made up of lots of different bones.
● Can recognise and name the skull, ribs and spine.
● Can understand why the skeleton is made of lots of different bones.
● Can make observations.

LINKS
PSHE: understanding of our own bodies.
Literacy: labelling a drawing.
Drama: exploring the movements of the body.
ICT: using digital/video cameras.

Lesson 3 ▪ A bag of bones

Objective
● To know that bones have some features that can be compared.
● To make close observations recorded as drawings.
● To raise questions.

Vocabulary
compare, difference, observe, question

RESOURCES

Main activity: An interesting sterilised bone, ideally an animal or bird skull, in a feely bag or box (a bag or box that a child can put their hand in to feel an object without seeing it).
Group activities: 1 A collection of sterilised bones including some bird and large fish bones as well as mammalian bones; a feely bag or box for each group, hand lenses, drawing materials, paper, cards with question words 'How?', 'Why?', 'Which?', 'What?', 'When?', strips of card. **2** Writing materials.

PREPARATION

Bones need to be sterilised by boiling for at least an hour before classroom use. Share the collection of bones between the feely bags. There should be at least one bone for each child.

BACKGROUND

Bones are sometimes seen as dead, solid objects. Close observation reveals that they have holes – some being large spaces inside the bone where the bone marrow was situated, some being small channels where blood vessels travelled, and some being sponge-like spaces that make the bones lighter. The ends of bones can be examined to see how they might fit together as joints. Different bones can be compared and suggestions made as to which animal or which part of an animal they might have come from.

STARTER

Explain to the children that in this lesson they are going to develop their observation skills and find out about different animals.

MAIN ACTIVITY

Show the children the feely bag and ask for a volunteer to feel what is inside. Tell the volunteer that they must not say what they think it is, but describe what it feels like. Ask several other children to do this. Then ask the other children: *What do you think it might be?* Ask the children who have felt the bone if they agree . Draw out the bone with a dramatic flourish!

Explain that each group has some bones to study and draw. Demonstrate how to use a hand lens to observe details.

GROUP ACTIVITIES

1. Members of each group should take turns to remove a bone from the feely bag, describing it to the rest of the group. Circulate and encourage the children to compare their bones by asking: *Is there anything the same about your bones? Is there anything that is different?* The children should then work individually to observe and draw their chosen bone. Ask the children to annotate their drawings with questions. If this is an unfamiliar activity then stop the whole class and model it by writing some examples on the board. Refer them to the question cards on the table for support. Make sure that all the children have had the opportunity to feel the skull or bone from the Main activity during this time. Leave it on display.
2. Ask the children to work in twos and threes to brainstorm descriptive words or phrases about the bones. These can include personal responses such as 'scary'. Ask the children to use these words as the basis for a poem or a piece of descriptive writing.

ASSESSMENT

Do the children's drawings show evidence of careful observation? Can they describe similarities and differences between the bones? Have they raised questions about the bones?

Differentiation
Encourage children who are having difficulty raising questions by modelling them, asking such questions as: *I wonder what animal this comes from? Why does this bone have a hole here?* For children who need literacy support, scribe their question on to a strip of card, then cut it up into individual words for the child to reassemble and copy.

Children can be extended in their questioning by challenging them to use all the question words twice.

PLENARY
Ask various children to tell the class one of their questions. Use a flipchart or piece of sugar paper to record a range of questions. Make sure that this includes: 'Do all animals have bones?' Ask: *How could we find out the answers to our questions?* (Use books or CD-ROMs, ask experts.) Explain that the children will be trying to find the answers in the next lesson.

OUTCOMES
● Can compare the features of different bones.
● Can make careful observational drawings.
● Can raise scientific questions.

LINKS
Art: observational drawing.
English: writing questions and descriptions.

Lesson 4 ◗ Animal skeletons

Objective
● To know that some animals have skeletons of bones and some do not.
● To use secondary sources to answer questions.

RESOURCES
Reference books (or CD-ROMs/websites) on bones and skeletons including dinosaurs; strips of card in two colours; marker pens, writing materials.

MAIN ACTIVITY
Write questions on cards for pairs of children to research (these can be duplicated). Examples of questions could include: 'Which animals have bones in their bodies?', 'What are bones made from?', 'How do we know that dinosaurs had bones?', 'Which part of the animal did the bone come from?' The children can research and make notes of the answers. Give them a time limit after which they need to be ready to report to the class.

ASSESSMENT
Can the children find the answer to their question? Can they give examples of animals that have bones?

PLENARY
Ask each child to present their information orally. Record their answers on different-coloured strips of card to make into a temporary display. Ask the children: *Can you give me an example of an animal that does have bones?* (Any mammal or bird, some reptiles and most fish.) Ask: *Can you think of any animals that don't have bones?* (Worms and caterpillars do not have bones.)

Differentiation
Match the questions and research materials to children's interests and their ability to access the text containing the answers.

OUTCOMES
● Can use secondary sources to answer a question.
● Can give examples of animals with skeletons of bones.
● Understand that not all animals have skeletons made of bones

Lesson 5 ◗ Planning a survey

Objectives
● To know that the skeleton grows from birth to adulthood.
● To plan a survey (on bone growth).
● To consider what sources of information they will use to answer questions.

RESOURCES ◎
Main activity: Photographs of people of different ages and bones from people of different ages, if available (hard copies or displayed on an interactive whiteboard); a model skeleton, an enlarged copy of photocopiable page 24 (also 'My skeleton' (red), on the CD-ROM), a flipchart.
Group activities: 1. Writing materials, copies of photocopiable page 25 for each group. **2.** Tape measures, scrap paper and pencils.

Vocabulary
bone, forearm, grow, survey

PREPARATION 💿
Photocopy page 25 for each group and enlarge it to A3 for display or copy it on to the flipchart for the Main activity (or display 'Planning a survey' on an interactive whiteboard).

BACKGROUND
It is important that children do not think that fair testing is the only form of enquiry that is valid in science. Surveys are an important part of the range of enquiry skills they need to develop, particularly when investigating living things that cannot be controlled in fair tests. The data produced needs to be handled in different ways and helps children to understand the variation that exists between organisms. The data to be collected needs to be discussed with the class, as suggested on photocopiable page 25.

STARTER
Show the children the photographs of people of different ages. Ask: *How do you think their skeletons have changed?* (In size, strength and shape.) Give the children the opportunity here to talk about any personal experiences that relate to bone growth by asking: *Does anyone have anything they want to tell us about how bones grow?*

MAIN ACTIVITY
Ask the children each to look at their own forearm. Show them the forearm bones on the model skeleton. Ask: *How do you think your forearm has changed since you were born? Do you expect it to change as you grow older?* (It should get longer and wider.) *How could we find out about how children's arms grow?* Introduce the idea of a survey.

Display the enlargement of photocopiable page 25 or the questions written on the flipchart for discussion. Read through the questions and explain that these are some of the things they may need to think about when planning their survey, but they may have other ideas too.

GROUP ACTIVITIES
1. Ask each group to go back to their table and discuss what they think about these questions, explaining that everyone's ideas will be taken into account, but the whole class will need to use the same method in the end.
2. Ask each child to measure the forearm of all the other children in their group and jot down the measurements on scrap paper. Ask: *Do you all have the same measurement for each person? Why?/Why not?* This will alert you to any children who need support with measuring and provide discussion points for the Plenary.

ASSESSMENT
Do the children realise that bones grow from birth to adulthood? Do the children contribute to planning the survey? Do any children need extra input or support with measuring in the next lesson?

PLENARY
Discuss the questions, recording the class's decisions next to each question on the flipchart. Ask: *Who shall we survey?* Emphasise that you will not be recording names so that people will not get embarrassed. Ask: *What ages shall we survey? Shall we survey boys, girls or both?* (Equal numbers.) *How many children?* (Ten from each year group?) *What information do we need to record?* (Age or year group, and length of forearm.) Ask: *How will we measure the forearm? Where from? Where to? Shall we measure the inside or outside of the arm? How accurate does our measuring have to be?* (To the nearest centimetre.) Ask: *What equipment do we need?* (Tape measures, paper and pencils for recording.) Explain that the children will carry out the survey in the next lesson all using the same method as agreed here.

Differentiation
Have mixed-attainment groups so that there are a variety of ideas discussed. Support any groups in need by asking questions such as: *Do you think all the children in Reception/Primary 1 have the same length forearms? How long would it take to measure the forearms of the whole class?*

OUTCOMES
- Can state that the skeleton grows from birth to adulthood.
- Has participated in the planning of the survey.
- Can consider the information that needs to be collected to answer a question.

LINKS
PSHE: understanding how our bodies grow as we get older.
Maths: data-handling and measurement of length.

Lesson 6 ◗ Bone-growth survey

RESOURCES
Main activity: Large sheet of paper.
Group activities: 1 Small cards (5×7cm) in a different colour for each year group (or use coloured Post-it Notes), writing materials, tape measures. **2** Small cards as for Group activity 1 with recorded data.

PREPARATION
Make sure you have arranged a time that is convenient to the other classes for your surveys.

BACKGROUND
The survey will produce data that is continuous – that is, the measurements could be anywhere along a continuous line. This kind of data is more difficult to handle than discrete data, for example, eye colour, that can be represented as simple block graphs. The children can begin to understand how the data is distributed by representing it as shown below. The range of the data is the spread from the lowest measurement to the highest.

STARTER
Remind the children of the decisions they made in the previous lesson by returning to the flipchart and reviewing their decisions about the process of data collection.

MAIN ACTIVITY
Allocate a year group for each group to survey. A good way for the children to record the data for later analysis is to record each person's data on a separate card, colour-coded for the different year groups.

Each group should measure one or two of its own members to form the data for Year 4/Primary 5 and to practise measuring and recording the information before leaving the classroom.

GROUP ACTIVITIES
1. Ask each groups to visit the class they have been assigned to collect their data.
2. Ask each group to put their cards in order from the shortest forearm to the longest forearm. Explain that this is the 'range'.

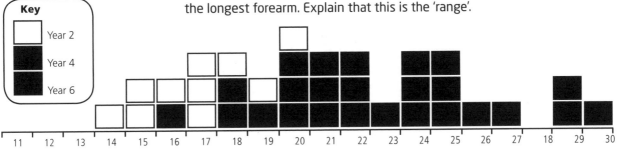

Length of forearm (cm)

Differentiation
Place the children in mixed-attainment groups for peer support.

ASSESSMENT
Have the children collected the data as agreed? Have they recorded it in the form that the class has agreed upon?

PLENARY
Ask each group in turn, starting with those who surveyed the youngest children, to come and write the length of the shortest and the longest forearm on the board. Ask the class to look at the numbers. Ask: *Do you notice anything about the numbers?* (They get bigger, but not in neat steps.) *Do all children who are in Year 6/Primary 7 have the same length of forearm?* (No.) *Why not?* (People are not all exactly the same, and they grow at different rates.) *Do you still think it is true that bones grow as children get older?* (Yes.)

The cards could then be made into a graph by writing the different forearm lengths along the bottom of a large sheet of paper (on the x axis). The children could stick the cards above these lengths to make a frequency graph. The spread of the different-coloured cards should show how the older children tend to have the longer forearms. This could form the basis of a display with questions around it such as: 'How long is the longest forearm in Year 5/Primary 6?', 'How many Year 6/Primary 7 children have a forearm longer than 20cm?'

OUTCOMES
● Can carry out a survey in collaboration with others.
● Can use the data from the survey to develop their ideas about bone growth.

LINKS
PSHE: understanding and accepting that people differ from one another.
Maths: data-handling.

Lesson 7 ▪ Science challenge

Objective
● To apply and develop survey planning skills
● To decide on appropriate measurements to answer the question
● To carry out measurements with a good degree of accuracy
● To work collaboratively
● To be introduced to scattergrams as a way of looking for trends in data.

Vocabulary
survey, trend, pattern, scattergram

RESOURCES
Group activity: Metre rulers, tape measures, writing materials, copies of class list (available for reference but not handed out), copy of photocopiable page 26 for each group (also 'Science challenge' (red), on the CD-ROM).

PREPARATION
Organise the children into small. Make copies of photocopiable page 26 for each group. Provide each group with a set of resources.

BACKGROUND
To find out whether people with the longest arms also have the biggest heads requires children to look for relationships between the two sets of measurements. Although this is a survey, not a fair test, they will still need to make decisions about where to start and end their measurement of the arm and what measurement of the head they will take. There are no right answers, but they should still be consistent within their own investigation.

A basic approach would be to see if the person with the longest arms also had the biggest head. A more sophisticated approach would be to look for a consistent correlation between arm length and head size. Children may not come to this independently. The main activity introduces scattergrams.

STARTER
Present the children with the question 'Do people with the longest arms have the biggest heads?'. Explain that there are different ways of answering

it and that you want each group to decide how they will answer it and then to take any measurements that they need. Give them a time by which they need to be ready to present their work to the rest of the class.

GROUP ACTIVITY

Arrange the children into small groups and ask them to plan and carry out their survey. If children have little experience of collaborative group work, you can help them to manage their time by giving them ten minutes to think about how they will answer the question, ten minutes to prepare how they will record their measurements, 15 minutes to carry out the measurements and then five minutes to decide how to present their findings to the class. The role of the teacher is to circulate, supporting groups as needed and taking the opportunity to observe and assess them.

MAIN ACTIVITY

If any of the groups decided to look for general trends in the data, then build on their ideas. If not, then introduce this approach as the next step on from what the children have already done. Select six children to enter their data on arm length and head size into a table drawn on a whiteboard or flipchart. You may wish to select children who need to become more secure in entering data into a table. If the measurements were taken in different ways, some children may need to be measured again so that there is a consistent approach.

Model choosing an appropriate scale to fit the data and write in the relevant numbers on the axes of a graph, using a whiteboard, or graphing software on an interactive whiteboard. Point out that it is the lines that are being numbered not the spaces. This is different from the bar charts that children may be more familiar with. Starting with nought will probably waste a lot of space so explain that it is acceptable in these circumstances to use the range of numbers in the data.

Invite the six children to come up one at a time and mark with crosses the points where their arm length and head size are shown. The scattergram may look something like the drawing below.

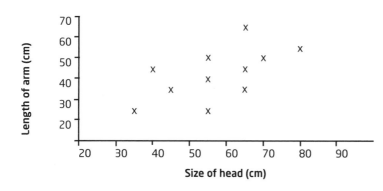

Talk about the data together: *Which cross shows the person with the biggest head? Which cross shows the person with the longest arm? Are they the same person? Is there a general trend (pattern) in the way the crosses are going? Are there any that don't fit in with the pattern?* Invite other children to come up and add on crosses for their arm and head size. *Does this change the pattern or make it clearer?* Make the point that the general trend is more important than looking at individual cases. Ask: *Suppose a child had an arm that was 43cm long, could you predict how big their head would be?*

PLENARY

Ask each group to feed back in turn. Ask: *Where did you start your measurement on the arm and where did you measure to? How precise were your measurements?* (Measuring to the nearest cm or half cm was probably sufficient for the task.) Discuss any differences in how the children carried out the task, such as how many children they surveyed and who they chose. *What answers to the question did the groups decide on? Did everyone agree?* Did the person with the smallest head have the shortest arm length? Did the person with the second longest arms have the second biggest head? Help the children to see the value of looking for a general trend rather than focusing on the extreme cases.

Differentiation

Plan to have groups containing children with a range of skills and attainment for mutual support. Circulate and ask groups about their plans. Support them as required by asking further questions about how many children they will plan to measure, what equipment they will use, what unit of measurement will they choose, and where they will write down the information. Supporting some groups in coming to a collective decision and helping them to resolve disagreements may also be important.

ASSESSMENT

Are the children using the data to justify their answer to the question? Are they making appropriately accurate measurements? Were the group able to agree on a plan and carry it out?

OUTCOMES

● Can plan and carry out a survey with as much independence as possible.
● Can identify scattergrams as a means of analysing survey data.

LINKS

Maths: data handling.

Lesson 8 ▪ Skeleton models

Objectives
● To know that a skeleton supports the body.
● To explore ideas by making models.

RESOURCES

Straws, pipe cleaners, cotton wool, scissors, adhesive.

MAIN ACTIVITY

Show the children how to join the straws together by using pipe cleaners cut in half. The children can then design their own skeleton for an imaginary animal using cotton wool stuck onto the skeleton to represent body parts. Ask children how their straw skeletons support the animal they are making.

ASSESSMENT

Can the children explain how a skeleton provides support?

PLENARY

Show the children's models and discuss how the straws act like a skeleton. Say: *Imagine how animals made from only cotton wool might look.* Ask: *Could they stand up? Why not?*

Differentiation
Mainly by outcome. Support less dextrous children with extra adult help.

OUTCOMES

● Can recognise that a skeleton provides support.
● Can use model making to explore ideas.

ENRICHMENT

Lesson 9 ▪ Inside our bodies

Objective
● To know that the skeleton supports and protects organs in the human body.
● To locate and name some of the organs of the body.
● To use secondary sources of information to answer questions.

RESOURCES

Main activity: A model of a human torso or a 'body apron': a tabard that a child wears with felt cut-outs of different body parts that are stuck on with Velcro; large labels for 'brain', 'heart', 'lungs', 'stomach', 'bladder', 'kidney', 'intestines'; Blu-Tack®; double-sided sticky tape or Velcro to attach labels.
Group activities: 1 Books on the body; prepared questions on cards, each inserted into the book that contains the answer. **2** Drawing materials.

PREPARATION

Have the resources for the Main activity to hand. Have the books and question cards ready on the tables. The exact questions will depend on the information available in the books provided for the groups. The following questions about some vital organs provide guidance:
● Make a list of things the brain helps us to do.
● How big is the heart and what does it do?
● What do we do with our lungs? What do we breathe?
● How long is the intestine?
● Whereabouts is your stomach?

Differentiation
Use groups based on literacy attainment. Support those with weaker literacy skills with teacher time; the brain is a good subject for them. Those with good literacy skills and good scientific understanding can research the kidneys, bladder or the lungs.
You can also support children by inserting cards at the right page. Other children will be able to use the index or practise skimming skills.

● How many kidneys have we got?
● What do we store in the bladder?

BACKGROUND

Children have existing ideas about what is inside their bodies, as will be evident from Lesson 1. Common ideas are that the heart is heart-shaped, and that food goes into the stomach and stops. Few children will have ideas about the intestine and kidneys by Year 4/Primary 5. This lesson is not intended to give the children a full understanding of the function of each of these organs, but to be a foundation for later work.

STARTER

Review the children's drawings from the initial assessment in Lesson 1. Ask the children what they think is inside their bodies. Make a list of the main organs (brain, heart, lungs, stomach, bladder, kidneys, intestines) on the board as the children suggest their ideas.

MAIN ACTIVITY

Look at the model/body apron, asking children if they can name any parts. Add the labels in the correct places. Discuss briefly what each organ does, but do not go into detail (see Preparation).

Explain that each group will study one organ and find out some information about it using books or CD-ROMs to report back to the class.

GROUP ACTIVITIES

1. Nominate one member of each group to act as scribe. Each group finds out the answers to the questions on the cards on their table. The question cards should be inserted into the books containing the answer.
2. Ask each group to present their findings as a simple poster with an annotated drawing. Make sure the poster is kept simple and is about communicating information, not decorative artwork - a time limit might help.

ASSESSMENT

Can the children locate the different organs on their own bodies and on a model? Can they explain how the skeleton protects them?

PLENARY

Take the labels off the model of the body and put them back as each group presents their information. Ask the children: *What might happen if our organs got damaged?* (They might not work properly; we could die.) Ask: *What is covering the organs that helps to protect them?* (Skin and the skeleton.) *Which part of the skeleton protects the brain?* (The skull.) *Which part of the skeleton protects the heart and the lungs?* (The ribs.) Ask the children to feel their own ribs and skull: *How do they feel? Can they move?* (The skull is limited to turning: the ribs can expand and contract.) *Why do the ribs need to move?* (To accommodate changes in breathing.)

OUTCOMES

● Can name and locate some of the organs of the body.
● Can describe how the skeleton protects some of the internal organs.

LINKS

PSHE: understanding that we need functioning organs to keep us alive.
Literacy: use of information texts; labelling diagrams.

Lesson 10 ▪ Muscles for moving

Objectives
● To know that the action of muscles helps the body to move.
● To observe their own bodies closely.

Vocabulary
bone, muscle, pull, stretch

RESOURCES
Main activity: Equipment for model of an elbow joint: two rulers with holes in one end, two pop socks, an elastic band cut open, strong sticky tape (see illustration below).
Group activities: 1. Mirrors, writing equipment. **2.** Equipment for model elbow as above.

PREPARATION
Have all the resources for the model elbow to hand.

BACKGROUND
Muscles are attached to bones by tendons. They contract (shorten), pulling on the bones to cause movement. They can contract on their own, but they cannot relax unless they are stretched out by another muscle shortening. This means that muscles are organised in 'antagonistic pairs'. Children at this stage do not need to know this term, but can begin to understand that when one muscle contracts, the other is stretched. Ligaments help to hold joints together.

STARTER
Ask the children to tell you some things they have learned about the skeleton. List on the board that it supports, protects and helps us to move. Ask the children what else we have that helps us to move (muscles).

MAIN ACTIVITY
Ask the children to hold their right upper arm with one hand to keep it still. Ask them to move their forearm. Ask: *What directions can you move it in?* (Up and down.) Show the children the two rulers and explain that these are like the bones in your forearm and upper arm. Tie the rulers together using a cut elastic band through the holes at the ends. Explain that you have made a joint, like the joint at the elbow. Show how the rulers can move, forming the 'elbow'.

Show the pop socks and explain that these are like muscles because they can stretch in length and return to being short again. Tape one pop sock several centimetres from one end of both rulers, explaining that your muscles are joined to your bones. Straighten out the rulers to represent a straight arm. The children can follow these movements with their own arms. Ask them to describe the pop sock 'muscle'. (It is stretched and long.) Explain that the muscle can make itself short and that this pulls up the forearm.

Explain that although the muscle can make itself short, it cannot then make itself long again. Ask: *Can you think of a way of bringing the forearm down again?* (Use another muscle.) Tape another pop sock onto the underside of the rulers and show how when this gets shorter the other 'muscle' is pulled long again and the forearm is brought down.

GROUP ACTIVITIES
1. Ask the children to feel what happens to their muscles as they move their arms. When the muscles feel hard, they are short and are working at pulling a bone. When they feel soft, they have been stretched out. Ask the children to write and draw how muscles and bones work together to make us move.
2. Ask the children to work in pairs to make their own model elbow joints. Making pairs of muscles can be difficult, so limit the task to making a model with a muscle to pull the arm up; extend it to a pair of muscles only if the first task has been successfully completed.

Differentiation
Group activity 1
For children who need literacy support, write out the key vocabulary as a wordbank. Expect more detailed descriptions from more confident children.

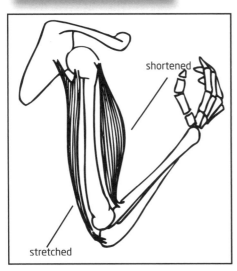

shortened

stretched

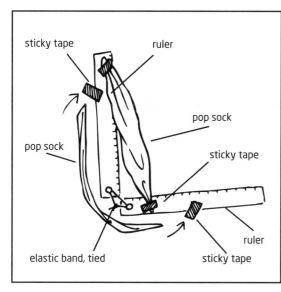

Labels in diagram: sticky tape, ruler, pop sock, pop sock, sticky tape, sticky tape, ruler, elastic band, tied

ASSESSMENT
In the children's work, do they show an understanding that muscles pull on bones to make them move?

PLENARY
Ask: *How does our skeleton help us?* (It gives support and protection and allows movement.) *How do our muscles help us to move?* (They pull on the bones.) *What tells the muscles to pull on the bones?* (Our brain.)

OUTCOMES
● Know that we need both skeleton and muscles to move.
● Know that muscles pull on the bones to move our limbs.
● Can observe themselves in a focused way.

LINKS
PE: movement.

Lesson 11 ◼ Exercising muscles

Objective
● To know that when muscles work hard in exercise they also affect the body in other ways.
● To relate their work in science to PE.

RESOURCES
A PE lesson.

MAIN ACTIVITY
Ask the children what they will be using to help them move. During the lesson, and as the children are cooling down, ask them to describe how they are feeling. (Tired, hot, out of breath and can feel the heart beating fast.)

ASSESSMENT
Are the children able to describe the changes to their bodies? Can they make connections between their science work and the PE lesson?

PLENARY
Back in class, ask the children: *When your muscles had to work hard to move you quickly, how did that make you feel? Does this link to anything else we have been learning about?* (The heart and lungs are working hard, too.)

Differentiation
Target questions to involve those children who are enthusiastic about sport and less so about science!

OUTCOMES
● Can describe how their body feels after exercise.
● Can relate their science work to PE.

ENRICHMENT
Lesson 12 ◼ How do minibeasts move?

Objectives
● To develop observation skills and recording of observations.
● To learn about the variety of ways that minibeasts move.

RESOURCES
Collecting pots, transparent tanks/containers, pooters, paint brushes, digital camera, digital microscope, wildlife programmes showing minibeasts moving.

MAIN ACTIVITY
Collect a range of minibeasts and ask the children to make careful observations of how they move. These could be recorded as annotated drawings photographs, or even as a commentary on a digital movie.

ASSESSMENT
Are the children able to describe the movements of the minibeasts and compare them? Are they able to record their observations in a suitable form?

Differentiation
Encourage children to record their observations in a format that will further develop existing strengths or tackle areas for development.

PLENARY

Share findings as a class and compare different speeds of movement, different kinds of 'legs', different patterns of activity. Watch the children's own video clips or clips from other sources and enjoy looking at close-ups of these amazing creatures!

OUTCOMES

● Have a greater knowledge of the diversity of life.
● Can make and record detailed observations.

Lesson 13 ▪ Short legs - short strides?

Objectives
● To decide what data to gather to answer a question.
● To carry out a survey and present the results.

RESOURCES

Rulers, tape measure, metre stick, stop clock, paper, pencils.

MAIN ACTIVITY

Do people with short legs take smaller strides than people with longer legs? Present this question as a collaborative group task. Suggest that the children think about their previous survey and how they could improve on it.

ASSESSMENT

Have the children chosen to collect data that will answer the question? Have any chosen to look for pattern in a large data set as modelled in lesson 7?

Differentiation
Allow children to work in groups of mixed skills for mutual support. As an additional challenge, ask children to investigate the question: *Does your stride length change when you walk fast?*

PLENARY

Invite groups to present their findings to the class. Discuss the outcomes. Was the same conclusion reached? What differences were there in the approaches taken? Evaluate the different approaches.

OUTCOMES

● Can make decisions about how to answer a question.
● Can conduct a survey and present their findings to the class.

Lesson 14 ▪ Sinking in the sand

Objective
● To model a situation in order to investigate it.
● To choose a suitable range of variables to test.

RESOURCES

Varied masses, card, sticky tape, sand and trays, lolly sticks, matchsticks, rulers.

MAIN ACTIVITY

Introduce the question 'Do animals with big feet sink into the sand as much as animals with small feet?' There are different possibilities for putting this in a meaningful context – you could discuss experiences at the beach or look at photos or video clips of desert animals. Ask the children to think about how they could investigate the question without having real animals in the classroom. Discuss possible ideas and then invite groups to carry out their investigations. Their findings could be presented in the form of a poem or even a song!

ASSESSMENT

Can the children suggest suitable models for the real-life question? Are they systematic in their planning, trying a sufficient range of feet and adopting a consistent approach?

Differentiation
Let children work in mixed ability groups, with adult support for those who need it.

PLENARY
Share findings and discuss any differences such as whether the size of the foot or the mass makes most difference. What further questions are raised? For example: *Does it matter whether the sand is wet or dry? What about animals that jump?*

OUTCOMES
- Can explain how the model was used to explore a real-life question.
- Can choose a range of variables in order to investigate a question.

Lesson 15 ▪ Assessment

Objectives
- To assess the children's knowledge and understanding of the skeletal system.
- To assess the children's ability to interpret survey data.

RESOURCES 💿
Assessment activities: 1 A copy of photocopiable page 27 for each child (also 'Assessment – 1' (red), on the CD-ROM), writing materials. **2** A copy of photocopiable page 28 (also 'Assessment – 2' (red), on the CD-ROM), for each child, writing materials.

ASSESSMENT ACTIVITY 1
Give each child a copy of photocopiable page 27. Act as a reader and scribe for any children who need this support. You may wish to discuss the answers immediately so that the children are able to assess their own progress, and any questions can be addressed on the spot.

ANSWERS
1. To support our body; To help us move; To protect some of our organs.
2a. The skull.
2b. The ribs.
2c. Labelled diagram.
3. It grows; The bones get bigger/longer.

LOOKING FOR LEVELS
Most children should be able to answer these questions correctly. Some may have difficulty remembering the correct vocabulary. Questions 1 and 3 are the most important in demonstrating understanding of the key ideas.

ASSESSMENT ACTIVITY 2
This activity focuses on assessing children's data interpretation skills. Give each child a copy of photocopiable page 28. Ask them to answer the questions on their own. Explain that you are looking for evidence of thoughtful explanation in questions 3 and 4, not the 'right' answer.

LOOKING FOR LEVELS
Most children should be able to answer questions 1 and 2. In question 3, some children may think that the children must be different ages because they have different-sized feet. Some may argue that Mark is younger because his feet are a lot smaller. Others may remember that there was a spread of forearm length in their earlier survey and so say that they could be the same age. These are all acceptable responses.

Children who suggest a reason for their are working at NC Level 3/ Scottish Level C. Those who give more sophisticated explanations relating to scientific knowledge and understanding are working at NC Level 4/ Scottish Level C/D in this aspect.

PLENARY
After Assessment 2, it would be good to discuss different interpretations of the data and allow the children to argue their point of view.

PHOTOCOPIABLE

My skeleton

◾ Label these bones on the drawing:

jaw
hip joint
collar bone
ribs
skull
spine

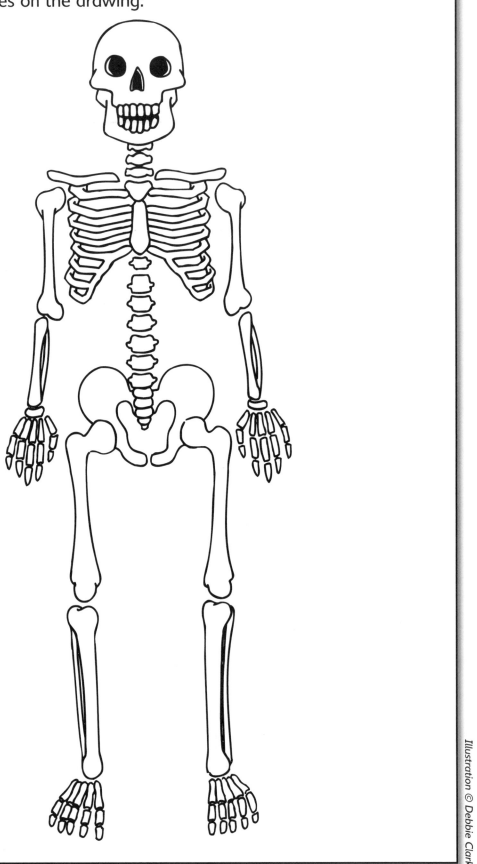

◤SCHOLASTIC

Planning a survey

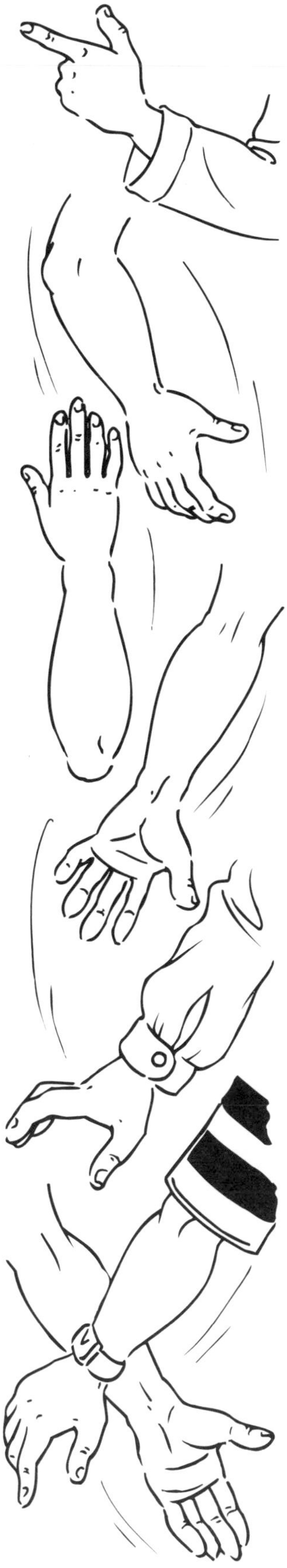

Do children's forearms grow as they get older?

_____

What ages shall we survey?

_____

Shall we survey boys, girls or both?

_____

How many children shall we survey?

_____

What information do we need to record?

_____

_____

How will we measure the forearm?

_____

_____

How accurate does our measuring have to be?

_____

_____

What equipment do we need?

_____

_____

_____

_____

_____

_____

Illustration © Debbie Clark

Science challenge

◼ You need to investigate this question:

Do people with bigger heads have longer arms?

Hints:
What measurements will you need to make?
How many people will you survey?
How will you record it?

Be ready to present your research to the science conference at

_____

Illustration © Theresa Tibbetts c/o Beehive Illustration

◤SCHOLASTIC

Assessment – 1

1. Why do we need a skeleton?

✓ Tick the answers you agree with.

☐ To support our body

☐ To help us move

☐ To make us tall

☐ To protect some of our organs

☐ To make us heavy

☐ To protect our muscles

2a. Which part of the skeleton protects the brain?

_____

2b. Which part of the skeleton protects the heart and lungs?

_____

2c. Now label those two parts (a) and (b) on the drawing of the skeleton.

3. What happens to your skeleton as you grow up?

_____

_____

_____

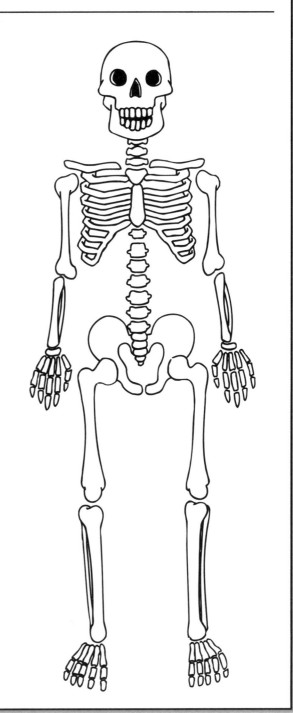

Illustration © Debbie Clark

Assessment – 2

■ A group of children measured the length of their feet. The results are in the table below.

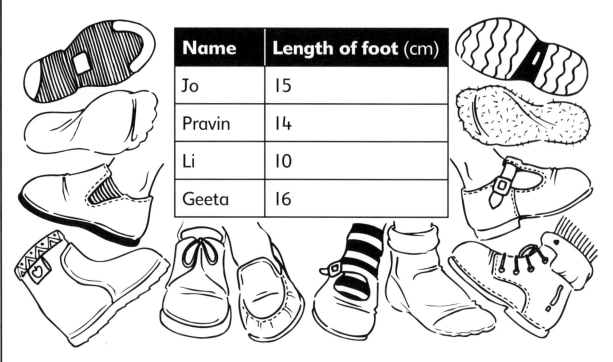

Name	Length of foot (cm)
Jo	15
Pravin	14
Li	10
Geeta	16

1. Who had the longest foot?

_____

2. Who had the shortest foot?

_____

3. Do you think these children are the same age?

_____

4. Explain why you think that.

_____

_____

_____

Illustration © Debbie Clark

■SCHOLASTIC

CHAPTER 2   Habitats

Lesson	Objectives	Main activity	Group activities	Plenary	Outcomes
Lesson 1 Living things	• To elicit children's ideas about living things. • To know that there is a wide variety of organisms on the planet. • To know that living things are called organisms.	Discussing what makes something 'living'. Sorting a collection of living things into animals and plants.	Sorting a collection into 'living' and 'not living'.	Discussing the breadth of living things that exist.	• Teacher is aware of children's existing ideas about living things. • Can give examples of a wide variety of organisms. • Can understand the term 'organism'.
Lesson 2 Habitat challenge	• To know what the term 'habitat' means. • To identify a variety of local habitats.	Discuss what living things need to stay alive and that they get them from their habitat.	Listing different habitats in the school grounds.	Considering the range of habitats within the school grounds.	• Can explain what the term 'habitat' means. • Can identify a variety of local habitats.
Lesson 3 Habitat investigators	• To identify different physical aspects of habitats. • To make observations and measurements of the physical conditions of two chosen habitats.	How to measure and record the physical nature of a habitat, such as light levels.	Observing and measuring physical nature of habitats within the school grounds. Presenting information as a book.	Discussing how the physical environment might affect the living things in a habitat.	• Can identify different physical aspects of habitats. • Can make observations and measurements of the physical conditions of two chosen habitats.
Enrichment Lesson 4 Water skeletons	• To know that some animals have a 'skeleton' of water.	Introducing the idea that some animals have a 'water skeleton' using a water-filled balloon.		Discussion on the limitations of a water skeleton.	• Can describe how water is used as a skeleton in some animals.
Lesson 5 Minibeasts	• To know how to collect animals sensitively. • To observe carefully. • To know that some invertebrates have soft bodies and some have a skeleton on the outside.	Introduce the idea of an 'outside skeleton'. Demonstration of techniques for collecting small animals.	Collection and observational drawing of small animals.	Grouping collected animals according to their skeleton.	• Can observe closely. • Can collect animals with respect for life. • Can group a collection of invertebrates according to observable features. • Can explain that there are different types of skeleton.
Lesson 6 Collecting animals	• To investigate the animals found in a particular habitat. • To suggest reasons why animals are found in a certain habitat. • To be able to choose appropriate equipment to collect an animal. • To learn to collect animals carefully.	Demonstration of how to collect animals sensitively.	Collecting animals found in different habitats in the school grounds.	Relating the animals found in a habitat to the physical environment.	• Can collect animals carefully without damaging them. • Can investigate the animals found in a particular habitat. • Can choose appropriate equipment to collect an animal. • Can suggest reasons why animals are found in a certain habitat.
Lesson 7 Classifying living things	• To elicit children's existing understanding of groups of living things. • To observe features of living things. • To group living things according to observable features. • To understand that a wide range of living things can be classified as animals or as plants.	Grouping pictures of plants and animals and identifying features common to each group.	Grouping and comparing photographs of living things.	Discussion on differences between plants and animals.	• Can sort living things according to observable features. • Can explain criteria used for grouping. • Can recognise the diversity of living things within the classification of plants and animals.
Lesson 8 Comparing animals	• To know that animals can be grouped according to whether or not they have a backbone. • To recognise similarities and differences between different groups of vertebrates. • To compare and group items according to different criteria.	Classifying animals into those with and without backbones and identifying the groups: mammals, birds, fish, reptiles and amphibians.	Recording similarities and differences between pictures of animals and classifying animals with backbones as mammals, birds, fish, reptiles and amphibians.	Discussing similarities and differences identified and clarifying the group animals belong to.	• Can explain that animals can be grouped into those with and without backbones. • Can recall the five different groups of animals with backbones. • Can describe features that characterise members of the five groups.

Lesson	Objectives	Main activity	Group activities	Plenary	Outcomes
Lesson 9 Identification keys	• To know how to use a simple key to identify vertebrates and plants. • To carry out observations.	Using a simple key to identify local birds. Collecting plants and making a simple key by describing them.		Presenting keys made to the class.	• Can use a key to identify local animals. • Can construct a simple key to identify local plants.
Lesson 10 Decision tree	• To know how a decision-tree key can be used to classify and identify animals.	Explaining how to use a decision tree to identify animals.	Using decision trees to identify pictures of animals.	Checking that the animals have been correctly identified.	• Can use a decision tree to identify invertebrates.
Lesson 11 Animal preferences	• To know how to investigate the behaviour of an animal species. • To understand the need for repeated tests. • To pose their own questions for investigation.	Planning how to test animal preferences using choice chambers.	Carrying out tests of preference and recording results. Writing about ' A day in the life of...' a particular animal.	Considering the need for repetition of tests.	• Can investigate the behaviour of an animal species. • Can explain the need for repeated tests. • Can put ideas for an investigation in the form of a question.
Enrichment Lesson 12 Bird behaviour	• To know how to investigate the behaviour of birds. • To make observations for a sustained period of time.	Observation of bird behaviour in a local area.		Discussing the most common behaviours observed.	• Can explain how to investigate the behaviour of birds. • Can make observations for a sustained period. of time.
Lesson 13 Animals	• To know that animals eat certain foods in a habitat. • To use secondary sources to find information. • To become familiar with a wider range of animals.	Explaining how to create a factfile card about animals in the UK and Ireland by using secondary sources of information.	Researching a particular animal using secondary sources. Wordsearch.	Children report their research to the class.	• Can use secondary sources to find specific information. • Can describe the eating habits of some animals found in the UK.
Lesson 14 What do they eat?	• To know that animals in certain world habitats eat certain foods. • To use secondary sources to answer questions.	Researching animals in world habitats using secondary sources.		Feeding back findings to the class.	• Can explain that animals in certain world habitats eat certain foods. • Can use secondary sources to research the answers to questions.
Lesson 15 Food chains	• To understand what is meant by a food chain. • To know what the terms 'producer' and 'consumer' mean.	Explanation of the concepts of food chains, producers and consumers.	Constructing food chains from information cards.	Reinforcing how food chains are represented with arrows.	• Can make a food chain with one link. • Can give examples of a producer and a consumer.
Lesson 16 Predators and prey	• To be able to construct food chains with two links. • To understand the terms 'predator' and 'prey'.	Reviewing ideas about food chains and identifying the prey and predator within examples of food chains.		Giving examples of prey and predators.	• Can construct food chains with two links. • Can explain the terms 'predator' and 'prey'.
Lesson 17 Food web	• To understand the terms 'carnivore' and 'herbivore'. • To understand that food chains are part of more complex food webs.	Explanation of the term 'food web'.	Constructing food webs from information on cards.	Discussing the complexity of food webs. Using terms 'carnivore', 'herbivore' and 'omnivore'.	• Can explain the terms 'carnivore' and 'herbivore'. Understand that food chains are part of more complex food webs.

Assessment	Objectives	Activity 1	Activity 2
Lesson 18	• To assess children's ability to group animals. • To assess children's understanding of food chains. • To assess children's understanding of habitats and how to study them. • To assess children's ability to interpret data in the form of tables.	Pencil and paper test assessing children's classification of plants and animals, their interpretation of data and understanding of the impact of humans on animal life.	Assessment of children's understanding of food webs and use of terms such as 'prey'.

SC1 SCIENTIFIC ENQUIRY

Minibeasts preference test

LEARNING OBJECTIVES AND OUTCOMES
- Plan an investigation.
- Check observations by repeating them.
- Ask questions that can be investigated.

ACTIVITY
After having a woodlouse choice chamber test modelled to them, children are asked to devise their own question about what conditions or foodstuffs a minibeast of their choice prefers. They plan and carry out the tests and are questioned about how reliable their test results are based on the number of animals they used or number of times they repeated it.

LESSON LINKS
This Sc1 activity forms an integral part of Lesson 11, Animal preferences.

Lesson 1 ▪ Living things

Objectives
- To elicit children's ideas about living things.
- To know that there is a wide variety of organisms on the planet.
- To know that living things are called organisms.

Vocabulary
animal, fungi, fungus, living, not living, organism, plant

RESOURCES
Group activity: A collection of living and non-living things for each group: a plant in a pot, the cut stem of a plant, a candle, a mushroom, a piece of wood, an apple, a stone, a crayon; pictures of a cat, a frog, a spider, a tree and a car.
Main activity: One collection of living things as described above; three hoops; card labels saying 'Living', 'Not living', 'Animal', 'Plant', 'Fungus'; flipchart and marker pens.

PREPARATION
Have the resources for the Main activity to hand. Put the collections for the Group activities on the tables.

BACKGROUND
Living things can be called organisms. Living things have the potential for growth, movement, feeding, respiration (using oxygen to get energy from food, which plants do as well as animals), excretion, sensitivity to stimuli (for example, a plant's response to light) and reproduction. It is not expected that the children should learn these as a list, but this will help inform your responses. Living things can be grouped into plants, animals, fungi and bacteria. At this stage children can focus on the groups of plants and animals, but can be introduced to the idea that fungi are a group on their own.

Children may use some of the characteristics to group items in a way that is not in line with the scientific definition of living, for example, they may group the car or the candle as living because they move and 'eat' petrol or wax. The apple may give rise to some discussion. It is living, because it contains seeds that are part of the life cycle of the apple tree.

Be aware that some children will not consider a tree to be a plant, as their idea of a plant may be that it is small, green and fleshy, not big and solid. Another common alternative idea is that only mammals are animals, so some children may incorrectly classify the spider and frog. The group discussion that will arise is the first way of questioning and challenging these ideas.

In this lesson, the Group activity comes first, as sorting the collection is important in orientating the children to the new topic and eliciting their existing ideas.

Differentiation
Have mixed-attainment groups to encourage cross-fertilisation of ideas. Where you identify ideas that are different from the scientific ones, intervene by questioning and explain the scientific view. Support children's recording in the Group activity by providing a wordbank with the names of the items in the collection. Extend children by asking them to pick out two items in the 'living' group and to list the things they have got in common.

STARTER

Explain that you are beginning a new topic and you want to find out what ideas the children already have to help you know what to teach them next. Explain that the topic is all about living things and the places that they live. Give the children several minutes to explore the collection generally before setting the task.

GROUP ACTIVITY

Ask the groups to each sort their collection into things they think are 'living' and things they think are 'not living'. (Do not use the term 'dead'.) Ask them to record how they have sorted them in their own way. If the children are using pictures to record, however, ensure that they draw quick sketches that will not take too long. Ask for a written response to the question: *How do you know these things are living?*

Observe how the children have made their decisions and ask: *What made you decide to put that object in the 'living' group? How do you know that object is not living?*

MAIN ACTIVITY

Bring the class to sit in a circle on the carpet. Have one of the collections in the centre. Choose a group to show the rest of the class how they sorted the collection, putting the items into the two labelled hoops. Ask: *Are there any items that other groups sorted differently?* Ask the children to explain the reasons for their choices. Encourage the children to discuss their ideas by asking: *Does anyone agree or disagree with that decision? Why?* Clarify ideas by explaining the reasons that scientists would use to decide which group they belong to.

Ask: *How do we know these things are living? What have they all got in common?* List the children's responses on the flipchart. Explain that all living things can be called 'organisms' and write the word on the flipchart. Put the non-living group to one side and ask: *Could we sort this 'living' group into smaller groups?* Let different children show the class how they would sort the collection. If it does not arise naturally, suggest that the collection could be sorted into 'plants' and 'animals'. At this point you may need to explain that the mushroom has a group of its own, and put it in the third hoop with the label 'fungi'. (You might also want to explain that 'fungus' is singular and 'fungi' plural.)

ASSESSMENT

Have the children sorted the collection according to the scientific classification? Can they give examples of how we know something is alive? (For example, it feeds or it moves.) Can they give examples of plants and animals?

PLENARY

Ask: *Can you give me an example of an organism?* Ask several children for their suggestions. Ask: *Can you explain how we know if something is living or not? Can you give me some examples of plants and animals?* Encourage a diverse range of responses by praising unusual contributions.

OUTCOMES

● Teacher is aware of children's existing ideas about living things.
● Can give examples of a wide variety of organisms.
● Can understand the term 'organism'.

LINKS

Maths: sorting and grouping.

Lesson 2 ▪ Habitat challenge

Objectives
● To know what the term 'habitat' means.
● To identify a variety of local habitats.

Vocabulary
habitat, organism

RESOURCES
Main activity: Flipchart and marker pen, the page from the flipchart from Lesson 1 of the list of characteristics of living things.
Group activity: Clipboards, writing materials, digital cameras (optional).

PREPARATION
Have the materials for the Main activity ready and the children sitting on the floor in front of you.

BACKGROUND
A habitat is the place where an animal or plant lives. Each type of living thing is adapted to suit the habitat it lives in. There are several aspects to studying a habitat: the physical conditions of the habitat itself, the animals and plants that live there, and the relationships between the physical environment and the different living things. This includes considering how the organisms are suited to that particular habitat and the relationships between the different organisms, such as food chains.

STARTER
Return to the list compiled in the previous lesson of characteristics of living things and review it with the class.

MAIN ACTIVITY
Now turn to a new sheet of the flipchart and, as a class, brainstorm a list of things that organisms need to stay alive, for example, food, water, warmth, shelter, safety, air (oxygen). Ask: *Where do you get all the things you need to stay alive?* (From home, school and at the shops.) *Where do you think other living things might get everything they need?* Encourage children to give more specific answers by asking about certain animals: *Where does a spider/shark/blackbird/daisy get what it needs to stay alive?*

Explain that the place where an animal lives and gets everything it needs to stay alive is called its habitat. Give some examples of different main habitats and ask children to add to the list. Organisms might live in a pond, in the sea, in a wood, high on a mountain.

Explain that these are 'big' habitats, but that there are little ones where different things may live too, such as under a rotting log, in a crack in a wall, on the branch of a tree. Tell the children that you are going to go for a walk around the school grounds and do the 'habitat challenge' – see how many different habitats they can find. Remember to set boundaries for exploration and agree a signal for when to regroup.

GROUP ACTIVITY
Ask the children to work in pairs to list on their clipboard as many different habitats as they can find. They could also take a photograph of each habitat.

ASSESSMENT
Can the children find examples of different habitats? Can they give examples of what an organism gets from their habitat to keep them alive?

PLENARY
Back in the classroom, ask the pairs to feed back some of their ideas to the whole class. This could involve sharing photographs on the interactive whiteboard. Keep a list of the children's ideas on the flipchart. As a class, go through the list and identify those which are 'tiny' habitats, such as under a leaf, and larger habitats such as the hedge. Choose several of the habitats and ask: *What might live here?*

Differentiation
Pair children so that at least one of the two has good writing skills to facilitate recording. Expect some children to identify more obvious habitats and others to be very imaginative. Help children who are finding this difficult by encouraging them to imagine that they are an ant, a beetle, a bird, and think about what the school grounds would be like from their point of view.

OUTCOMES
● Can explain what the term 'habitat' means.
● Can identify a variety of local habitats.

LINKS
Citizenship - Environmental issues: an awareness that different animals live in specific habitats.

Lesson 3 ◗ Habitat investigators

Objectives
● To identify different physical aspects of habitats.
● To make observations and measurements of the physical conditions of two chosen habitats.

Vocabulary
dark, habitat, light, moisture, sheltered, temperature

RESOURCES ◉
Main activity: An electronic light sensor; an electronic temperature sensor, data-logging equipment or thermometers; the page of flipchart from Lesson 2, digital cameras.
Group activities: 1 Clipboards; copies of photocopiable page 55 (also 'Habitat investigators' (red), on the CD-ROM); writing materials. **2** Writing materials, sugar-paper books (see Group activity 2).
ICT link: PowerPoint, or other presentation software; digital camera.

PREPARATION
Copy photocopiable page 55 for each group. Have card booklets made up so that the children can see the form in which their work will be presented.

BACKGROUND
In this series of lessons, the children will study and compare two easily accessible habitats.

The range of measuring equipment used will depend on what is available in each school, but this is an excellent opportunity to use data-logging equipment and electronic sensors to measure temperature and light levels.

Photographs provide a good record and means of communicating ideas about the habitats as they can be presented in the book with captions. Constraints on resources may mean that some groups use equipment such as thermometers or devise scales of their own (see Main activity).

STARTER
Return to the flipchart from Lesson 2 and ask: *What do we mean by the word 'habitat'?* (It is a place where an organism lives.) Explain that in this unit the children are going to find out as much as they can about two habitats in the school grounds.

MAIN ACTIVITY
Ask: *What might we notice or measure about the different habitats?* You may need to provide some examples to stimulate ideas (such as how dark or light it is, how damp or dry, how warm or cold, how windy, how sheltered or open, how low or high above the ground).

Demonstrate how to use the measuring equipment and digital camera. This will vary according to the precise equipment being used. (See Unit 4C, Lesson 2 for a specific lesson on learning to use a thermometer.) As equipment is likely to be limited, explain that the different groups will take turns. Where specific measuring equipment is not available, the children could devise a scale, for example 0 = complete shade, 5 = full sunshine, so that they are beginning to quantify their observations.

GROUP ACTIVITIES
1. Ask each group to choose two different habitats within the school grounds to study. Each group needs to gather information about their two chosen habitats. Photocopiable page 55 may be used to support this

process. It is also a good idea to take some photographs of the habitats. Circulate, ensuring that the measuring equipment is fairly shared and helping the children to use it. It may be best to move around with any particularly vulnerable equipment if this is the children's first experience with it. Ask questions such as: *Do you think the temperature will be the same all day? What might cause changes in the amount of light? Do all parts of your habitat have the same amount of shelter?*

2. Each group can then decide how best to present the information in a book. This might include mounted pictures and photographs with captions, questions and answers in speech bubbles. So page 1 might begin: 'What is it like in the hedge?' and continue with a description, photos and measurements. Page 2 might begin: 'What lives in a flower bed?', which could be added to the book as a result of Lesson 6.

ICT LINK
Children could present their work using PowerPoint and include digital photographs.

ASSESSMENT
Can the children describe physical aspects of their chosen habitat? Can they make measurements of some of these aspects? How accurate are their measurements? Can they begin to make suggestions as to how the physical aspects of the habitat may have an impact on the organisms that live there?

PLENARY
Ask the groups to feed back to the class what they have found out about one of their habitats. Encourage them to think about how the physical conditions might affect living things by asking questions such as: *How might the wind affect the plants that grow there? What do you think the shelter does for the plants and animals that live there? What sorts of living things might be suited to living in your habitat? Did one habitat have more light than the other? Will this affect the things that can grow there?*

OUTCOMES
● Can identify different physical aspects of habitats.
● Can make observations and measurements of the physical conditions of two chosen habitats.

LINKS
Maths: measurement.
Citizenship: environmental awareness.
Literacy: recording information.
ICT: digital photography, PowerPoint presentation.

ENRICHMENT
Lesson 4 ◗ Water skeletons

RESOURCES
Snails, worms and slugs in transparent containers; long balloons filled with water; hanging masses, trays, writing materials.

MAIN ACTIVITY
The purpose of this lesson is to introduce the children to some of the variety in the biology of different 'minibeasts'. Some invertebrates (animals without backbones) have a hydrostatic, or 'water skeleton' instead of bones or a hard outer shell (exoskeleton). Review the children's ideas about skeletons from Unit 4A 'Moving and growing'. Ask the children if they can think of any animals that might not have bony skeletons (jellyfish, spiders, ants, worms

Differentiation
Support children by providing a bank of key words. Expect some children to offer more sophisticated explanations of how the water skeleton works.

and so on). Explain that today they are going to focus on certain groups of animals without backbones: worms, slugs and snails. Give the children time to observe the animals. Ask them to think about how they move and what they might have instead of a bony skeleton. Discuss the children's ideas. Introduce the idea that these animals have a 'water skeleton'. Demonstrate how a balloon can be given a firm structure by filling it with water.

Give the children time to feel the water-filled balloons and to try putting masses (weights) on them to show how water skeletons can support them. Ask the children: *Why do you think the snail has a shell too? Discuss their ideas.* Ask the children to record their ideas about worms, slugs and snails as annotated drawings. Then release the creatures where they were found.

ASSESSMENT
Can the children describe how a worm keeps its shape? Can they name some other animals that have a water skeleton?

PLENARY
Ask the children: *Could humans have a water skeleton?* Discuss the limitations of a water skeleton: no joints, small range of movement, size and shape. *Which animals take advantage of the lack of protection?* (Birds.)

OUTCOMES
● Can describe how water is used as a skeleton in some animals.

Lesson 5 ▪ Minibeasts

Objectives
● To know how to collect animals sensitively.
● To observe carefully.
● To know that some invertebrates have soft bodies and some have a skeleton on the outside.

Vocabulary
ant, beetle, caterpillar, centipede, insect, millipede, 'outside skeleton', slug, snail, spider, worm.

RESOURCES ◉
Main activity: A pooter, a paintbrush, a transparent container.
Group activities: 1. Transparent collecting containers, pooters, paintbrushes, hand lenses or other magnifiers, drawing and writing materials, digital microscope. **2.** Copies of photocopiable page 56 (also 'Minibeasts - 1' (red), on the CD-ROM) and 57 (also 'Minibeasts - 2' (red), on the CD-ROM), several dice (optional).

PREPARATION
Have the resources for the Main activity to hand. Put the resources for the Group activities on the tables.

BACKGROUND
In Lesson 4, the children explored animals with 'hydrostatic' or water skeletons. In this lesson they will be introduced to the idea that other invertebrates, such as spiders, millipedes and beetles, have an 'exoskeleton' - an 'outside skeleton'. The exoskeleton has joints. The children don not need to use the technical vocabulary - 'water' and 'outside' skeleton are sufficient at this stage. However, they may enjoy the way in which the prefixes change the meaning. An internal skeleton of bones is known as an 'endoskeleton'.

STARTER
Ask: *What do we have that supports us and helps us to keep our shape?* (We have a skeleton.) *What is our skeleton made of?* (Our skeleton is made of bones.) *Ask: How do worms keep their shape?* (Worms have a water skeleton.) Tell the children that we divide animals into two groups: those with and those without a backbone. Ask: *Do slugs have a backbone?* (No, slugs have a water skeleton.) *What about beetles, do you think they have a backbone? How do you think beetles keep their shape?* Allow the children to express their ideas and make suggestions.

MAIN ACTIVITY

Introduce the idea that a beetle has a skeleton on the outside. It has a hard 'crunchy skin'. Explain that the class is going to collect some animals and look at them carefully to think about the kind of skeleton that they have.

Demonstrate how to use a pooter or the tip of a paintbrush to collect small creatures without damaging them. Discuss with the class how they should treat animals with respect. Set your expectations of behaviour and boundaries for where they can go to collect.

GROUP ACTIVITIES

1. Ask the children to collect one or two animals per group and return to the classroom to study them. Ask them to draw their animal carefully, using magnifiers to look at details. Some children could use the digital microscope for a more detailed look. They can then write down any observations they have made, such as the colour, type of 'skin' and number of segments. Ask them to record the kind of skeleton they think their animal has. Release the animals close to where they were found.
2. Give the children a copy each of photocopiable page 56 which asks them to give descriptions of the pictures of animals using the word bank provided. An alternative or additional activity is for the children to play a game of 'Beetle' using photocopiable page 57.

ASSESSMENT

Do the children treat the animals with respect? Do they refer to the type of skeleton in their descriptions? Are the drawings good representations?

PLENARY

Bring the class together and share any images collected on the digital microscope and/or use it to look closely at the segments and joints of different animals. Write the names of the different animals that have been collected on cards and stick them to the board. Ask the class: *Which of these animals could be grouped together?* Move the cards according to the children's suggestions. Make sure that one of the groupings is according to the kind of skeleton the animals have. Ask: *Can you tell me some of the ways in which animals support their bodies?* (Some animals have a bone skeleton, some have a water skeleton, some have an outside skeleton.)

OUTCOMES
● Can observe closely.
● Can collect animals with respect for life.
● Can group a collection of invertebrates according to observable features.
● Can explain that there are different types of skeleton.

LINKS
Art: observational drawing.

Lesson 6 ◗ Collecting animals

Objectives
● To investigate the animals found in a particular habitat.
● To learn why animals are found in a certain habitat.
● To be able to choose appropriate equipment to collect an animal.
● To learn to collect animals carefully.

RESOURCES 💿
Main activity: A pooter, a paintbrush, a flipchart and marker pen or interactive whiteboard.
Group activities: 1. Photocopiable page 58 (also 'Collecting animals - 1' (red), on the CD-ROM); pooters, paintbrushes, nets; collecting pots, preferably transparent with magnifying lids; magnifiers; white scrap paper; books or keys for identifying 'minibeasts'; a range of drawing materials, digital camera, digital microscope (optional). **2.** Photocopiable page 59 (also 'Collecting animals - 2' (red), on the CD-ROM), writing materials.

Vocabulary
ant, aphid, beetle, butterfly, caterpillar, fly, ladybird, magnifier, millipede, moth, pooter, slug, snail, spider, woodlice, woodlouse

PREPARATION
Have the resources for the Main activity and Group activities to hand.

BACKGROUND
It is important that during this activity the children have a proper regard for the animals they collect, so that they do so sensitively and without damaging them. A paintbrush can be used to lift small creatures, and a pooter can be used to collect even smaller ones. The children themselves should return the animals to where they found them.

Drawing helps to focus observation and should be done with good quality materials, such as a range of pencils. The photocopiable page will structure note-taking, but is not intended to provide the end product which will be the book or PowerPoint presentation group started in Lesson 3.

STARTER
Ask the children to think about their two habitats and predict what different animals they might find there. This provides an opportunity to remind individuals that insects, birds, and so on are all animals. Ask: *Why do you think you will find (snails) there?* (There is food for them; they have somewhere to hide from birds; they have been seen there before.)

MAIN ACTIVITY
Remind the children that if they are going to investigate animals it is important that they think about how they will treat the animals. Ask: *Can you tell me some things we should do, and some things we should not when we look at animals?* On the flipchart or interactive whiteboard compile a list of 'Dos' and 'Don'ts'.

Show children again how to use a pooter and a paintbrush to pick up a small animal without touching it. Demonstrate how to sweep a net across a pond, hold the neck closed and shake the contents gently into a container.

Explain that first the children should observe the habitat and make notes about any animals they see there, and then each child can choose one animal to bring inside to observe carefully and draw.

GROUP ACTIVITIES
1. Give each child a copy of photocopiable page 58. Ask the children to make observations of their habitats and complete the list of animals they find before choosing an animal to collect and selecting suitable collecting equipment. The animals can be brought inside to draw carefully. Encourage the children to use the magnifying equipment for closer observation. Digital cameras and microscopes can also be used to take images that can be labelled. This leads to a different kind of focused observation, therefore children should ideally experience both drawing and photographing as a means of recording during the topic. When the animal cannot be easily recognised, direct children to the keys and books to identify them. Remember to return the animals to the places they were taken from.
2. Give the children a copy of photocopiable page 59 and ask them to illustrate their own version of 'Dos' and 'Don'ts' with a picture of children collecting and handling animals carefully using the equipment demonstrated. They may wish to add their own rules.

ASSESSMENT
Do the children show sensitivity in their treatment of the animals? Can they describe the animals found in their chosen habitat? Are their observational drawings reasonably accurate? Can they make suggestions about why the animals may live in that particular habitat?

PLENARY
Sit the children in a circle holding their drawings. Ask a few children to

Children who have difficulty recording in writing can make quick sketches of the animals instead of listing them in words. They could also use 'Collecting animals - 1' (green), from the CD-ROM, a simplified version of the core sheet. You can also support children by asking questions such as: *How many legs has it got? Can you see any wings? Can you describe its head? How does it move?* Some children could be extended by using magnifiers to do detailed observational drawing of particular parts of the animal.

describe their animals. Ask: *Why do you think you found a (snail) there? Where else might you find (snails)? What might that habitat give them that they need to stay alive? How is the animal suited to live in that habitat?*

Play 'Silly habitats' – take it in turns to suggest an animal and an unlikely habitat, for example: *'I know a fish that lives in a tree!' 'I know a lion that lives in a pond!'* and so on.

OUTCOMES
- Can collect animals carefully without damaging them.
- Can investigate the animals found in a particular habitat.
- Can choose appropriate equipment to collect an animal.
- Can suggest reasons why animals are found in a certain habitat.

LINKS
Environmental issues: respect for other living things.
Art: observational drawing.
ICT: making a PowerPoint presentation.

Lesson 7 ▸ Classifying living things

Objectives
- To elicit children's existing understanding of groups of living things.
- To observe features of living things.
- To group living things according to observable features.
- To understand that a wide range of living things can be classified as animals or as plants.

Vocabulary
animal, group, plant, sort

RESOURCES
Main activity: A collection of photographs of living things with the name of the organism written clearly on the back (include a range of plants such as a small flowering plant, a fruiting deciduous tree such as an apple tree, a fruiting bush such as a blackberry; corn or grass, a vegetable plant, a fir tree, moss and a fern; and animals such as a snail, cow, spider, worm, snake, fish, bird, human), two labels of the words 'Plants' and 'Animals', two hoops.
Group activities: 1 Each group needs a set of photographs as above. (There are commercially produced photopacks or you can collect your own from magazines and the internet.) **2** Writing and drawing materials.

PREPARATION
Have the sets of photographs ready on the tables. It is a good idea to colour-codesets with a sticky label on the back in case they get mixed up. Have the card labels to hand.

BACKGROUND
Living things can be classified into 'kingdoms'. The two main kingdoms are plants and animals (fungi and bacteria are additional kingdoms). Children often have their own meanings for these categories. For example, they may not see a tree as a plant, because their understanding is that a plant is something smaller. In everyday language the word 'animal' is frequently used to mean mammal, so children may not consider fish, birds, and insects as animals. Sometimes children do not realise that humans are animals too.

This lesson is planned to find out what existing ideas the children have about classifying living things and to begin to develop and challenge these, so the Group activities come before the Main activity. Ideas about classification will continue to be developed throughout this unit.

STARTER
Hold up one photograph. Ask: *What can you tell me about this?* Accept all the children's ideas. Help them to focus on making careful observations by asking: *Can you describe the colours? What might it feel like?* Explain that you want them to look very carefully and thoughtfully at some photographs and to sort them into groups. Stress that there are no right answers and that they can group them as they choose.

Differentiation
Let the children work in mixed-attainment groups so that they support each other through discussion. Some children may need individual questioning to help them to make careful observations and to group the photographs. Ask: *What do you notice about this photograph? Is there another photograph that you would put with it? Why have you chosen that one?* Some groups may need support to resolve disputes – explain that scientists often disagree with each other, but need to listen and try out each other's ideas.

GROUP ACTIVITIES

1. Ask the children to take one photograph from the collection, look carefully at it and describe to the rest of their group what they observe. Then ask them to sort the collection of photographs into groups. Circulate, asking the groups to explain why they have grouped them as they have and encouraging them to find different ways of grouping them, for example, by colour, size, where they are found and so on.

2. Ask the children to record one of the ways they have sorted the collection in their own way.

MAIN ACTIVITY

Have the class sitting in a circle on the carpet. Put out the two hoops and spread all the photographs around them. Explain that you are going to focus on one particular way of grouping the photographs. Put the label 'plants' by one hoop and the label 'animals' by the other. Ask a child to choose a photograph to put in one of the hoops and to explain why they think it goes in that hoop. Continue, asking different children to do this, discussing reasons. You may need to introduce the idea that a snail, for example, is an animal and that a tree is a plant. Ask the children: *What have the animals got in common?* (For example, parts to help them move, parts to help them eat.) *What have the plants got in common?* (For example, green colour, they stay in one place.) If you have electronic versions of the photographs this could be done by dragging them into groups on the interactive whiteboard.

ASSESSMENT

Are the children able to explain how they have grouped the photographs? Can they correctly group the living things as plants or animals?

PLENARY

Ask the children to recap the different ways in which they sorted the photographs. Ask: *What did you need to do to sort them?* (Look carefully at each one.) Collect up all the photographs and go through them one at a time, at a fast pace, asking the children which hoop it should go into.

The collection of photographs sorted into plants and animals could be displayed on the wall as a record of the discussion and for the children to refer to.

OUTCOMES

- Can sort living things according to observable features.
- Can explain criteria used for grouping.
- Can recognise the diversity of living things within the classification of plants and animals.

LINKS

Maths: sorting and grouping.

Lesson 8 ▪ Comparing animals

RESOURCES ⊙

Main activity: A collection of photographs as in Lesson 7; card labels of 'Animals with backbones', 'Animals without backbones', 'Reptiles', 'Amphibians', 'Birds', 'Fish' and 'Mammals'; a picture of a skeleton showing a backbone (perhaps in a book); additional photographs of animals from each of the five vertebrate groups - mammals, birds, fish, amphibians, reptiles.
Group activities: 1 Sets of photographs for each group (as in Lesson 7); writing materials; the writing frame from photocopiable page 60 (optional; also 'Comparing animals - 1' (red), on the CD-ROM). **2** Photocopiable page 61

(also 'Comparing animals – 2' (red), on the CD-ROM), writing materials.
ICT link: 'Comparing animals' interactive on the CD-ROM.

PREPARATION
Remove the display of grouped pictures of animals and plants from Lesson 7 and put the photographs out on a table.

BACKGROUND
The animal kingdom is subdivided into animals with backbones (vertebrates) and animals without backbones (invertebrates). The vertebrates are subdivided again into mammals, birds, fish, amphibians and reptiles. Children can begin to become aware of these different groupings and how they help scientists to understand different animals.

Mammals are characterised by the fact that they give birth to live young rather than laying eggs, they suckle their young and are often hairy. Birds have feathers and wings and beaks. Fish have scales and can 'breathe' underwater. Amphibians, such as frogs, can live both in water and on land. Reptiles, such as lizards and snakes, have a scaly skin and mostly lay eggs; they breathe on land.

STARTER
With the children sitting in a circle ask them to think back to when they sorted all the photographs into animals and plants. Explain that you want to focus on animals again today, but when you took the display down all the photographs got muddled up. Ask: *Can you help me to pick out all the animals from the collection?* Briskly hold up each picture, allowing the children to call out 'animal' or 'plant'. Put the plants to one side and spread the animal photographs out in the middle of the circle.

MAIN ACTIVITY
Ask: *What can you tell me about bones?* Listen to the children's answers, clarifying them if necessary.

Ask different children to point to an animal they think does have bones, then one they think does not have bones. Ask one child to sort the picture collection into those with and without bones. Ask the other children if they agree, and intervene to correct the groups if needed. Put the labels 'Animals with backbones' and 'Animals without backbones' on the relevant groups.

Explain that scientists are particularly interested in whether or not animals have a backbone. Show the class a picture of a skeleton and point out the backbone. Ask them to feel their own backbones and then each other's. Explain that today you are going to concentrate on the animals with backbones, and put the group without backbones to one side. Ask the children if they can name any of the photographs - they may use the family name 'bird', for example, or give its common specific name, such as 'kingfisher'. Explain that at the moment you are interested in the family name. Focus on each group in turn, putting the card with the correct family name by the photograph(s). Ask the children to describe the animal there (for example: 'It has feathers/is scaly/lives in the water'). You may need to introduce the terms 'amphibian' and 'mammal', and add to the children's descriptions by asking: *Does this animal lay eggs? Where does it live?* This may well generate questions to which you and the class don't know the answer. Note them down and treat them as good starting points for research. Hold up the new photographs one by one and ask: *Which family does this belong to? How do you know that?*

Ask a child to choose two different photographs. Write the names of the two animals on the board or flipchart. Ask: *Can you tell me something that is different about the animals?* Write: 'They are different in that ...'. Then ask: *Can you tell me something that is the same?* Write: 'They both ...'. Explain that the children will all be looking for similarities and differences between

---

Objective
● To know that animals can be grouped according to whether or not they have a backbone.
● To recognise similarities and differences between groups of vertebrates.
● To compare and group items according to different criteria.

Vocabulary
amphibian, backbone, bird, fish, mammal, reptile

Differentiation

Group activity 1
Expect a different number of pairs of photographs to be compared according to the speed at which the children can work. Expect simple descriptions from some children and more sophisticated comparisons from others. Those with limited writing skills could record their comparisons on 'Comparing animals - 1' (green), which provides a word bank and allows children to include drawings to back up their writing.

Group activity 2
For children who need support, use 'Comparing animals - 2' (green), from the CD-ROM, which asks the children just to match the animals to their groups. To extend children, use 'Comparing animals - 2' (blue) which asks the children to research which group other animals belong to and to explain why.

the animals in their group work, and recording it in the way you have just demonstrated.

GROUP ACTIVITIES

1. Ask the children to work in pairs. They should choose two photographs and record similarities and differences in the way that you showed them. Photocopiable page 60 provides a writing frame.

2. Distribute copies of photocopiable page 61 and ask the children to identify which groups each of the animals belongs to and explain why, then to draw an animal with a backbone. The children can work individually or in twos and threes.

ICT LINK

Children could use 'Comparing animals' interactive on the CD-ROM. This activity requires them to match the animal with the correct group.

ASSESSMENT

Can the children give examples of some animals that have backbones and some that do not? Can they describe similarities and differences between different animals? Can they describe the main features of each vertebrate group?

PLENARY

Ask pairs of children to hold up the photographs they compared and tell the class the similarities and differences they noted. Ask them to say which of the five groups their animals belong to. Ask the class to describe distinctive features of fish, reptiles, amphibians, birds and mammals. The set of pictures can be returned to the wall display with the new sub-groups shown.

OUTCOMES

● Can explain that animals can be grouped into those with and without backbones.
● Can recall the five different groups of animals with backbones.
● Can describe features that characterise members of the five groups.

LINKS

Maths: sorting and grouping.

Lesson 9 ▪ Identification keys

Objectives
● To know how to use a simple key to identify vertebrates and plants.
● To carry out observations outside the classroom.

RESOURCES

A local park or similar space; a simple key on local birds that requires children to match the bird with a picture and short description; sandwich bags for collecting plant material; adult helpers. (It is a good idea to visit the area in advance and to prepare a key that matches the range of birds that are actually found there.)

MAIN ACTIVITY

Review the classification system so far understood – from animals to animals with backbones, to birds and so on, and explain that the next step is to identify particular sorts of birds.

Explain how to use the key, and that features such as colour, beak shape and size are important indicators.

Visit the local park or suitable outdoor space. Ask the children to sit quietly and identify the birds that they see using the key. Gather the class and review which birds have been spotted. Ask whether any were difficult to identify.

Differentiation
The keys can be differentiated by changing the number of birds. Adult support can be provided for children needing extra guidance.

Give out the bags. Ask the children to collect six different sorts of plants within a group, for example, leaves from different trees or flowers from different grasses, that they will use to make their own key later. Give clear guidance on any plants that are *not* to be collected.

Back in the classroom, the children can tape their specimens to a piece of paper and write a brief description (the shape if there are seeds or flowers, the number of leaves/petals and how they are arranged). If the name is known then that can be included, but it is not essential – children could make up their own names.

ASSESSMENT
Can the children use keys to correctly identify birds? Can they construct their own simple key?

PLENARY
Children present their keys to the class. If you have access to a colour photocopier, a permanent record can be made by putting the paper with samples directly on to the copier. Digital cameras could also be used to record findings.

OUTCOMES
● Can use a key to identify local animals.
● Can construct a simple key to identify local plants.

Lesson 10 ● Decision tree

Objective
● To know how a decision tree key can be used to classify and identify animals.

RESOURCES
Starter: A decision tree copied on to a board or flipchart, as shown on the left, but modified to fit photographs from the collection used in Lesson 7.
Main activity: Three cards with 'Yes' written on and three cards with 'No' written on; thin strips of card to represent lines; enlarged pictures from photocopiable page 62 (also 'Decision tree - 1' (red), on the CD-ROM).
Group activity: Copies of photocopiable page 63 (also 'Decision tree - 2' (red), on the CD-ROM).
ICT link: 'Decision tree' interactive and diagram from the CD-ROM.

PREPARATION
Enlarge the pictures from photocopiable 62 onto card. Have the children sitting in a circle, but able to see a flipchart. Have the resources for the Starter and Main activity to hand.

BACKGROUND
Decision trees are fairly easy to use, but surprisingly difficult to construct, so, in this lesson, the process of making a decision tree is done as a whole class and then the children use it to identify animals.

STARTER
Show the children the decision tree on the flipchart or whiteboard. Say that you are thinking of an animal, for example: a snake, a fox, a sardine or a jellyfish, and they have to work out which one, using the decision tree. Tell the class to read out the first question: 'Does it have a backbone?' and answer 'Yes' or 'No'. Continue in the same way until they have identified the animal you were thinking of. Repeat this so that the children understand the structure. Ask one of the children to think of an animal and repeat it again.

MAIN ACTIVITY
Put the pictures of the worm, the beetle, the spider and the slug from

Differentiation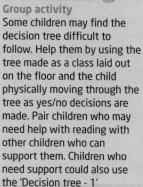
Group activity
Some children may find the decision tree difficult to follow. Help them by using the tree made as a class laid out on the floor and the child physically moving through the tree as yes/no decisions are made. Pair children who may need help with reading with other children who can support them. Children who need support could also use the 'Decision tree - 1' interactive (see ICT link).

Extend children by asking them to make their own decision trees using the 'Decision tree - 2' interactive (see ICT link). Alternatively, they could make a decision tree from scratch for four animals of their choice.

photocopiable page 62 out on the carpet or display them on the interactive whiteboard. Explain that you are going to make a decision tree together. Ask a child to sort the pictures into two groups. Ask: *What is the difference between those groups?* Ask the children if they can think of a question with a yes/no answer to separate the groups. (They may need you to do this at first.) Write the question on a card and put thin strips of card running to 'Yes' and 'No' cards. For each picture, ask the question and place it in the appropriate group. Go to the smallest group and together think of another question that could separate the animals. Write it on the card and represent the tree on the carpet with card strips as before. Repeat this process for the other group, until each animal is identified separately and the pictures are all laid out. Now pick up the pictures and ask a child to take one of them. Together move through the decision tree to identify the animal.

GROUP ACTIVITY
Give each pair of children the decision tree on photocopiable page 63. Ask them to work in pairs, with one child asking the questions and the other answering. They change over roles each time an animal has been identified.

ICT LINK
Children can use the 'Decision tree' interactive to add questions to a decision tree. This could be used as an extension activity, or at the end of the lesson as part of the plenary.

ASSESSMENT
Can the children successfully identify the animals using the decision tree? Can any construct their own decision tree?

PLENARY
Discuss each animal on photocopiable page 63 as a class to check that everyone agrees. Share any decision trees that children have designed themselves and test them as a class.

OUTCOME
● Can use a decision tree to identify invertebrates.

LINKS
Maths: data-handling.

Lesson 11 ▪ Animal preferences

Objective
● To know how to investigate the behaviour of an animal species.
● To understand the need for repeated tests.
● To pose their own questions for investigation.

Vocabulary
behaviour, choice, prefer, respond

RESOURCES
Main activity: A transparent container with one end containing dry sand and one end containing wet sand; a separate container of woodlice.
Group activities: 1 Containers such as ice-cream tubs; card and sticky tape; water, soil or sand; a range of foodstuffs, for example apple or lettuce; a range of 'smells', for example peppermint, vanilla essence, lavender oil (diluted with water, as undiluted essential oils could damage children's skin), antiseptic liquid (for example Dettol diluted with water); cotton buds. **2** Writing materials.

PREPARATION
Have the resources for the Group activities prepared, but keep them to one side where the children can collect them. Have the resources for the Main activity to hand.

BACKGROUND

Investigating living things has particular issues associated with it. For
ethical reasons, the tests that can be done on animals must not involve
cruelty and should keep disturbance to the animal to a minimum. The tests
suggested here can be carried out quickly and the animals returned to their
natural environment at the end of the lesson.

STARTER

Revise the code of conduct for how to collect and treat animals, reminding
the children that they should be treated with respect.

MAIN ACTIVITY

Show the children the container with wet and dry sand. Explain that you are
investigating: 'Do woodlice prefer wet or dry conditions?' Write this question
on the board or flipchart. Put one woodlouse into the container and ask the
children to observe it. Ask: *What do you notice about it?*

When the woodlouse has made some movement, perhaps to the dry sand,
ask: *Can we say that woodlice prefer dry conditions from this test?* (No, it
may be chance that the woodlouse went to one end; other woodlice may
behave differently.) Ask: *How could we improve this test so that we can be
more sure of our results?* (Try it with more woodlice and observe over a
longer period of time to see if they stay in one area.)

Explain that the children will be able to carry out their own tests of this
kind on animals that they collect. Give the children some examples of other
preference tests they could try, such as sorts of food or whether dark or
light is preferred. Suggest that they might like to try out some of their ideas
about their chosen habitats from Lesson 2. For example, if they think there
are snails there because they like the grass, they could try putting grass and
some other sorts of leaves in and see which the snails prefer.

GROUP ACTIVITIES

1. Small groups collect animals and bring them back to the classroom. The
groups set up and carry out their tests. Ask the children to record their
results as follows:
Our question:
Drawing of our test:
What we found out:
2. Ask the children to choose an animal to write about 'A Day in the Life of...'
from the animal's point of view, for example, 'My name is Sammy Snail.
When I woke up this morning I felt hungry, so I set off to find a leaf to
munch. On the way...'

ASSESSMENT

Can the children carry out an investigation into animal behaviour? Can they
give a reason for repeating the test or having more than one animal? Have
they put the focus for their investigation in the form of a question?

PLENARY

Ask each group what their question was, then ask: *What was the answer to
your question?* Some groups may not have reached a definite answer, and
may need reassurance that this is a normal part of the process of science.

OUTCOMES

- Can investigate the behaviour of an animal species.
- Can explain the need for repeated tests.
- Can put ideas for an investigation in the form of a question.

LINKS

PSHE: ethics of using animals in scientific tests.

ENRICHMENT
Lesson 12 ▸ Bird behaviour

Objectives
● To know how to investigate the behaviour of birds.
● To make observations for a sustained period of time.

RESOURCES
An area where birds can be observed, such as a local park; clipboards and writing materials; an identification guide to common birds (optional); prepared observation sheets like the one below (one for each child and some spares, plus an enlarged copy to use in the Main activity).

Name of bird:

Behaviour	How often
feeding	
preening	
singing	
flying	

There are some spaces for your own ideas.

MAIN ACTIVITY
Review the ways used to explore the behaviour of small animals. Ask: *Could we use the same approach to finding out about birds?* (No, it would be cruel and impractical: it is better to observe birds in their natural environment.) Ask: *How could we find out about bird behaviour?* (Observe and make notes.) Explain that one way of being more focused is to decide in advance what the bird might be doing and have a list to tick as we watch.

Show the children the enlarged recording sheet and explain how it is to be used. Explain the meaning of terms such as 'preening'. The blank spaces are for the children's own ideas. Discuss the need to be very quiet and still and to have good concentration. Children go outside and observe a bird for up to 10 minutes. If the bird flies away another sheet can be started.

ASSESSMENT
Are the children able to make sustained observations? Is their own behaviour conducive to making observations? Can they explain why they have taken this approach to investigating bird behaviour?

Differentiation
Some children will benefit from sitting near and observing alongside the teacher. More confident children could be shown how to use tally marks instead of ticks on the record sheet.

PLENARY
The children can feed back to the class the most common behaviours they observed. Discuss what they have seen.

OUTCOMES
● Can explain how to investigate the behaviour of birds.
● Can make observations for a sustained period of time.

Lesson 13 ▸ Animals

Objectives
● To know that animals eat certain foods in a habitat.
● To use secondary sources to find information.
● To become familiar with a wider range of animals..

Vocabulary
See lists of animals in Preparation section.

RESOURCES 💿
Main activity: An A5-sized ring binder, 'factfile' headings written on a flipchart.
Group activities: 1 A range of books and resources about animals in local habitats; relevant CD-ROMs; 'factfile' pages made from photocopiable page 64 (also 'Animals – 1' (red), on the CD-ROM), writing materials. **2** Photocopiable page 65 (also 'Animals – 2' (red), on the CD-ROM), writing materials.
ICT link: 'Animals' interactive from the CD-ROM.

PREPARATION
Make the factfile pages by copying photocopiable page 64 onto card, cutting in half and hole-punching. Put some of the cards into the ring binder and put the rest on the tables for the Group activities. Write the headings of the factfile cards on the board or flipchart for the Main activity. The following

For children who need support, use 'Animals - 1' (green) from the CD-ROM, which asks them to find fewer facts. The animal lists have been ordered from more difficult to easier on the basis of familiarity. However, the main means of differentiation is the matching of the level of text difficulty with the reading level of the children in each group. Some children may need you to identify a particular text and animal that they have responsibility for researching. Other children could gather information from several sources and draw it together and compare it. Some children may research more than one animal; others could be invited to make an index or design a cover for the file.

are possible lists of animals:
- dragonfly, frog, minnow, newt, otter, pike
- grasshopper, ladybird, slug, snail, spider, woodlouse
- adder, hare, kestrel, slow-worm, squirrel, weasel
- bat, fieldmouse, grass snake, shrew, toad, vole
- blackbird, blue tit, cuckoo, robin, sparrow, thrush
- badger, fox, hedgehog, mole, owl, rabbit.

These lists need to be checked against available resources, and written on cards for each table. Put the relevant secondary sources on the table with the appropriate list. Identify any texts particularly suitable for strong readers/those who need support with reading and put them near the children they will be best matched to.

BACKGROUND
It is important that the use of secondary sources is focused so that children process information rather than merely repeat it. The lesson described here could be integrated into a Literacy Hour (in England and Wales) if the learning objectives are appropriate, or attention could be drawn to skills learned in the Literacy Hour that could be applied in the science lesson. Preparation in matching secondary sources to the children's reading level will be required, but this will ensure that children do not become frustrated during the lesson and that they have a positive experience of using information texts.

Children are often very enthusiastic about miniature factfiles, and this activity gives them the chance to make their own.

STARTER
Show the children the folder for the factfile and explain that they are each going to make a page on a particular animal. If any children have factfiles of their own, they could show them to the class.

MAIN ACTIVITY
Look at the layout of the factfile card. Explain that the children will first need to find out information by using the secondary sources and making notes, then they will carefully write the information on to the factfile card. If appropriate, revise skimming and scanning a text for information and the use of contents and index pages with one example such as the rabbit.

Explain that each table will have a selection of animals to choose from to make sure that the same animal is not researched twice.

GROUP ACTIVITIES
1. Ask the children to make notes on scrap paper as they find the answers to the questions and any interesting facts. Encourage skimming to identify the food and habitat, and then more careful reading for interesting information.

Once the information has been gathered it can be written onto the factfile (in sentences) and lastly, a picture of the animal can be drawn in the box.

2. The wordsearch on photocopiable page 65 may be useful as an independent activity, releasing you to support particular groups in their research.

ICT LINK
Display 'Animals' interactive on an interactive whiteboard and complete as a whole-class activity.

ASSESSMENT
Can the children use the secondary sources to locate information about their animal? Can they describe the eating habits of their chosen animal?

PLENARY

Ask each child to briefly report back to the class what they have discovered about their chosen animal. Put their card into the factfile as they report. The factfile can be made available for individual reading and may be drawn upon in subsequent lessons.

OUTCOMES
● Can use secondary sources to find specific information.
● Can describe the eating habits of some animals found in the UK.

Lesson 14 ▶ What do they eat?

Objectives
● To know that animals in certain world habitats eat certain foods.
● To use secondary sources to answer questions.

RESOURCES

A range of secondary sources: books, CD-ROMs and so on; writing materials.

MAIN ACTIVITY

Explain that in this lesson the children will be learning about animals anywhere in the world.

Draw three columns on the flipchart and put the headings: 'What I already know'; 'My question'; 'What I have found out' on the columns. Model the process by choosing an animal, for example the tiger, and asking the class: *What do you already know about tigers?* Write their response in the first column. Next ask: *What would you like to find out about tigers? What questions about tigers have you got?* Write these in the second column. Include 'What do tigers eat?' Model skimming and scanning to try to answer the questions. Explain that the children may not be able to answer all the questions, but should find the answers to those they can.

Ask the children to work in pairs or threes to list what they already know and raise questions. Ask the children to include 'What do they eat?', even if they think they already know. Each group researches their animal and records what they have found in the last column of the grid. This could be carried out as a group activity in a Literacy Hour to reduce the demand on resources.

ASSESSMENT

Can the children give examples of foods eaten by animals from around the world? Can they use secondary sources to try to answer their questions?

PLENARY

Ask the groups to feed back what they have found out about what the animals eat. Ask: *Why do you think different animals eat different food?*

OUTCOMES
● Can explain that animals in certain world habitats eat certain foods.
● Can use secondary sources to research the answers to questions.

Lesson 15 ▶ Food chains

Objectives
● To understand what is meant by a food chain.
● To know what the terms 'producer' and 'consumer' mean.

RESOURCES 💿

Main activity: A loaf of sliced bread; samples or pictures of flour, wheat and corn; flipchart and marker pens.
Group activities: 1 Writing materials; copies of photocopiable page 66 (also 'Food chains' (red), on the CD-ROM). **2** Musical instruments (optional).
ICT link: 'Food chains' interactive from the CD-ROM.
Plenary: Card labels saying 'Consumers' and 'Producers' and Blu-Tack®.

Vocabulary
consumer, food chain, producer

PREPARATION
Copy photocopiable page 66. Cut the slices of bread into quarters.

BACKGROUND
Some children may not yet have been introduced to the idea that plants make their own food, so they may find that there are some difficult concepts in this lesson. The idea that plants make their own food is introduced, but this does not require a discussion of photosynthesis. These ideas will be further developed in Year 6/Primary 7. Focus instead on the idea of the green plants being the first living thing in every food chain – they do not 'eat' anything. This lesson also introduces the idea that plants get their energy from the Sun, relating this to previous work on plant growth when the children became aware of a plant's need for light. The terms 'food chain', 'producer' and 'consumer' are introduced. All green plants are producers, because they make their own food by photosynthesis. Other living things get their energy by eating other living things, so they are called consumers.

This lesson draws together a great deal of prior knowledge and children will vary in their understanding about what different foods are made from and how they are produced. Discussing experiences of cooking can help them relate the ingredients to the end product.

STARTER
Give each child a piece of bread to eat. As they eat it ask them to think about where their food comes from. (Be aware of and sensitive to children with specific dietary needs, such as coeliacs needing gluten-free bread.)

MAIN ACTIVITY
Ask: *Where do we (humans) get our energy from?* (We get energy from our food.) *What different things do we eat?* List children's suggestions on the flipchart. Take one of the suggestions and trace it backwards along its food chain until you reach a green plant (for example: hamburger, cow, grass). Record this on the board as you go along. (Do not show arrows at this stage as this may cause confusion when proper food chains are constructed.) To help children understand the processes in food production show them samples of flour, wheat and corn as these are mentioned.

Ask: *What does a chicken eat to get its energy?* (It eats corn or wheat.) *Does the wheat eat anything to get energy?* (No, wheat gets its energy from the Sun and makes its own food.) Ask: *What is cheese made from?* (Cheese is made from milk.) *Where does the milk come from?* (Milk comes from a cow, or a sheep or a goat.) *What does the cow eat to get its energy?* (A cow eats grass.) *Does the grass eat anything to get its energy?* (No, grass gets its energy from the Sun and makes its own food.) Repeat this for various different foods.

Go down the list and ask: *What is at the beginning of this chain?* Draw a circle around each of the producers. Ask: *What have these got in common?* (They are all plants.) Explain that following the food as it goes from plants into animals and then into other animals is called a 'food chain'. Draw a food chain on the board in the form: corn ➤ chicken ➤ human. Ask: Which direction are the arrows going in? Explain that they always go that way because they are showing the journey of the energy in the food.

GROUP ACTIVITIES
1. Give the children the information cards (photocopiable page 66) and ask them to draw their own food chains using the information provided.
2. Ask groups to represent one of the food chains through drama. They could mime the different plants and animals or play a musical instrument for each organism, adding a new instrument as something eats it. The resulting composition will show how there is a part of each living thing within its consumer.

Differentiation
Work in groups where at least one child has good writing skills and can act as scribe for the group. Target texts for more- and less-confident readers appropriately. Expect some groups to answer only one or two questions at a basic level and others to have a range of detailed answers.

Differentiation
Group activity 1
For children who need support, use 'Food chains' (green) from the CD-ROM, which includes fewer animals than the core sheet. To extend children, give them 'Food chains' (blue), which asks them to carry out research to make the food chains longer.

ICT LINK
Children can use the 'Food chains' interactive from the CD-ROM to create a series of food chains on the computer.

ASSESSMENT
Can the children construct a simple food chain, using the arrows correctly? Can they give examples of producers and consumers?

PLENARY
Go through each card asking children to feed back their responses, showing on the flipchart the correct way to write the food chain. Write them one above the other. Ask children to add any that they have found from their own research.

Explain that the green plants are all known as producers because they produce their own food. Blu-Tack® the card with the word 'producers' on it above the list of green plants. Explain that the animals are all called consumers because they eat (or consume) the green plants. Blu-Tack® the card with 'consumers' written on it above the list of animals. Alternatively, use the interactive whiteboard activity to drag the labels to the animals, involving the children by inviting them to come up and move the labels.

OUTCOMES
- Can make a food chain with one link.
- Can give examples of a producer and a consumer.

LINKS
PSHE: choices about eating, animal welfare – how are animals reared commercially for food fed?

Lesson 16 ▪ Predators and prey

Objective
- To be able to construct food chains with two links.
- To understand the terms 'predator' and 'prey'.

RESOURCES
Writing materials; a set of pairs of cards for each group: 1. Foxes eat rabbits, Rabbits eat grass; 2. Common bats eat flies, Flies eat dead plants; 3. Hedgehogs eat slugs, Slugs eat plants; 4. Otters eat fish, Fish eat pond weed; 5. Badgers eat mice, Mice eat seeds; 6. Grass snakes eat frogs, Frogs eat flies.

MAIN ACTIVITY
Recap the previous lesson by looking at the flipchart from the Plenary and asking the children to give examples of a producer and a consumer. Explain that in this lesson they will be learning about more complicated food chains. Put the following example of a food chain on the board or flipchart: corn → vole → owl. Ask: *Which is the producer?* (The corn is the producer.) *Which are the consumers?* Explain that there are now two sets of consumers. Introduce the terms 'prey' and 'predator'.

Ask the children to write food chains using the six sets of cards as sources of information. Ask them to identify the prey and predator in each case and write 'predator' or 'prey' in brackets near the right animal. Remind them that the predator eats the prey, and to use arrows to show where the food is going.

ASSESSMENT
Can the children construct the food chains accurately from the information given? Can they correctly identify prey and predators?

PLENARY
Go through the examples of food chains on the cards, asking the children to identify the prey and predators in each case. Card 6 may give rise to interesting discussion as the frog is both prey and predator.

OUTCOMES
- Can construct food chains with two links.
- Can explain the terms 'predator' and 'prey'.

Lesson 17 ◗ Food web

Objectives
- To understand the terms 'carnivore' and 'herbivore'.
- To understand that food chains are part of more complex food webs.

Vocabulary
carnivore, food web, herbivore, omnivore

RESOURCES 💿
Group activity: Sets of cards from photocopiable page 67 (also 'Food web' (red) on the CD-ROM); sugar paper, pencils, glue, felt-tipped pens.
Plenary: Flipchart or board and marker pens.

PREPARATION
Copy photocopiable page 67 onto card and cut out the cards. Each group needs a set. (It helps prevent sets being muddled if each is copied on to different-coloured card. The sets could be laminated for future use.)

BACKGROUND
Food chains can be very complex, as many animals have more than one common source of food. In any habitat there will be complex food webs, rather than simple chains that show the feeding relationships between all the living things in a habitat. This lesson provides an important basis for understanding how all the elements of a habitat are interrelated so that later they will consider how changing one element will have an impact on all the others. The terms 'carnivore' (eats meat only), 'herbivore' (eats only plants) and 'omnivore' (eats a mixed diet) are introduced.

This lesson depends on the children's experiences in the Group activity, so the Main activity is short but the Plenary is long.

STARTER
Ask: *What do we mean by a food chain? Can anyone give us any examples of a food chain?* Ask a number of children to respond to get a good variety of living things.

MAIN ACTIVITY
Ask: *Are some animals eaten by more than one predator? What different living things eat slugs?* (Birds, foxes, hedgehogs, badgers and so on.) *What different living things eat grass?* (Deer, rabbits, cows, sheep, and so on.) Explain that although food chains are a useful idea, the real picture is more complicated. Introduce the term 'food web' to describe the complicated links between the different feeding relationships. Explain that the task the children are going to do may seem frustrating at times, but this will help them to understand what is going on in a habitat and they should persevere.

GROUP ACTIVITY
As a collaborative Group activity, using the cards provided on photocopiable page 67, ask each group to work out the food web provided and represent it by showing arrows to link the food with what eats it. This is best done by spreading the cards out on sugar paper and drawing the links in pencil first, only gluing down the cards and marking the arrows in pen when the children are satisfied of the correct links. Suggest that all the cards that do not 'eat' anything (producers) are lined up across the bottom of the sugar paper.

Differentiation
Let the children work in mixed-attainment groups so that they can support each other.

ICT LINK
Children can use the 'Food web' interactive to classify living things as carnivores, omnivores, herbivores and producers.

ASSESSMENT
Can the children give examples where a living thing provides food for more than one consumer? Can they find examples of carnivores, herbivores and omnivores?

PLENARY
Ask the groups to show their sheets of sugar paper. Reassure them that there is more than one correct way of setting it out. Ask: *What made that activity difficult to do?* (It is complicated.) Us the interactive whiteboard activity to create the food web. Ask the children to pick out food chains within the web, for example, berries are eaten by mice, which are eaten by snakes, which are eaten by badgers.

Explain that some animals eat only plants – they are called herbivores; some animals eat only meat – they are called carnivores; and some animals eat a mixture of both – they are called omnivores. Write these terms on a board or flipchart.

Ask the children if they can pick out examples of each type using their food webs (for example, the fox and the grass snake are carnivores; the vole and the rabbit are herbivores; and the badger is an omnivore). *Can you think of any other examples from your general experience?* (For example, lions are carnivores; cows are herbivores.) Ask: *What are humans?* (Humans are omnivores.)

OUTCOMES
● Can explain the terms 'carnivore' and 'herbivore'.
● Understand that food chains are part of more complex food webs.

LINKS
Environmental issues: awareness of the dependence of animals on plants.

Lesson 18 ◗ Assessment

Objectives
● To assess children's understanding of the main groups of living things
● To assess children's understanding of food chains
● To assess children's understanding of habitats and how to study them.
● To assess children's ability to interpret data in the form of tables.

RESOURCES
Assessment activity 1: A copy of photocopiable page 68 (also 'Assessment – 1' (red), on the CD-ROM) for each child, scissors, blank paper, glue, writing materials.
Assessment activity 2: A copy of photocopiable page 69 (also 'Assessment – 2' (red), on the CD-ROM) for each child, writing materials.
Assessment activity 3: A copy of photocopiable page 70 (also 'Assessment – 3' (red), on the CD-ROM) for each child, writing materials.

PREPARATION
These assessment activities should be considered alongside the ongoing assessment opportunities indicated throughout the unit when making a judgment about which level a child is working at. If you are unsure what a child means by their response to a question then discuss it with them afterwards.

ASSESSMENT ACTIVITY 1
Give each child a copy of photocopiable page 68 and ask them to cut out the pictures. Tell them to look carefully at each animal and then to sort the animals into groups by thinking about what their bodies are like. You may want to give further help to less confident children by suggesting them to

look at the number of legs they have, or whether they have fur, scales or feathers. Explain that there is more than one way to do the task. Ask the children to glue down the pictures and label each group to explain how they sorted them.

LOOKING FOR LEVELS
Most children will be working at NC Level 3/Scottish Level C - they will have used observable features of the animals and clearly explain the criteria they have used for sorting them.

If they have used criteria based on personal experience, for example: I like these/I don't like these, or have used very broad criteria such as big/small, this indicates working at NC Level 2/Scottish Level B.

Children working at NC Level 4/Scottish Level C/D will show that they have applied their scientific knowledge and understanding of animals, for example by classifying the animals according to whether or not they have backbones or using the family groups. The correct classification would be: without backbone - snail, spider, ladybird, slug, worm, wasp; with backbone - rabbit, fox, elephant, baby (mammals), frog (amphibian), crocodile, snake (reptiles).

ASSESSMENT ACTIVITY 2
Give each child a copy of photocopiable page 69 to work through on their own.
Answers:
1. snails
2. ladybirds
3. 5
4. 3
5. accept sensible suggestions e.g. shelter, more food, less trampled.
6. accept sensible suggestions e.g. protection from birds, food plants grow there.
7. accept sensible suggestions e.g. Don't hurt the animals, put them back where you found them.

LOOKING FOR LEVELS
The majority of children would be expected to get questions 1 to 4 correct, achieving NC Level 3/Scottish Level C. Correct answers indicate a good understanding of data in tables and poor performance in these questions signals the need for more work on this. Questions 5 and 6 require some understanding of relationships in habitats and detailed responses indicate they are working at NC Level 4/Scottish Level C/D. Most children will be able to show a respect for living things. Some may take this further and relate it to food chains or wider environmental issues.

ASSESSMENT ACTIVITY 3
Work with a group of children at a time using photocopiable page 70. Ask them to work through the first question individually, then give them time to look at the food web. This part of the assessment should be completed as a whole-class discussion activity.

Ask the following questions and note the children's responses. Target questions at specific children rather than allowing more confident individuals to dominate. If you need to explain terms such as 'predator' then do so, noting when the concept is secure but the appropriate vocabulary is not yet being used. Repeat the questions with different animals to give different children the opportunity to respond.

What sort of diagram have you got in front of you? (food web - chain is acceptable but less accurate.)
What does the ... eat?
Name a predator of ...

Can you tell me one producer?
Can you tell me the name of one consumer?
Can you give me an example of a carnivore/herbivore?
Suppose all the nettles died – what would happen to the blue tits?

LOOKING FOR LEVELS

Most children should be able to distinguish between an animal and a plant; less confident children may find it difficult to differentiate between a plant and fungus.

For the questions about the food web, if the children can describe feeding relationships and recognise that food moves up the chain from green plants, but are not necessarily using the correct terminology then this indicates NC Level 3/Scottish Level C. Children working below this level may recognize that animals need to eat, but find it hard to understand links in the food chain that are not direct such as the relationship between the blue tit and the nettle. If they understand that there are complex relationships in the web and can use the terminology correctly then this indicates they are working at NC Level 4/Scottish Level C/D.

PLENARY

Assessment 1: Ask the children to show each other the different ways in which they grouped the animals and discuss these. Help the children to recognise the usefulness of the scientific classification by asking questions such as: *Will everyone know what you mean by big? What other things do these animals have in common?*

Assessment 2/3: Go through the test questions giving the correct answers. The children could self/peer mark questions with one correct answer. When necessary explain why an answer is correct. Ask the class as whole to give some other examples of food web relationships they have learned during the topic.

Ask the children to reflect on their learning during the topic. Have they changed any of their ideas? What helped them to learn more? Explain that scientists are always learning and that scientists need to keep changing their ideas too.

When going through the answers to the assessments, you may want to display the assessment worksheets on an interactive whiteboard to complete, using the tools provided, or discuss as a class.

Habitat investigators

◾ Collect information about your chosen habitats.

	Habitat 1	Habitat 2
Description (for example, recently mown grass on a playing field)		
Amount of light (for example, whether it is shaded or in the sun)		
Temperature (for example, how warm or cold it is)		
Moisture (for example, how damp or dry it is)		
Shelter (for example, whether it is in the wind or sheltered)		

◾ The last two rows are left blank for your own ideas.

Minibeasts – 1

◼ Use the word bank to help you describe the animals. Remember to write in sentences.

feelers segments shell legs eyes body wings pattern head stripes spots tail water skeleton outside skeleton one two three four five six seven eight

The ladybird has _____

_____

_____

The wasp has _____

_____

_____

The grasshopper has _____

_____

_____

The snail has _____

_____

_____

Minibeasts – 2

◼ Take turns to roll the dice. You must draw the body first so you need a 6 to start. Then add the other parts as you throw the right number. You can only put the feelers and eyes on when you have a head, and you need to have the right number to draw the part.

◼ The first person to draw a whole beetle shouts "Beetle!". Then you all stop and add up your total score for that game.

	Game 1	Game 2
1 each eye · 2 each feeler · 3 each leg · 5 head · 6 body · 4 tail · **Total 39**		
Game 3	Game 4	Game 5
Game 6	Game 7	Game 8

Collecting animals – 1

■ Investigate some animals in your chosen habitats.

	Habitat 1	Habitat 2
Animals I found there		
Animal I have chosen to collect		
Where exactly the animal was found (for example, on the stem of the bush in the hedge)		
Notes about the animal		
Drawing of the animal		

Collecting animals – 2

Do handle animals carefully so you don't damage them.

Do put them back where you found them.

Don't keep the animals too long.

Don't hurt them in any way.

Illustration © Theresa Tibbetts c/o Beehive Illustration

PHOTOCOPIABLE

Comparing animals – 1

My two animals are _____ and _____

They are different because _____

_____

_____

_____

_____

They are alike because they both _____

_____

_____

_____

_____

◀ SCHOLASTIC

Comparing animals – 2

| mammal bird fish reptile amphibian |

The python belongs in the _____ group

because _____

_____

The mouse belongs in the _____ group

because _____

_____

The duck belongs in the _____ group

because _____

_____

◀ Draw your own animal with a backbone and decide which group it belongs to.

The _____ belongs in the _____ group

because _____

Decision tree – 1

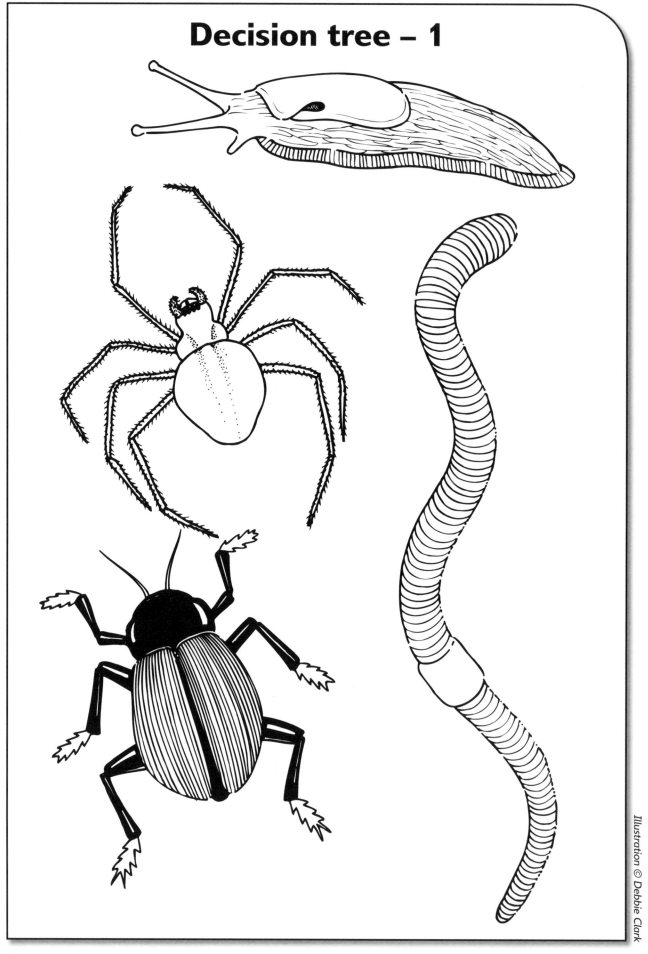

Illustration © Debbie Clark

▲SCHOLASTIC

Decision tree – 2

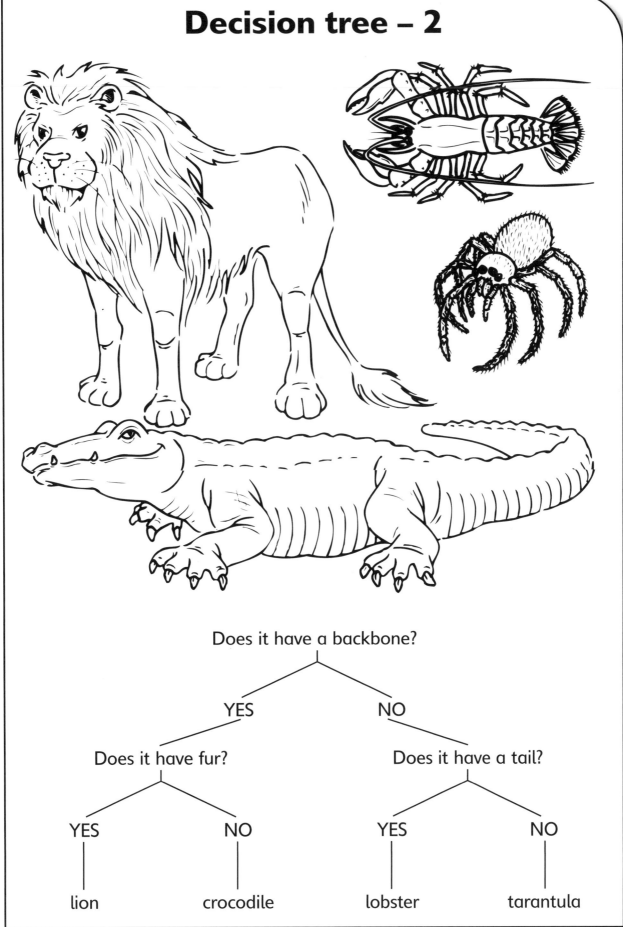

Does it have a backbone?

YES — NO

Does it have fur? — Does it have a tail?

YES — NO — YES — NO

lion — crocodile — lobster — tarantula

Illustration © Debbie Clark

PHOTOCOPIABLE

Animals – 1

Animal:

Where does it live?

What does it eat?

An interesting fact about this animal:

This page was compiled by:

Animal:

Where does it live?

What does it eat?

An interesting fact about this animal:

This page was compiled by:

◢◣ SCHOLASTIC

Animals – 2

◼ Find the names of these animals in the grid.

ant	earwig	mole	snail
badger	fly	moth	spider
bee	fox	mouse	squirrel
beetle	grasshopper	owl	woodlouse
bug	hawk	shrew	worm

E	A	R	W	I	G	W	Y	L	F	R	
G	R	A	S	S	H	O	P	P	E	R	
S	Y	F	O	X	Q	R	H	T	O	M	
Q	M	O	L	E	S	M	N	R	E	B	
U	B	E	E	X	H	A	A	E	S	E	
I	W	L	W	O	R	P	A	D	U	E	
R	B	A	D	G	E	R	N	I	O	T	
R	P	L	H	A	W	K	T	P	M	L	
E	W	O	O	D	L	O	U	S	E	E	
L	B	U	G	Z	L	I	A	N	S	X	

Illustration © Debbie Clark

Food chains

◾ Make a food chain with one arrow for each of these animals. The first one has been done for you.

Rabbits eat grass.

grass ⟶ rabbits

Bullfinches eat berries.

_____

Deer eat shoots from trees.

Red squirrels eat hazelnuts.

_____

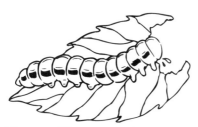

Caterpillars eat leaves.

Voles eat corn.

_____

Fish eat pondweed.

Slugs eat green plants.

_____

Illustration © Debbie Clark

◾ SCHOLASTIC

Food web

I am a fox.
I eat slugs, rabbits, hedgehogs, voles, frogs and snakes.

I am a grass snake. I eat fish and mice.

Green plants

I am a badger. I eat voles, frogs, hedgehogs, snakes and acorns.

I am a snail. I eat green plants.

Dead plants

I am a slug. I eat green plants.

I am a beetle. I eat dead plants.

Dead animals

I am a rabbit. I eat grass and other green plants.

I am an earthworm. I eat dead plants.

Grass

I am a hedgehog. I eat snails and worms and beetles.

I am a fly. I eat dead animals and plants.

Acorns

I am a vole. I eat beetles and flies.

I am a fish. I eat pond weed.

Berries
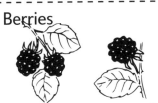

I am a frog. I eat flies, worms and slugs.

I am a mouse. I eat berries and seeds.

Seeds

Pondweed
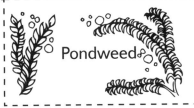

Illustration © Debbie Clark

PHOTOCOPIABLE

Assessment – 1

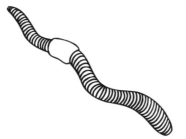

Cut out these pictures and put the animals into groups. Stick them down and write next to each group why those animals go together.

Illustrations Debbie Clark, Theresa Tibbetts c/o Beehive Illustration

SCHOLASTIC

Assessment – 2

◼ Gemma, Matthew and Sunita studied a wall and an area of concrete in their playground. They recorded their information in a table.

Animals	How many we found on the wall	How many we found on the concrete
snails	8	1
woodlice	6	2
ants	5	6
ladybirds	1	0
spiders	4	0

1. Which animals were there most of on the wall? _____

2. Which animals were there least of on the wall? _____

3. How many different sorts of animals did they find on the wall?____

4. How many different sorts of animals did they find on the concrete?

_____

5. Why do you think there were more different animals on the wall than on the concrete?

_____

6. The snails were found in the cracks in the wall. Why do you think they were there?

_____

7. The children decided to take some animals back into the classroom. Write down a rule they should follow when they collect the animals.

_____

Illustration © Debbie Clark

Assessment – 3

Tick the box ✓ to say whether the living thing is a plant, animal or a fungus.

	Plant	Animal	Fungus
oak tree			
owl			
mushroom			
ant			
human			
dandelion			
fox			
woodlouse			
toadstool			
moss			
grass			

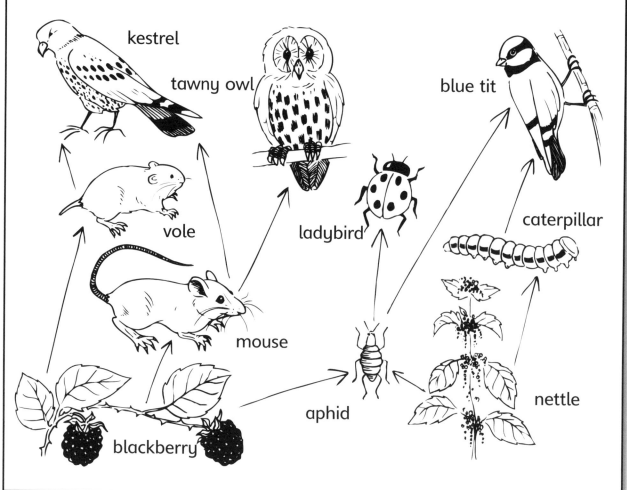

kestrel

tawny owl

blue tit

vole

ladybird

caterpillar

mouse

aphid

nettle

blackberry

Illustration © Debbie Clark

■ SCHOLASTIC

CHAPTER 3 Keeping warm

Lesson	Objectives	Main activity	Group activities	Plenary	Outcomes
Enrichment Lesson 1 What do we know about materials?	• To elicit children's existing understanding about materials. • To develop observation and sorting skills.	Exploring a collection of items and considering the materials they are made from and their uses.	Choosing items from the collection and describing them in detail.	Discussion about 'big ideas' that this unit focuses on.	• Teacher awareness of children's existing ideas about materials. • Can observe and sort a collection.
Lesson 2 Measuring temperature	• To know that the thermometer is an instrument for measuring temperature. • To measure temperature using standard units with an appropriate degree of accuracy.	Demonstration of how to measure temperature using a thermometer.	Measuring the temperature of different things. Reading temperatures from thermometer illustrations.	Discussion about the measurements taken and suggestions about the reasons for differences in temperature.	• Understand that temperature is a measure of hotness and coldness. • Realise that temperature can be measured using a thermometer. • Can read a thermometer with a reasonable amount of accuracy. • Can read a pictorial representation of a thermometer.
Lesson 3 Room temperatures	• To know that there are variations of temperature in a room. • To use thermometers in an investigation. • To describe and suggest explanations for findings.	Measuring the temperature in different parts of the room.		Suggesting reasons for their findings.	• Can use thermometers in the context of an investigation. • Can describe their findings using appropriate vocabulary. • Can suggest possible explanations for variations in temperature.
Lesson 4 Hot and cold	• To learn how to use the data logger to take snapshot measurements of temperature. • To understand the difference between snapshot and continuous measurements. • To begin to understand that a hot object will gradually cool to room temperature.	The children learn how to take snapshot measurements using the data logger and decide on a sensible time interval. Set up a data logger to take continuous measurements throughout the lesson too.	Measuring the temperature of a hot jacket potato at agreed intervals. Answering questions about keeping food hot and cold.	Comparing the continuous line graph and the bar chart made by one of the groups.	• Can use a data logger to take snapshot measurements • Are aware of the potential of data loggers to make both continuous and snapshot measurements of temperature and can give some examples of the advantages and disadvantages of each.
Lesson 5 Ice cubes	• To know that the heat insulation property of materials can be compared by investigation. • To know how to express predictions. • To know how to record in a simple table. • To know how to transfer information from a table to a bar chart.	Discussion about how to slow down the melting of an 'ice pop'. Support in planning a fair test and presenting results as a bar chart.	Planning and carrying out a test to find which material is best for slowing the melting. Presenting results as a bar chart.	Generalise from results about what materials are good insulators.	• Understand that different materials have different insulating properties and that these can be investigated to make predictions. • Know what 'insulator' means in relation to materials and temperature. • Can construct their own tables and bar charts from a model provided. • Can make predictions and suggest explanations.

Lesson	Objectives	Main activity	Group activities	Plenary	Outcomes
Lesson 6 Keeping liquids warm	• To know that the heat insulation property of materials can be compared by investigation. • To design a table to record results. • To carry out measurements with a reasonable degree of accuracy and record them in a table. • To compare the results of two investigations.	Model the process of giving reasons for predictions about which material will keep water hot the longest.	Carrying out a fair test, devising a table to record results and considering results against predictions. Choosing appropriate fabrics for wear on hot or cold days.	Relating materials which were good at keeping the ice cold to materials which were good at keeping the water hot.	• Can devise a table independently. • Can compare the results of two investigations. • Understand that some materials are better thermal insulators than others.
Lesson 7 Spoon test	• To know that different materials conduct heat differently. • To observe using the sense of touch. • To consider fair testing. • To be able to identify possible safety risks. • To relate the properties of materials to their uses. • To work collaboratively.	Predicting what would happen to different spoons put in hot water. Fair testing. Considering safety aspects of the test.	Testing what happens to spoons of different materials in hot water. Exploring a collection of other protective items such as oven gloves. Design a safety poster.	Discuss how the properties of the materials are related to their use.	• Know that heat can travel through some materials more easily than others and to know some examples of this. • Understand how the test was made fair. • Are aware of some risks associated with heat and can suggest action that can be taken to reduce the risk. • Can work collaboratively in a group.
Lesson 8 Conduction and insulation	• To know that materials with good thermal conduction or insulation properties can have uses.	Write and draw about examples of everyday items that make use of thermal insulation properties.		Reinforce the idea that heat can travel through some materials more easily than others.	• Can describe some uses of materials with good thermal conductivity. • Can describe some uses of materials with poor thermal conductivity.
Enrichment Lesson 9 Protective clothing	• To apply ideas about insulation in a real-life context. • To use the internet to research ideas.	Researching how divers and astronauts keep warm, and how vulcanologists keep cool.		Pairs feed back their findings.	• Can use the internet to research questions. • Can relate their scientific understanding to contexts in the wider world.

Assessment	Objectives	Activity
Lesson 10	• To assess children's understanding of thermal insulation properties of materials. • To assess children's ability to read the scale on a thermometer. • To assess children's ability to interpret a bar chart.	Pencil and paper test assessing reading a thermometer and uses of materials for thermal insulation.

SC1 SCIENTIFIC ENQUIRY

Keeping water warm

LEARNING OBJECTIVES AND OUTCOMES
- Make comparisons and identify patterns in their own observations and measurements of data.
- Use a table to record results.
- Make systematic observations and measurements.
- Compare the results of two investigations.

ACTIVITY
In this activity the children compare how well two different materials keep a container of hot water warm. They make their own table of results and are supported in phrasing predictions and drawing conclusions. The results are compared with those for keeping an ice cube cold.

LESSON LINKS
This Sc1 activity forms an integral part of Lesson 6, Keeping liquids warm.

ENRICHMENT

Lesson 1 ▶ What do we know about materials?

Objectives
- To elicit children's existing understanding about materials.
- To develop observation and sorting skills.

Vocabulary
fabric, glass, materials, metal, paper, plastic, wood

RESOURCES
Main activity: Board or flipchart, marker pens.
Group activities: 1 Collections of items made from different materials (one collection per group), though they do not need to be the same; a bin-liner per group.

PREPARATION
The collections should include a wide range of items, for example, a metal saucepan, a woollen glove, a plastic beaker, aluminium foil, a cereal box, a paper fastener, a plastic glove, cotton wool, a plastic bottle, a reel of thread. Try to include a few particularly interesting items, such as a glass pebble, a soft toy, an African wooden spoon. Put each group's collection into a bin-liner and put them out on the tables.

BACKGROUND
This activity will help you to find out what the children's existing ideas about materials are. It will help the children to make links with previous ideas and provide a thought-provoking starting point to the unit. The word 'material' is commonly used to mean fabric. This lesson also provides an opportunity for children to learn/revise how the term 'material' is used in science.

STARTER
Ask the groups to explore their collection by taking it in turns to take out an item from the bag and describe it to the rest of the group. Encourage children to go beyond the obvious by saying three things about each item. Then ask the groups to sort their collection in as many different ways as they can, for example, things used in the kitchen, things made from metal. Ask each group to choose one item and bring it to the carpet.

Differentiation

As this is an initial assessment, the differentiation will be mainly by outcome. However, some children may want to begin with the item that has already been discussed. Also, children with poorer writing skills can be supported by your scribing of their ideas.

MAIN ACTIVITY

Sit the children in a circle and ask each group to put their item in the centre. Pick one object and ask: *Can you tell me anything about this?* If these ideas do not arise from the children's comments, then follow up by asking: *What material is this made from? What do you think it is for? Why might it be made of that material?* Repeat this for each of the other objects.

Explain that in science the word 'material' means the 'stuff' that something is made from, such as glass, plastic, metal, or cotton.

GROUP ACTIVITIES

1. Ask each child to choose one item at a time from their collection, do a sketch of it and write down everything they can about it. This could be in the form of a table as shown.

2. Ask the children to work in groups of three or four. The children take turns to think of an item and the others have 20 questions to work out what it is. Encourage them to ask questions about the materials it is made from and what it is used for.

Object	My ideas about it
Woollen glove	This is a glove. It is good for keeping your hand warm when it is winter. It is knitted.

ASSESSMENT

Some children may give a limited description of the materials the objects are made from, such as 'it's metal'. For these children, an important part of subsequent lessons will be helping them to observe different properties of materials. Others may be able to describe some of the properties, such as, 'it's hard, it's heavy'. These children can be targeted with questions to help them think more about the ways in which people use different materials to perform different functions. Other children may already be making links between the properties of the material and its use, and for them, the unit will broaden their experiences and help them to learn about specific properties such as insulation which they may not be aware of.

PLENARY

Explain that for the rest of the unit you are going to be finding out more about different materials and that there are three big questions to keep in mind when the children are learning about materials. Write these on the board or flipchart:
- What are the materials like?
- What do they do?
- How can we use them?

OUTCOMES
- Teacher awareness of children's existing ideas about materials.
- Can observe and sort a collection.

LINKS
English: description.
Maths: sorting.

Lesson 2 ▪ Measuring temperature

Objectives
● To know that the thermometer is an instrument for measuring temperature.
● To measure using standard units with an appropriate degree of accuracy.

Vocabulary
Celsius, cold, degrees, hot, temperature, thermometer

RESOURCES

Main activity: Several ice cubes; a covered hot water bottle (not too hot); a spirit-filled thermometer (avoid clinical mercury thermometers; not only is mercury poisonous, but they will break at temperatures above 40°C); a picture of a giant thermometer drawn on a flipchart (see below) and a red marker pen; a transparent plastic container.

Group activities: 1. Spirit-filled thermometers; a thermos flask of hot, but not boiling, water; tap water; ice cubes (to add to the water); woolly fabric; containers; photocopiable page 87 (optional; also 'Measuring temperature - 1' (red), on the CD-ROM). **2.** Photocopiable page 88 (also 'Measuring temperature - 2' (red), on the CD-ROM).

ICT link: 'Measuring temperature' interactive, from the CD-ROM.

BACKGROUND

Temperature can be understood by considering the idea that all matter is made of tiny particles. Temperature is a measure of how fast the particles are moving, of how much energy they have; the faster they are moving, the more energy and the higher the temperature. Children often think that coldness is a property itself, rather than thinking about it as an absence of heat.

Children do not need to know about particles at Key Stage 2, but having this understanding may help you avoid using phrases such as 'letting the cold air in', which are scientifically untrue.

Temperature is measured in degrees Celsius (°C). The melting–freezing point of water is 0°C and the boiling point is 100°C. Room temperature is generally around 23°C and everything in a room will be at room temperature unless it has its own heat source. One source of confusion is that when we feel things by touching them, they may feel cold or warm, even though they are actually at room temperature. This is because some materials, like metals, conduct the heat from our bodies away quickly, leaving our skin feeling cold. In comparison, a material like polystyrene – which is a good insulator – feels warm, as little of our body heat is drawn away.

A thermometer works by the liquid inside it, for example, spirit or mercury, expanding as it is heated and contracting as it cools.

PREPARATION

Draw the thermometer opposite on the flipchart and have it where the children can see it clearly. Make copies of photocopiable pages 87 and 88 for each child.

STARTER

Have the children sitting in a circle. Pass around some ice cubes and a covered hot water bottle. Ask the children to describe what they feel like. Introduce the word 'temperature' and ask the children what they think it means. Ask the children how they could measure the temperature of the ice and hot water, introducing the idea of a thermometer if necessary. Help the children to relate their own experiences of thermometers, such as when they were ill. Explain that in this lesson they will learn to use thermometers, and this will help them to investigate materials.

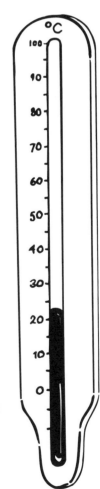

MAIN ACTIVITY

Show the children a spirit-filled thermometer, explaining that it is fragile and must be handled with care.

Using the drawing of the thermometer show the children how the scale is arranged and explain that temperature is measured in degrees Celsius. Draw a red line up to 10°C and ask the children what temperature that represents. Increase the line to 30°C and ask again. Draw the line to 35°C and help them to work out what it would represent. Do the same for approximately 47°C and further examples.

Pour some warm water from the thermos flask into a transparent container and show the children that you need to wait for the line to stop moving and keep the thermometer in the water while you read the temperature. Remember that this is different from what they will have experienced with clinical thermometers. Point out that you do not have to shake the thermometer to make the line go down again.

GROUP ACTIVITIES

1. Give the children copies of photocopiable page 87 and, working in pairs, ask them to find the temperatures of the different things on the sheet. Encourage them to feel the items with their fingers as well. While they are doing the first few items you can put out containers of warm and icy water. Children can take ownership by trying out some ideas of their own, but warn against putting thermometers in their mouths.
2. Give each child a copy of photocopiable page 88. Ask them to read the temperatures indicated on the drawings.

ICT LINK 💿

Children can use the 'Measuring temperature' interactive to read and record temperatures on the computer. The children have to drag the correct temperature label to each thermometer.

ASSESSMENT

Observe the accuracy of the children's practical measurement skills. Most should be able to read to the nearest 10°C, and many will be able to read to the nearest 5°C. Are their readings from the pictures of the thermometers correct? Can the children demonstrate their understanding of temperature by predicting whether it will go up or down when the thermometer is moved between substances?

PLENARY

Ask what the children think the word 'temperature' means. Ask: *Were there any surprises?* (Perhaps that the woolly fabric isn't warm.) *What temperature was the icy water?* (Should be 0°C if the thermometers are accurate.) *Can it ever get colder than 0°C?* (Below 0°C, it will be ice.) *Did everyone get exactly the same measurements?* (Probably not.) *What might affect the accuracy?* (Thermometers, care with reading or letting the level of spirit adjust.) Ask: *How could you change the temperature of something?* (For example warming with an oven or radiator.)

OUTCOMES

● Understand that temperature is a measure of heat.
● Realise that temperature can be measured using a thermometer.
● Can read a thermometer with a reasonable amount of accuracy.
● Can read a pictorial representation of a thermometer.

LINKS

Maths: measurement, using scales.

Lesson 3 ▪ Room temperatures

RESOURCES
Thermometers (ideally both spirit thermometers and other types such as strip thermometers).

MAIN ACTIVITY
Review how to use a thermometer. Make predictions about the room temperature. Ask the children: *Do you think the room will be the same temperature all over? What parts of the room could we try?*

The children take temperatures in different parts of the classroom, for example, in the Sun, near the door, near a radiator. They measure the temperature in the same place during the course of the day and record their measurements.

ASSESSMENT
Have the children been able to use the thermometers independently? Can they describe their findings? Can they suggest possible explanations that are consistent with their findings?

PLENARY
Look at the measurements taken during the day. First ask the children to describe what they found and then to suggest possible explanations for their findings.

OUTCOMES
● Can use thermometers in the context of an investigation.
● Can describe their findings using appropriate vocabulary.
● Can suggest possible explanations for variations in temperature.

Lesson 4 ▪ Hot and cold

RESOURCES ◉
Data loggers with temperature probes (at least two), data logging software on computers, potatoes, access to a traditional or microwave oven, oven gloves or mitts (or equivalent) to handle the hot potatoes, ice, kettle, water, containers, copy of photocopiable page 89 (also 'Hot and cold' (red), on the CD-ROM) for each group.
ICT link: Graphing tool from the CD-ROM.

PREPARATION
Set up the data loggers. Put the potatoes into the oven or microwave to cook. Prepare pots of water at different temperatures (but not boiling). Prepare copies of photocopiable page 89 for each group.

BACKGROUND
There are various types of data loggers, but most will make continuous, ongoing readings over a period of time, and can also be used to take snapshot readings at a particular moment. The data is either stored or fed directly to a computer and can be used to draw graphs. The snapshot measurements can be used to create a bar chart, which the children are likely to be familiar with, but an advantage of data logging is that it provides a way of understanding line graphs as they are generated in real time in front of the children.

Differentiation

It may be helpful to teach a group of children how to use the data loggers in advance of the lesson so that they can act as expert technicians and help the other children. This would be an opportunity to boost the self-esteem and confidence of the selected children.

Ask a child with confident writing skills to act as scribe for the group and another who needs to practise telling the time to act as time keeper (perhaps with peer support).

STARTER

Ask the children to think about what happens to their hot food when it leaves the kitchen and is served up on a plate. (It cools down). Explain that today you will all be using hot baked potatoes to explore how things cool down. Ask: *How long do you think it might take for a hot baked potato to cool down completely?* Record the different predictions that children make. Ask: *How will we know when it has finished cooling down?* Children may suggest measuring its temperature, in which case you might follow up by asking them to suggest what the temperature might be when it has cooled down. At this stage there is no need to discuss cooling to room temperature unless it emerges naturally from the discussion – the children's ideas can stay as speculations to be informed by the investigation.

In front of the class, set up the data logger to make continuous measurements of temperature of a baked potato. Ideally display this on an interactive whiteboard so that the children can see the changes while they work on other activities. At points during the Group activities you might want to stop the class to draw attention to the current temperature and invite observations and comments: *Can anyone say what is happening here?*

MAIN ACTIVITY

In the main activity you need to show the children how to take snapshot measurements with the data logger. The precise instructions for this will depend on the kind of data loggers being used. Demonstrate how to use the data logger first to measure air temperature. Use the pots of water at different temperatures to give as many different children as possible the opportunity to come up to the front and explain out loud how they are taking the measurement.

Decide together on a reasonable interval of time between each measurement and how the measurements will be recorded. Depending on the kind of equipment being used, and whether groups are sharing data loggers between them, it may be appropriate to show how a bar chart may be formed as you go along, or you may want to do this later when different readings have been recorded on paper or stored in the data logger.

GROUP ACTIVITY 💿

Provide each group with a hot potato, oven mitts and a data logger or organise how the data loggers will be rotated between groups. Ask them to record the temperature of the potato at intervals as agreed. Ask the groups to make sure that every child has a turn using the data logger. Circulate and check that every child is able to use the data logger. You may wish to record this information.

While the children are waiting between measurements ask them to discuss the questions on photocopiable page 89 and for one child to scribe the group's responses.

If the data-logging equipment has not already been set to generate bar charts then it may be appropriate to invite a group at a time to come to the computer and do this. Additional adult help would be very useful here. Alternatively, children could use the graphing tool available on the CD-ROM to create a line graph or bar chart of their results.

ASSESSMENT

Can each child use the data logger to make a snapshot measurement of temperature? Can the children explain the difference between the snapshot and continuous measurements and suggest some advantages of each?

PLENARY

Look at the line graph generated by the cooling potato set up at the start of the lesson. Invite the children to describe the line. *Is it the same all the way along? Where is it steepest? What temperature was the potato at 2.10?*

Ask: *How cold do you think the potato would get if we left it for longer?* Encourage a debate about this. Introduce the idea that it could not get colder than room temperature. Ask: *How could we make it colder than the room?* (Put it in a fridge or freezer.)

Compare the continuous graph with a bar chart made by one of the groups using their snapshot data. Ask: *What are the differences? What are the similarities? Which one do you think is most useful? Are there any disadvantages with using that one?*

OUTCOMES
● Can use a data logger to take snapshot measurements.
● Are aware of the potential of data loggers to make both continuous and snapshot measurements of temperature and can give some examples of the advantages and disadvantages of each.

LINKS
ICT - using data loggers.
Maths - data-handling.

Lesson 5 ● Ice cubes

Objectives
● To know that the heat insulation property of materials can be compared by investigation.
● To know how to express predictions.
● To know how to record in a simple table.
● To know how to transfer information from a table to a bar chart.

Vocabulary
bar chart, frozen, insulator, material, melt, table.

RESOURCES ●
Main activity: A frozen 'ice pop', two ice cubes, a large wad of newspaper, a small piece of fabric, equal-sized pieces of newspaper and fabric.
Group activities: 1 A collection of materials including fur fabric, woolly fabric, bubble wrap, foil, newspaper, plastics, timers, hand lenses, ice cubes (use very small ice cubes if you want to speed up the test!) **2** Optional copies of photocopiable pages 90 and 91 (also 'Ice cubes - 1' (red) and 'Ice cubes - 2' (red), on the CD-ROM). **3** Reference books or copies of photocopiable page 92 (also 'Ice cubes - 3' (red) on the CD-ROM.
ICT link: 'Ice cubes' interactive and the graphing tool from the CD-ROM.

BACKGROUND
Different materials have different thermal insulation properties. Because of their own, everyday experiences of putting on more clothes when it is cold, children often think that covering something will make it warmer. They may need teacher intervention to help them distinguish things that produce their own heat from things that do not. Even those who have grasped how, for example, wrapping a baked potato keeps it warm for longer, can have their ideas challenged by wrapping an ice cube, because they expect the wrapping to warm it up. For some children, the explanation of their results will be that the wrapping keeps the cold *in*, rather than the scientific version that the wrapping keeps the heat of the room out. Be prepared for a long wait - a well-wrapped ice cube can take over an hour to melt!

In this lesson, whole-class interactive teaching is interspersed with two practical Group activities for the children. This enables the teacher to keep a tight focus on the skills being taught, modelling them step by step.

STARTER
Show the children a frozen 'ice pop'. Ask them to imagine that they had bought an ice pop to give to their friend, but their friend lived quite a long way away. Ask the children what might happen to the ice pop on the way, allowing them to use their own words. This will provide formative assessment of the children's existing ideas for the teacher to build on.

MAIN ACTIVITY - PART 1
Can the children think of anything that could help stop the ice pop from

Differentiation
Some children may be able to devise their own recording sheets rather than using the photocopiable sheets.

melting? The children can draw on their own experience to make suggestions. Say that people sometimes used to wrap ice-cream blocks up in newspaper to take them home from the shops. Do the children think that would work? What else could they try?

Explain that ice pops are too big and expensive to use for a test, but that the children can test their ideas using ice cubes. Wrap one ice cube in a huge wad of newspaper and another in a tiny piece of woolly fabric. Ask: *Is that a good test?* Remind the class of the importance of fair testing. Now wrap the ice cubes in similar-sized pieces of the two materials. Ask different children to predict which ice cube they think will take the longest to melt. Ask them to give a reason for their answers. On the flipchart or board, model predicting with a reason: *'I think that the ice cube wrapped in _____ will melt fastest because _____. I think that the ice cube wrapped in _____ will melt slowest because _____.'*

GROUP ACTIVITIES

1. Ask the children, in groups of three, to select from a range of materials the three that they would like to test. Ask them to record their predictions with reasons as you have shown. Have hand lenses available to encourage close observation of the materials.

MAIN ACTIVITY - PART 2

Bring the class back together. Ask the children to feed back their predictions and give their reasons. Ask the children how they will know how long the ice cubes take to melt. Discuss the use of timers. How often will they check the ice cubes? Ten minute intervals would be appropriate. Together, devise a table to record this or use photocopiable page 90.

```
T A M E I C E Z E S Y T
F E B E R N K X Q L J A
A G M N A L S D C O W B
R M S P M S C U j W B L
G T A F E Q U L L Y P E
D A F T P R K R C A I X
L B R O E M A H E I T V
O S O D M R L T T R I E
C Z Z E F N I I U M G L
T T E M E L T A P R J H
U O N W R S U Q L V E N
T H E R M O M E T E R O
```

GROUP ACTIVITIES

2. Ask the children to carry out the test, either using photocopiable page 90 or devising their own table to record their results.
3. It may be useful to have another simple ongoing activity during this time, perhaps reading relevant non-fiction books on materials or doing the wordsearch provided on photocopiable page 91. The solution is shown opposite.

MAIN ACTIVITY - PART 3

Explain to the class how to represent their results as a bar chart (based on photocopiable page 92 if required). Each child can then construct their own using squared paper or a copy of the photocopiable.

ICT LINK 💿

A small group of children can complete the science wordsearch on the computer using the 'Ice cubes' interactive from the CD-ROM.

A bar chart can be created to record the results of the ice cube experiment using the graphing tool on the CD-ROM.

ASSESSMENT

Have the children expressed their predictions and explanations clearly? Have they been able to construct and use the table accurately? Can they transfer their own results to a bar chart?

PLENARY

Ask the groups to report back to the class on their findings. Were their results as they predicted? Ask the children to explain why some materials were better than others, for example they were thicker, they trapped air.

Can any generalisations be made? Introduce the term 'a good insulator'. Ask the children to explain how they think the materials slow down the melting.

OUTCOMES
● Understand that different materials have different insulating properties and that these can be investigated to make predictions.
● Know what 'insulator' means in relation to materials and temperature.
● Can construct their own tables and bar charts from a model provided.
● Can make predictions and suggest explanations.

LINKS
Unit 4F Circuits and conductors: comparing thermal insulators with electrical insulators.
Maths: data-handling.

Lesson 6 ◖ Keeping liquids warm

Objectives
● To know that the heat insulation property of materials can be compared by investigation.
● To design a table to record results.
● To carry out measurements with a reasonable degree of accuracy and record them in a table.
● To compare the results of two investigations.

Vocabulary
insulator, material, table

RESOURCES
Starter: A baby's bottle containing warm milk.
Main activity: A collection of materials including fur fabric, woolly fabric, bubble wrap, tin foil, newspaper, plastics and timers.
Group activities: 1. Thermometers or data loggers; a collection of materials as above; hot (not boiling) water; bottles to put the hot water in, such as small plastic fizzy drink bottles; containers to stand the bottles in, such as plastic beakers; hard lenses/x20 magnifiers. **2.** A collection of assorted fabrics (a rag bag) with varying insulating properties; scissors; glue.
Plenary: Digital microscope, if available.
ICT link: digital microscope; data loggers.

PREPARATION
The recording could be made into a sugar-paper class book, with each group contributing one A4 page. Prepare the book in advance so the children have some idea of the end product.

BACKGROUND
Different materials have different thermal insulation properties. A good insulator does not allow much heat to travel through it so the heat tends to stay where it is. This means that a good insulator will keep hot water hot and keep ice cold. Children may not find this an easy concept. By comparing the results of this investigation into which material is best at keeping things warm, with the results of the previous investigation in Lesson 5 – keeping an ice cube cold – they will begin to see that what appears to be two different properties of materials is actually the same thing. Be careful with your own language and do not talk about 'keeping the cold out'; instead say 'keeping the heat in'.

STARTER
Show the class a baby bottle with some warm milk in it. Explain that the baby's dad wants to take the baby out on a trip on a cool day, but the baby will need some warm milk when they are out. Ask the class: *What will happen to the warm milk dad has prepared?* (It will cool down.) Say: *He doesn't have a thermos flask or camp stove.* Ask: *We are going to think of a way dad can keep the milk warm for longer.* Ask the children: *How would you keep yourselves warm on a cold day?* (Wear warm clothes.) *What materials do you think would be best for keeping the baby's milk warm?* The children may draw on other experiences such as polystyrene foam or aluminium dishes that they have had take-away meals in.

Differentiation
For some children, recording the temperature of one bottle of water will be sufficiently demanding practically. Some may need support in drawing up a table of results. Those previously identified as needing support with the accuracy of their measurement can be targeted for help with their measuring skills.

Children with more advanced investigative skills could compare three samples of materials to test a more sophisticated hypothesis. (For example: *We think thick materials are better than thin ones.*) The explanations expected from some children will be at a higher level by being based on the nature of the material rather than previous experience. (For example: *I think this bubble wrap is good because of the air trapped inside it.*) This can be supported by providing hand lenses or ×20 magnifiers to encourage the children to consider the structure of the material more closely.

MAIN ACTIVITY

Show the class the collection, and ask several children to select a material they think would be good and give a reason for their choice. Model writing on the flipchart: *I think the woolly fabric will be good because jumpers keep you warm.*

Show the class the bottles they are going to use for the test. Demonstrate how the small bottle will be stood in the container, the chosen material put around it, and then the bottle filled with hot water. Ask the children: *How could you measure the temperature of the water?* (With a thermometer.) Explain that you want them to devise their own tables for recording their results, remembering what they have done in previous investigations. Stress that there is more than one right way of doing this. If you are making a class book, show the children where their work will be stuck in.

GROUP ACTIVITIES

1. The children can work in pairs or threes. Ask them to choose one material from the collection that they think will be good at keeping the water warm and one that they think will not be so good. Ask them to record their choices in this format: *I think that the _____ will be good at keeping the water warm because _____ and the _____ will not be as good because _____ .*

The children should then set up their two bottles. When they are ready and they have designed a table to record the results, help them to put hot water in the bottles and they can begin recording the temperature.

Ask the children to write what they found out in the format: *We found out that the _____ kept the water hot for longer than the _____ . We think this is because _____. This is/is not what we predicted.*

2. Ask the children in their groups to draw pictures of children on a hot day and a cold day, wearing appropriate clothes. They choose swatches of fabric from the collection and stick these alongside the drawing with arrows to indicate which item of clothing they would be suitable for. They should explain in terms of their insulating properties whether heat is being kept in or out.

ASSESSMENT

Are the children able to construct and use a table that is appropriate for the experiment? Can they relate this test to the previous one on ice cubes?

PLENARY

Ask each group which material kept the water warm the longest and which cooled the most quickly. Record these answers in two lists on the board or flipchart. Pointing to the first list, ask the class: *Is there anything you notice about this?* (The same materials are repeated; they are thicker; they have air spaces.) Do the same for the other list. It may be possible to make some generalisations. (For example: *We found that thick fabrics are better than thin ones, except for the newspaper, but that was scrunched up.*)

Ask the children to think back to the investigation into keeping an ice cube frozen. Which material was best at keeping the ice cube cold? It is likely that the best materials in each case are the same. Ask the children: *Why could these materials be good at keeping things hot and keeping them cold?* The children may respond by saying that coldness and heat can not get through these materials. This is a good basis for developing ideas about insulation, and for some children that is enough. Develop their ideas by explaining that coldness is not a separate thing, but that things are cold when they have not got much heat - we do not have a separate way of measuring coldness, a thermometer measures the amount of heat. If heat cannot get through a material very well (for example, a material that was a good thermal insulator in both experiments), then the heat is kept in the hot water, or the room cannot warm up the ice.

Using a digital microscope to take a close-up look at some of the materials together can lead to further suggestions about how the structure of the material is related to its insulation properties. For example, knitted fabrics have air pockets.

OUTCOMES
- Can devise a table independently.
- Can compare the results of two investigations.
- Understand that some materials are better thermal insulators than others.

LINKS
Design and technology: choosing appropriate materials.

Lesson 7 ◗ Spoon test

Objectives
- To know that different materials conduct heat differently.
- To observe using the sense of touch.
- To consider fair testing.
- To be able to identify possible safety risks.
- To relate the properties of materials to their uses.
- To work collaboratively.

Vocabulary
cold, heat, hotter, less hot, metal, plastic, travel, warm, wood

RESOURCES
Main activity: A collection of spoons made from different materials.
Group activities: 1 Stable bowls for hot water; collections of various spoons made from different materials – you can include different spoons made from the same material (do test the spoons first – some plastic ones melt at surprisingly low temperatures. You will need to show the children how to carry out the test safely.); a source of hot (not boiling) water; sugar paper and felt-tipped pens; strip thermometers (if available). **2** Drawing materials and paper.

PREPARATION
Set up the tables for the Group activities, keeping one collection of spoons to hand. Sit the children around you.

BACKGROUND
Heat can travel through some materials more easily than others. Those materials that heat can travel through easily, for example metal, are known as good thermal conductors (and poor thermal insulators). Those that heat cannot travel through easily are poor conductors (and good insulators), for example wood and plastic. Helping children to make the connection between these two apparently different properties of conduction and insulation will help to develop their understanding of heat, as well as their experience of materials.

The investigative focus is on fair testing and so, to limit the number of things the children need to think about, the temperature of the spoons is judged by touch, rather than measured. However, if you have strip thermometers available, these could be used to extend the activity.

Using hot water could pose a safety risk, so it is important that safe ways of conducting the test are made clear.

STARTER
Show the children the collection of spoons. Ask a child to choose one spoon and describe it, if necessary asking questions to prompt: *What is it made of? What would you use it for?* Ask different children to do the same for other spoons from the collection. Ask the children: *Why do we need to have different sorts of spoons?* This will help to set the activity in a real context so the children can relate it to their previous experience. It will also enable you to find out what ideas they already have, so these can be developed and particular children targeted during the activity.

MAIN ACTIVITY

Ask the children: *What do you think would happen if we put these spoons into hot water?* The children may draw on previous experience to answer, for example, knowing that a spoon gets hot in a cup of tea. Ask the children: *Will the same thing happen to all the different spoons?* Again the children may draw on previous experiences of cooking. Help them to focus on what will happen to the temperature of the handles. Ask: *How could we test that?* (Put them in hot water and feel how hot they get.) Ask: *How can we make sure it is a fair test?* (Put all the spoons in the hot water at the same time.)

Explain that the children will work in groups. Ask them to record their predictions of what will happen to each spoon and then test and record what does happen. Remind the children how to record results in the form of a table. Explain that each group will feed back to the rest of the class what they have found out.

Ask the children: *Are there any dangers with this test?* (Hot water might injure; hot spoons might burn skin.) *How can we make sure that we are safe?* (Have sensible behaviour; just lightly touch each spoon rather than grabbing it.) Demonstrate how they should quickly and lightly touch each spoon until they are sure it is not too hot.

GROUP ACTIVITIES

1. The children work in groups of up to six children, recording on sugar paper what they predict will happen to each spoon, then testing and recording it. Circulate, asking groups to give reasons for their predictions, focusing on those who did not participate earlier. Check that they are working safely. Encourage *all* children to feel the temperature of the spoon handles.
2. Ask the children to make a safety poster by drawing things in the home that might be very hot and should not be touched.

ASSESSMENT

Are the children able to relate the property of thermal insulation to different materials, comparing them with each other? Do they show understanding of the need for a fair test? Have they worked collaboratively? Can they relate the property of thermal conductivity to thermal insulation? Can they suggest any safety tips for cooking?

PLENARY

Each group will feed back to the class. Discuss whether everyone found the same thing. To summarise, ask: *Which materials let the heat through really easily? Which materials didn't let much heat go through them? What material would you use to make a handle for a spoon to stir a pot of soup? Why do you think teaspoons are often made of metal?* (Metal is easier to shape – can be made smaller, with a hollowed part.) *What could we do to be safer in the kitchen?* (Don't leave metal spoons in hot things.)

To finish, play a game: in a circle each child suggests a nonsense item, such as a paper saucepan or a metal scarf. This is a fun way of making the point that materials can be used for particular purposes because of their properties.

OUTCOMES

● Know that heat can travel through some materials more easily than others and to know some examples of this.
● Understand how the test was made fair.
● Are aware of some risks associated with heat and can suggest action that can be taken to reduce the risk.
● Can work collaboratively in a group.

LINKS

PSHE: collaborative working; safety in the home.

Lesson 8 ▪ Conduction and insulation

Objective
● To know that materials with good thermal conduction or insulation properties can have uses.

RESOURCES
An oven glove, a scarf, a cool box, a sock, a wooden spoon, a table mat, a tea cosy, a radiator in the room, a metal saucepan.

MAIN ACTIVITY
Review Lesson 7 on thermal conductivity of different spoons. Discuss other occasions when we might need to keep something cold or hot. Use the resources to stimulate and discuss ideas, encouraging children to contribute their own experiences.

Ask children to choose two items and draw them, writing to explain how they work to keep/make something hot or cold.

ASSESSMENT
In their writing, do the children show that they are aware that different materials have different thermal properties? Do they refer to heat being able to get through/not get through different materials?

Differentiation
Support children with poorer writing skills by scribing for them or providing words. Extend children who are secure with the idea that different materials have different thermal properties by asking them to suggest reasons why some materials may be better than others at keeping heat in.

PLENARY
Ask several children to read what they have written. *Does everyone agree?* Reinforce the idea that heat can travel through some materials more easily than through others, and we can use this to help us.

OUTCOMES
● Can describe some uses of materials with good thermal conductivity.
● Can describe some uses of materials with poor thermal conductivity.

ENRICHMENT

Lesson 9 ▪ Protective clothing

Objectives
● To apply ideas about insulation in a real-life context.
● To use the internet to research ideas.

RESOURCES
ICT link: Internet access; PowerPoint.

MAIN ACTIVITY
Divide the class into three groups and explain that each will have a different research focus for the lesson. Introduce the real-life problems faced by divers and astronauts in keeping warm, and vulcanologists in keeping cool. Together discuss some strategies to search for the information such as key words to enter in a search engine. Ask the children to present their findings as a PowerPoint slide with one or two key ideas and a URL (link to a website) inserted into it.

ASSESSMENT
Are the children able to identify appropriate web pages to find information? Can they make links between their previous work on insulators and their research findings?

PLENARY
Invite pairs to feed back their findings. Take opportunities to make links back to previous lessons, such as the kind of materials that are chosen as insulators.

Differentiation
Pair the children so that those with good literacy and internet research skills can support their peers.

OUTCOMES
● Can use the internet to research questions.
● Can relate their scientific understanding to contexts in the wider world.

Lesson 10 ▢ Assessment

Objectives
● To assess children's understanding of thermal insulation properties of materials.
● To assess children's ability to read the scale on a thermometer.
● To assess children's ability to interpret a bar chart.

RESOURCES 💿
Assessment activity: A copy of photocopiable page 93 (also 'Assessment' (red), on the CD-ROM) for each child.

PREPARATION
This Assessment activity should be considered alongside the ongoing assessment opportunities indicated throughout the unit when making a judgement about the level the child is working at.

ASSESSMENT ACTIVITY
Give each child a copy of photocopiable page 93. Ask them to do the test on their own. If you are unsure what a child means by their response to a question, then discuss it with them afterwards.

ANSWERS
1a. 40°C
1b. 60°C
1c. 35°C
3a. The one wrapped in newspaper.
3b. 50°C
3c. Aluminium foil, because it has good insulation properties and does not allow the heat to escape.

LOOKING FOR LEVELS
Most children will be able to correctly answer 1a to 1c, though they may have some problems with 1d. They will make sensible suggestions about what to make the hat and saucepan out of and be able to offer a reason, for example, a winter hat made out of wool because it keeps you warm, a saucepan made out of metal because it will not burn on the cooker. They will have correctly interpreted the bar chart. This would indicate that they are working at NC Level 3/Scottish Level C.

Some children may have made errors in reading the thermometers and interpreting the bar chart. They may have been able to suggest a material for the items but not given a reason. This would indicate NC Level 2/Scottish Level B.

Other children may correctly read and interpret the bar chart. They may offer more sophisticated explanations linked to the properties of materials, for example, the saucepan made of metal will get hot and heat the food up but not so hot that the pan melts.

PLENARY
Go through the answers to the questions, discussing the children's ideas in response to the more open-ended questions. Ask the children what new skills they have learned in this unit.

Measuring temperature – 1

◼ Use a thermometer to measure the temperature of these things. Remember to write °C after the number to show that it is degrees Celsius. Find some more things and measure their temperatures.

What I am measuring	Temperature
Inside my fist (gently!)	
The air	
Woolly fabric	
Tap water in a container	
Warm water	
Icy water	

Measuring temperature – 2

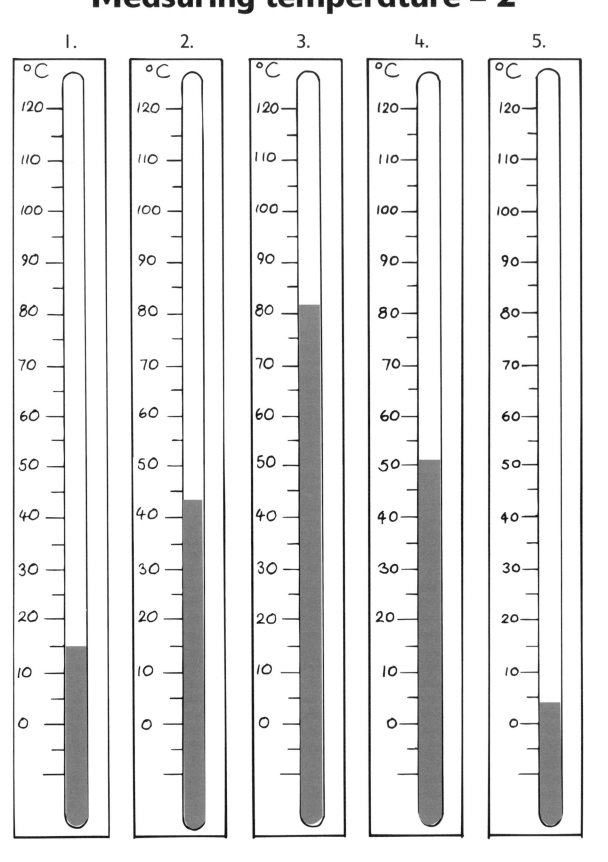

SCHOLASTIC

Hot and cold

◼ Discuss these questions in a group and make notes of your ideas. For each question, think about foods at home, at school, and out and about.

1. What are the different ways of keeping food warm?

_____

_____

_____

2. What are the different ways of keeping food cool?

_____

_____

_____

3. Write down the names of some foods we try to keep hot and some that we try to keep cool.

Keep it hot	Keep it cool

PHOTOCOPIABLE

Ice cubes – 1

■ Check the ice cube every ten minutes and put a tick in the box to show you have checked it.

■ When there is no ice left, put a cross in the box. Add any notes of your own below.

Time (minutes)	10	20	30	40	50	60	70	80	90	100	110	120	130	140	150	Total number of minutes
Cube 1																

Illustration © Debbie Clark

Ice cubes – 2

◼ Find these words in the grid.

cold	ice	measure	table
frozen	insulate	melt	temperature
hot	material	slow	thermometer

T	A	M	E	I	C	E	Z	E	S	Y	T
F	E	B	E	R	N	K	X	Q	L	J	A
A	G	M	N	A	L	S	D	C	O	W	B
R	M	S	P	M	S	C	U	J	W	B	L
G	T	A	F	E	Q	U	L	L	Y	P	E
D	A	F	T	P	R	K	R	C	A	I	X
L	B	R	O	E	M	A	H	E	I	T	V
O	S	O	D	M	R	L	T	T	R	I	E
C	Z	Z	E	F	N	I	I	U	M	G	L
T	T	E	M	E	L	T	A	P	R	J	H
U	O	N	W	R	S	U	Q	L	V	E	N
T	H	E	R	M	O	M	E	T	E	R	O

Ice cubes – 3

■ A bar chart to show which material is the best at slowing down the melting of the ice cube.

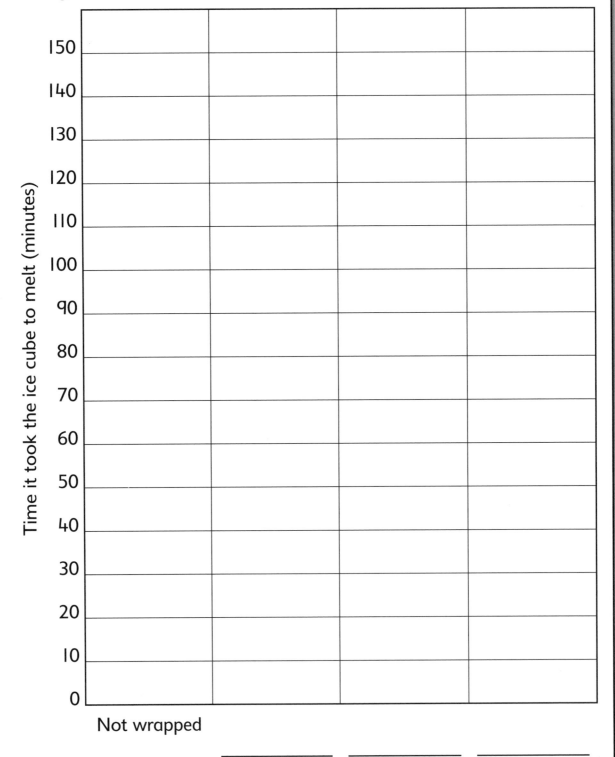

■ Write the name of the material the ice cube was wrapped in on the lines.

Assessment

1. Write down the temperature shown on the thermometers.

a. 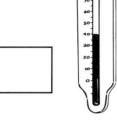 b.  c.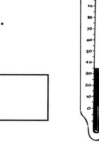

2. Finish these sentences by putting in your ideas.

I would make a winter hat out of _____

because _____

I would make a saucepan out of _____

because _____

3. Dad wanted to keep his baked potatoes warm to eat later so he tried wrapping them in different materials. This bar chart shows the temperatures of the potatoes when he unwrapped them later on.

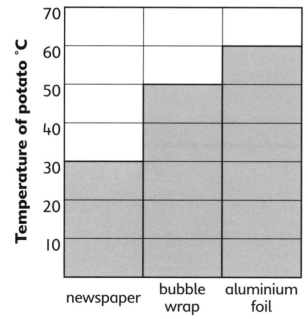

a. Which potato was the coldest?

_____

b. How hot was the one in bubble wrap?

_____

c. Which material was best for keeping the potato hot?

_____

Can you suggest why this was?

_____

Illustration © Debbie Clark

CHAPTER 4 Solids and liquids

Lesson	Objectives	Main activity	Group activities	Plenary	Outcomes
Enrichment Lesson 1 Solids and liquids	• To know that some materials can be classified as solids and some as liquids. • To be able to describe some of the properties of solids and liquids. • To record classification as a Venn diagram.	Comparing two materials: water and wood.	Sorting the collection of solids and liquids and recording as a Venn diagram.	Considering the meaning of the terms 'solid' and 'liquid'.	• Can group solids and liquids. • Can explain the criteria for sorting solids and liquids. • Are aware of the terms 'solid' and 'liquid'.
Enrichment Lesson 2 Science through drama	• To reinforce ideas about the properties of solids and liquids using drama. • To work collaboratively.	Miming Plasticine being pulled and pushed to form new shapes.		Performing mimes to each other.	• Understand the difference between solids and liquids in terms of flow and holding shape. • Can work collaboratively in a group.
Lesson 3 Measuring volume	• To know that a liquid has a constant volume, but that its shape depends on that of its container. • To be able to measure the volume of a liquid.	Demonstration and experience of measuring the volume of an amount of liquid.		Discussion about liquids maintaining volume while being poured into different containers.	• Can measure volumes of liquids accurately. • Understand that the volume remains constant, even though the shape changes.
Lesson 4 Solids that act like liquids	• To know that solids made of very small particles behave in some ways like liquids.	Observation of sugar and flour being poured. Are they solid or liquid?	Pouring different solids with small particles. Observation of particles using magnifiers. Making annotated drawings.	Clarification that some solids with small particles can be poured, but they are not liquids.	• Know that solids made of very small particles behave in some ways like liquids.
Lesson 5 Reversible or irreversible	• To know that a solid can be changed into a liquid by melting. • To know that a liquid can be changed into a solid by freezing. • To know that melting and freezing can be reversed, and are the reverse of each other. • To make predictions. • To practise observation skills.	Demonstration of how to heat materials safely.	Observation of how materials change as they are heated and then left to cool.	Introduction of the idea of a reversible change.	• Can describe how water can be turned into ice and ice into water. • Can describe how some materials have to be warmed to melt. • Can make predictions. • Can observe carefully.
Lesson 6 Melting solids	• To know that different solids melt at different temperatures. • To know that some solids will melt at very high temperatures. • To be able to raise questions. • To use secondary sources of information to answer questions.	Use of secondary sources to consider examples of solids (for example, metal/rock melting at a very high temperature).		Discussion about different materials melting at different temperatures.	• Can recognise that different materials melt at different temperatures. • Can recognise that metal needs a high temperature to melt and rock an extremely high temperature to melt. • Can raise questions. • Can use secondary sources to research answers.
Lesson 7 Mixing and separating	• To know that materials can be mixed together and separated. • To know that mixtures can be separated by using differences in properties of materials.	Demonstration of different ways to separate mixtures by using a magnet, sieving and floating.	Children are challenged to separate different mixtures. Listing recipe ingredients.	Discussion on how knowledge of differences in properties of the materials allows them to be separated.	• Can recognise that some materials can be mixed. • Can devise ways to separate materials. • Can explain how sieving, floating and magnets can be used to separate materials.

Lesson	Objectives	Main activity	Group activities	Plenary	Outcomes
Lesson 8 Dissolving	• To know that changes occur when some solids are added to water. • To know that some solids dissolve in water and some do not. • To devise and carry out a fair test. • To apply skills of measurement of volumes of water.	Observing salt dissolving. Introducing a test to find out which materials dissolve. Using a table to record predictions and test results.	Carrying out investigations into which materials dissolve.	Modelling how to present findings clearly.	• Can recognise that some materials dissolve when mixed with water and some do not. • Can devise a test. • Can record predictions and findings.
Lesson 9 Filtering	• To know that an undissolved solid can be separated from a liquid by filtering. • To present findings and suggest explanations.	Demonstration of filtration with kitchen paper.	Groups investigate the best papers to filter a mixture of sand and water. Recording focuses on suggesting explanations for their results.	Imagining that the filter paper might have very small holes in it that let the water through.	• Can recognise the properties of a material that make it a good filter. • Can recognise that filtering is a way of separating an undissolved solid from a liquid. • Can suggest explanations for their findings.
Lesson 10 Dissolved substances	• To know that a dissolved substance cannot be separated from water by filtering. • To be able to suggest possible explanations.	Filtering salt and sugar solutions and tasting to show the sugar/salt is still there.		Suggesting reasons why the sugar and salt were not filtered out.	• Can recognise that a dissolved substance cannot be separated from water by filtering. • Can suggest explanations based on previous experience and ideas.
Enrichment Lesson 11 Properties of liquids	• To plan and carry out an enquiry. • To explore properties of liquids.	Looking at a variety of liquids and ordering them according to transparency and viscosity.		Feeding back their findings and thinking why the viscosity of a liquid might be important.	• Can carry out a scientific enquiry and feed back their findings orally. • Have experience of variation in the properties of liquids.

Assessment	Objectives	Activity 1	Activity 2
Lesson 12	• To assess children's understanding of properties of materials. • To assess their understanding of how to carry out a fair test.	Children identify things that are 'unfair' about a test you have set up to investigate which sweets dissolve most quickly.	Pencil and paper test assessing separating mixtures.

SC1 SCIENTIFIC ENQUIRY

Does it dissolve?

LEARNING OBJECTIVES AND OUTCOMES
● Use observations to draw conclusions.
● Make a fair test by changing one factor and observing the effect while keeping other factors the same.
● Make systematic observations and measurements.

ACTIVITY
The children are asked to devise a test to see which of a collection of solids dissolve in water. They are asked to think about how to make the comparisons fair, for example by using the same amount of water, solid and stirring. They are supported with drawing tables to record predictions and results. The conclusions are summarised as a whole class.

LESSON LINKS
This Sc1 activity forms an integral part of Lesson 8, Dissolving.

ENRICHMENT
Lesson 1 ▷ Solids and liquids

Objectives
● To understand that some materials can be classified as solids and some as liquids.
● To be able to describe some of the properties of solids and liquids.
● To record classification as a Venn diagram.

Vocabulary
hard, liquid, pour, runny, shape, soft, solid

RESOURCES
Main activity A block of wood; a cup of water and container to pour it into; two card labels with the words 'Solid' and 'Liquid' written on them; Plasticine, a paper clip.
Group activities: 1 and **2** Each group needs a collection of solids and liquids for example, washing-up liquid, golden syrup, orange squash, water, bubble bath, vegetable oil, paper, card, rigid and flexible plastics, wood, stone, metal (for example, a paper clip), a glass marble, fabric, a sponge, chalk; transparent containers for liquids; plastic hoops; sugar paper; marker pens; drawing materials.

PREPARATION
Set up a collection of solids and liquids on each group's table. Have the wood and water for the Main activity to hand. Have the names of the materials in the collection written as a word bank for the children – either on the board or on cards.

BACKGROUND
Materials can be classified as solids, liquids and gases. Gases are difficult to understand at Year4/Primary 5, as they cannot be observed directly, so the focus here is on solids and liquids. Solids keep their shape; liquids can be poured and take up the shape of their containers. Children sometimes find it hard to grasp that solids do not have to be 'solid' in the everyday sense of the word – so paper and sponge are solids. They may find it hard to classify viscous liquids such as golden syrup, which pour slowly. Old church windows are thicker at the bottom than at the top and scientists are debating whether this is because glass is actually a very viscous liquid!

Although Key Stage 2/Primary 4-7 children do not need to know about particle theory, it is useful for a teacher to know that in a solid the particles are held together by strong bonds and they are organised into a particular structure. In a liquid, although there is some attraction between the particles, they are free to move around and are not held together in particular ways. Drama can be used to model this without going into detail (see Lesson 2).

Differentiation
Children with poorer writing skills can record pictorially, or use the wordbank to support their writing. Extend children who manage this task easily by encouraging them to add their own suggestions of objects that could go into each group, using a different coloured pen.

STARTER
Pass around the block of wood and the water. Ask the children: *What words can you use to describe the wood/water?* (Rough, hard, wet.) *What differences are there between the wood and the water?* (Runny/hard, strong/weak.)

MAIN ACTIVITY
Explain that you will be asking each group to sort their collection of materials in different ways, looking for things the different materials have in common and for differences between them.

GROUP ACTIVITIES
1. Ask the children to sort the collection in as many ways as possible, for example by colour, where they come from, their uses. They may well decide on solid/liquid as a category independently. If not, then ask the group to consider it by asking: *What happens to the materials when you move them about? Could you sort them according to those you can pour?* Encourage the children to use the hoops to sort the items into two groups. Ask the children to record this on the sugar paper as a Venn diagram.
2. Ask the children to choose two items from the collection and record ways in which they are different and ways in which they are similar.

ASSESSMENT
Can the children group the items according to whether they are solid or liquid? Can they explain the criteria for sorting as solid or liquid? Can they record in the form of a Venn diagram?

PLENARY
Bring the children together in a circle on the carpet. Put out the two hoops and place two liquids in one and two solids in another. Invite children to put another two objects in each. Ask them: *What do all these solids have in common?* (They have a certain shape; they cannot be poured.) *What do all these liquids have in common?* (They take the shape of the container; they can be poured.) These criteria could be made more explicit by writing them up on a board or flipchart. Explain that there are names – 'solid' and 'liquid' – that describe these groups and put the relevant name card by each hoop. Ask the children: *Were there any things in your collection that you were not sure about?* Discuss their ideas, for example, about fabric or golden syrup, ensuring that they are classified correctly. Explain that 'solid' has a special meaning in science that is different from its everyday meaning. Ask the children: *Can you think of any more things we could put in the solid/liquid groups?* If possible, they can get the objects and put them in the appropriate hoops. Show the children some Plasticine and ask them: Which hoop should this go in? Ask them to give reasons. Explain that you can change the shape of a solid by pushing or pulling it. Demonstrate this with the Plasticine and also with a piece of wire such as a paper clip.

OUTCOMES
- Are aware of the terms 'solid' and 'liquid'.
- Can group solids and liquids.
- Can explain the criteria for sorting solids and liquids.

LINKS
English: descriptive vocabulary.
Maths: classification, Venn diagrams.

Lesson 2 ▫ Science through drama

Objectives
● To reinforce ideas about the properties of solids and liquids using drama.
● To work collaboratively.

RESOURCES
Time in the hall; either the collection of solids and liquids as in Lesson 1 or cards with the names of the items in the collection; two contrasting pieces of music (optional).

MAIN ACTIVITY
As a warm-up, in pairs, one child mimes being a ball of Plasticine being pulled and twisted into a new shape by their partner. Groups then make solid shapes suggested by the collection of objects then, still in groups, mime liquids being poured: first golden syrup, then water. Use music to support this, if appropriate.

ASSESSMENT
Do the movements of the groups demonstrate an understanding of the properties of solids and liquids? Can the children work collaboratively?

Differentiation
Groups who manage this successfully could be extended by adding relevant vocabulary as a chant. Children who find collaborative work difficult will benefit from pairing and grouping with supportive children.

PLENARY
Groups perform one of their mimes for a solid or liquid - the rest of the class guess which one. Review the characteristics of solids and liquids.

OUTCOMES
● Understand the difference between solids and liquids in terms of flow and holding shape.
● Can work collaboratively in a group.

Lesson 3 ▫ Measuring volume

Objective
● To know that a liquid has a constant volume, but that its shape depends on that of its container.
● To be able to measure the volume of a liquid.

RESOURCES
Water; a variety of containers including calibrated beakers or measuring cylinders; water baths/tanks.

MAIN ACTIVITY
Demonstrate to the children how to measure out a particular volume of water with a good degree of accuracy and how to measure the volume of water held by a container. Introduce units of measurement of volume – cubic centimetres.

Ask the children to measure out a certain volume of water (this will need to be appropriate for the containers available) and explore pouring it into different containers. They should check that the volume has not changed by measuring it again.

ASSESSMENT
Can the children explain that the volume remains the same, even though the water is poured into different containers? Can they measure the volume with a reasonable degree of accuracy?

Differentiation
Expect different degrees of accuracy in measurement according to mathematical attainment. Some children may need to measure in non-standard units, such as 'up to the line'.

PLENARY
Discuss the process, asking children what happened to the shape and volume of the water as they poured it between the various containers.

OUTCOMES
● Can measure volumes of liquids accurately.
● Understand that the volume remains constant, even though the shape changes.

Lesson 4 ◼ Solids that act like liquids

Objective
● To know that solids made of very small particles behave in some ways like liquids.

Vocabulary
container, liquid, pour, shape, solid

RESOURCES

Main activity A collection of solids and liquids as in Lesson 1; two hoops; two card labels with 'Solid' and 'Liquid' written on them; flour, sugar, lentils in transparent containers; other containers to pour into.
Group activities: 1 Flour, salt, rice, sand, lentils in containers; other containers to pour into; hand lenses; ×20 magnifiers; digital microscope (if available). **2** Writing and drawing materials.

PREPARATION

Have the resources available to one side. Have the children sitting in a circle.

BACKGROUND

In previous lessons, the characteristic of liquids as materials that can be poured is an idea that has been developed with the children. Sometimes solids can be poured too, when they are made of small particles, such as sugar or flour. This can be a source of confusion for children when classifying solids and liquids.

STARTER

Put the two hoops in the centre and place one of the card labels 'Solids' and 'Liquids' by each. To review previous learning, go around the circle asking each child to take an item from the collection and put it in the relevant hoop. Ask the children: *What can you tell me about a solid/liquid?* Make sure that the idea that liquids can be poured is raised.

MAIN ACTIVITY

Show the class some flour. Pour it from container to container and ask: *Which hoop should this go in?* Ask the children to explain the reasons for their answers. Leave the question unresolved and show the children some sugar, pouring it between containers. Ask: *Which hoop should this go in?* Again invite suggestions and reasons from the children. Then show the children one lentil and ask: *Is this a solid or a liquid?* The children will probably say 'a solid'. Then pour lentils between containers and ask which hoop they should go in. Put them into the 'Solids' hoop and then go back to the sugar, then the flour, putting them all into the 'Solids' hoop. Explain that sometimes solids can be poured when they are in lots of small pieces.

GROUP ACTIVITIES

1. Give the children time to explore pouring different solids between containers for themselves. Circulate and ask the children to describe how the solids fall into the container: *Do they take its shape? Do they go into all the corners?* Have hand lenses/×20 magnifiers/digital microscope available so that the children can look in detail at the flour and sugar.
2. Ask the children to do an annotated drawing of two of the solids describing their observations and explaining how they pour.

ASSESSMENT

In their annotated drawings, are the children clear that it is a solid that is being poured?

PLENARY

Gather the children together. If you have a digital microscope available look at the sugar and flour together and note how they are made up of small, solid particles. Pour some water into a transparent container and ask the children to observe carefully. Then do the same with one of the 'pourable' solids. Ask: *What differences did you notice between the two?* (The solid

Differentiation
Some children may need support with writing. Some children could be extended by inviting them to imagine the particles made from smaller and smaller pieces, as a precursor to particle theory.

settled in a cone shape in the bottom of the container, while the liquid took the shape of the container.) Finish by holding up each 'pourable' solid and asking if it is a solid or a liquid.

OUTCOME
● Know that solids made of very small particles behave in some ways like liquids.

Lesson 5 ▪ Reversible or irreversible?

Objectives
● To know that a solid can be changed into a liquid by melting.
● To know that a liquid can be changed into a solid by freezing.
● To know that melting and freezing can be reversed, and are the reverse of each other.
● To make predictions.
● To practise observation skills.

Vocabulary
freeze, heat, liquid, melt, reversible, solid, solidify

RESOURCES 💿
Main activity A chocolate bar that has been allowed to melt and solidify again; chocolate, butter, ice cubes, candle wax, a heating system (these are commercially available or you can devise your own using tealights on saucers; the materials to be heated are put in foil dishes resting on a cylinder of chicken wire, or held in spoons with insulated handles. Ensure that the class follow safety instructions, as the foil dishes or spoons get very hot); matches (kept by the teacher); flipchart; interactive whiteboard.
Group activities: 1 Chocolate, butter, ice cubes, candle wax, a heating system as above, matches (kept by the teacher). **2** Photocopiable page 109 (also 'Reversible or irreversible?' (red) on the CD-ROM).

PREPARATION
Set up the tables for the Group activities. It is a good idea to have the materials to be heated ready-sorted, but kept in a cool box until the last moment. Have a flipchart or board ready to draw the table of results.

BACKGROUND
At a particular temperature, called the freezing point or melting point, some solids change into liquids or some liquids change into solids. To melt a solid it has to be given more energy (heat), and to freeze a liquid it has to have energy taken away. Children may need plenty of practical experience to appreciate that the substance is the same material, but in a different state. Often melting and dissolving are confused. When something melts, heat makes the particles vibrate faster and breaks down the bonds between them. They are still held together, but much more weakly. When something dissolves, a solvent (such as water) gets in between the particles. The children do not need to know about particle theory, but this may be helpful in clarifying your own understanding.

STARTER
Show the children the misshapen chocolate bar and ask them what they think might have happened to it. Ask the children what other experiences they have had of melting (for example, ice, snow, ice-cream, candle wax, butter). Draw out the role of heat in each example.

MAIN ACTIVITY
Explain that the children are going to explore how different materials melt. Show them the materials in the collection. Demonstrate how to use the heating system safely. Ask the children to draw up a table with four columns to record the name of the material, their prediction of what will happen to each material and a description of what actually happens. The last column is for a description of what happens to the material as it cools.

GROUP ACTIVITIES
So that each group's heating materials can be closely supervised, a second Group activity is provided. Alternatively, extra adult support (classroom

assistants) could each work with a group.
1. The children make their prediction, then heat each material in turn, recording their observations. The materials can then be left to cool and further observations recorded.
2. Ask the children to complete photocopiable page 109.

ASSESSMENT
Can the children describe how these materials need heat to melt? Can the children describe how ice can be turned into water and water into ice? Are their observations detailed and clearly recorded?

PLENARY
Consider each material and discuss the children's observations of what happened when it was heated and left to cool. Ask: *What has changed about the materials after cooling and what has stayed the same?* Emphasise that although the shape may have changed the material is still the same. If they got too hot some materials may have burned instead of melting and this may need clarification. Ask the children: *How could we get the water back into an ice cube?* Introduce the term 'reversible'.

OUTCOMES
● Can describe how water can be turned into ice and ice into water.
● Can describe how some materials have to be warmed to melt.
● Can make predictions.
● Can observe carefully.

LINKS
Design and technology: cooking activities.

Lesson 6 ▪ Melting solids

Differentiation
Group activity 2
To support children, use 'Reversible or irreversible?' (green), from the CD-ROM, which provides a range of answers for children to choose from.

Objectives
● To know that different solids melt at different temperatures.
● To know that some solids will melt at very high temperatures.
● To be able to raise questions.
● To use secondary sources of information to answer questions.

RESOURCES
A metal object; a rock (preferably an igneous rock such as granite); video clips showing volcanoes and metal in a molten state poured into moulds and solidifying; secondary sources (such as books, CD-ROMs, web pages) on processing metals and volcanic activity.

MAIN ACTIVITY
Ask the children whether the rock and metal are solid or liquid. *Could they be melted into a liquid? How?* Discuss the children's ideas. Divide a flipchart into two columns. Down one side, list questions that the children raise as a result of the discussion. Keep the questions focused on melting/freezing of rocks and metals.

Show the video clips. Ask: *What was needed to melt the metal and the rock?* (Very high temperatures.) If you are able to answer any of the questions from the video clips, then record the information in the second column.

In groups, ask the children to use other secondary sources to try to answer the other questions. These could be presented in the form of 'question and answer' speech bubbles and made into a wall display.

ASSESSMENT
Can the children offer explanations for how metal objects might be made that show an awareness of melting at high temperatures and moulding? Can they state that even rock can melt at high enough temperatures?

PLENARY

Feed back any answers that have been found. Reinforce the idea that most things can melt, but that some need very high temperatures to do so. Can the children suggest how coins might be made? (They are discs cut out of warm sheet metal and stamped with the design.)

OUTCOMES

● Can recognise that different materials melt at different temperatures.
● Can recognise that metal needs a high temperature to melt and rock an extremely high temperature to melt.
● Can raise questions.
● Can use secondary sources to research answers.

Lesson 7 ▪ Mixing and separating

Objectives
● To know that materials can be mixed together and separated.
● To know that mixtures can be separated by using differences in properties of materials.

Vocabulary
colander, float, magnet, mixture, separate, sieve, sink

RESOURCES 💿

Starter: A puppet character.
Main activity A mixture of flour and pins; a magnet; a mixture of macaroni and rice; a colander; a mixture of gravel and lentils; a tank or bowl of water, a sieve.
Group activities: 1 Mixtures of: flour, rice and beans; dried peas and sand; pieces of plastic and paper clips; a good selection of sieves and colanders; a tank or bowl of water; a magnet. **2** Children's recipe books; question cards, for example 'What goes together to make a flapjack?' 'What goes together to make a chapatti?'(according to the content of the recipe books); writing materials and paper.
ICT link: 'Mixing and separating' interactive, from the CD-ROM.

PREPARATION

Set up the tables for the Group activities. Ensure the resources for the Main activity are to hand and all the children can see. Perhaps they could sit in a circle and the demonstrations could take place in the centre.

BACKGROUND

Different materials can be put together. If they can be separated again, for example muesli, then it is a mixture. This is unlike when different materials have been combined to make new materials, like a cake, when the individual parts cannot be separated. In order to separate a mixture you need to know the different properties of each material. For example, magnetic materials can easily be separated from non-magnetic materials by using a magnet. Particles of different sizes can be separated by sieving and filtering. In filtering, the liquid goes through the holes, but any solid stays behind in the filter. If one substance floats and the other sinks, that provides another means of separation.

STARTER

Introduce the children to a puppet character. Tell them this 'naughty puppet' has mixed together lots of different things. Could the children help to separate them again?

MAIN ACTIVITY

First demonstrate how to separate flour and pins using a magnet. Tell the children that the naughty puppet put pins in his Granny's flour jar as a joke, but this was very dangerous. Imagine what would happen if his Granny had made a cake with it! Show the children the equipment you are going to use and ask them: *How could we use this to separate this mixture?* When you have separated the mixture ask: *What was different about those materials*

Differentiation
Some children may need suggestions to prevent them becoming frustrated. Children who have successfully completed the task could be challenged to think of a mixture for other children to sort out – they must have a method in mind!

that helped us to separate them?

Then demonstrate how to separate macaroni and rice using a colander. Tell the children that the puppet hates rice pudding, but loves macaroni cheese, so he thought he would try mixing them and see if he liked that! Show the children the equipment you are going to use and ask them: *How could we use this to separate this mixture?* When you have separated the mixture, ask: *What was different about those materials that helped us to separate them?*

Lastly, demonstrate how to separate gravel and lentils by floating and sinking. Tell the children that the puppet spilled the lentils outside, scraped up the mixture of lentils and gravel and put it back in the jar hoping no one would notice! Again, show the children the equipment you are going to use and ask them: *How could we use this to separate this mixture?* When you have separated the mixture, ask: *What was different about those materials that helped us to separate them?*

GROUP ACTIVITIES

1. Challenge the children to separate different mixtures: flour, rice and beans; dried peas and sand; pieces of plastic and paper clips. Let them find their own solutions – there is more than one possibility. Ask them to record in drawing and writing how they separated the mixtures.
2. Ask the children to take a 'What goes together to make...' card and list all the ingredients on paper.

ASSESSMENT

Can the children devise ways to separate the mixtures? Can they explain how their methods work by using the properties of the materials?

PLENARY 💿

Ask the groups to feed back some of the methods they used to separate the mixtures. Focus on the properties of the materials by asking questions such as: *How did the sieve separate the flour and rice? Why did putting the plastic and paper clips into water separate them?* Use 'Mixing and separating' interactive from the CD-ROM to start the discussion.

Ask the class if they can think of any real-life situation in which mixtures may need to be separated. If it doesn't arise, ask them to consider how rubbish could be sorted for recycling.

Ask if we can always separate materials from a mixture. (No, for example cakes or chapattis.)

OUTCOMES
● Can recognise that some materials can be mixed.
● Can devise ways to separate materials.
● Can explain how sieving, floating and magnets can be used to separate materials.

LINKS
Design and technology: cooking activities.

Lesson 8 ▪ Dissolving

RESOURCES
Main activity A transparent container of salty water; a transparent container of water; salt; a spoon; drinking straws cut into four.
Group activity: Transparent containers; calibrated beakers/measuring cylinders; spoons; labelled samples of salt, granulated sugar, sand, cornflour, wax flakes (available for batik from craft suppliers) and rice.

Objectives
● To know that changes occur when some solids are added to water.
● To know that some solids dissolve in water and some do not.
● To devise and carry out a fair test.
● To apply skills of measurement of volumes of water.

Vocabulary
dissolve, settle, solid, volume

PREPARATION
Have the resources for the Group activity ready on the tables and have the resources for the Main activity to hand.

BACKGROUND
Some solids dissolve in water - they are soluble. When it has dissolved you can no longer see the solid. The water molecules have got between the particles of the solid and it is dispersed through the water. Children may describe the solid as having 'disappeared', and it is a good idea to explore their ideas about where they think it has gone. Sometimes, most of the solid will dissolve, but some will be left on the bottom of the container. Sometimes, the solid will mix with the water, but not dissolve, forming a cloudy 'suspension' (school paint, for example). If a solid does not dissolve, it is insoluble in water. Because of these factors it is not always easy for children to decide if the solid has truly dissolved and this may need some discussion during the investigation.

Confusion between melting and dissolving is common, and children may well articulate ideas that express this. Focus their attention on the differences between the two - dissolving needs a liquid (usually water) and melting needs heat.

STARTER
Show the children a transparent container of the salt solution. Ask them to describe it. (It is watery, clear, transparent.) Now pass it around and ask each child to taste it by dipping in a cut up bit of a drinking straw (not by sucking!) Ask them to describe what it tastes like. (It tastes salty.) Ask: *What do you think might be in the water?* (There is salt in the water.) *Why can't we see it?* This is an opportunity to elicit the children's ideas about dissolving in order to develop them.

Tell the children that for safety reasons they must not taste clear liquids to find out what they are in normal circumstances - a clear liquid is not always water.

MAIN ACTIVITY
If the children have not already used the term 'dissolve', then introduce it. Show the children some salt and ask: *What do you think would happen if we poured some water on this?* (The salt would dissolve.) Pour the water on and allow the children to observe the salt dissolving. Ask a child to give a 'commentary' on what they observe happening. Ask: *Can you think of anything else that dissolves in water?* (Sugar dissolves in tea.) *Can you think of anything that doesn't dissolve when you put water on it?*

Explain that the children are going to investigate the question: 'Which materials dissolve in water and which do not?' Write this question on the board. Explain that you want the children to decide how to carry out the investigation for themselves, but that you will be looking out to see if they have made it a fair test, and that you expect them to record their predictions and what happens. Show them how to use tables to record their predictions and results, drawing a table on the board as a model.

Do not at this stage discuss how to make it a fair test; this will be part of the Group activity.

GROUP ACTIVITY
To enable all the children to consider the planning of the test they need to work in small groups: pairs or threes. Allow the children to begin discussing and carrying out their test. They are not expected to record the rest of their planning for the whole test in detail, as this would take too long. Circulate and ask: *How are you making this a fair test?* (By using the same amount of water and solid.) Intervene to help the children adjust their test if necessary, repeating parts if they need to.

ASSESSMENT

Can the children keep variables constant to make it a fair test? How independently can they do this? Make notes about this as you circulate and question each group. Can they use the recording system for predictions and their results? Do they use the equipment to measure volumes of water?

PLENARY

Discuss each item in the collection – did it dissolve or not? If there are any disagreements then ask each group to explain why they think they are right. Summarise by writing on the board: *We found out that_____dissolves in water and does not dissolve in water.* This models how to present findings.

OUTCOMES

● Can recognise that some materials dissolve when mixed with water and some do not.
● Can devise a test.
● Can record predictions and findings.

LINKS

Maths: measurement of volume.

Differentiation

For some children, it will be enough to keep just one variable constant, for example they may put in the same amount of water, but not consider having the same amount of solid. For children who need extension, you can ask them to consider how to keep a wider range of variables constant (to include the way they are stirring and for what length of time).

Some children may judge the amount of water by eye, others will measure it more accurately using the equipment provided. More accurate measurements of the amount of solid can be made by using level teaspoonfuls.

Lesson 9 ▪ Filtering

Objectives

● To know that an undissolved solid can be separated from a liquid by filtering.
● To present findings and suggest explanations.

Vocabulary

filter, filter paper, funnel, liquid, solid

RESOURCES

Main activity A sieve; a mixture of flour and lentils; a mixture of sand and water.
Group activities: 1 Containers; funnels; a collection of materials, including J-cloths, kitchen paper, loosely woven fabric, washed nylon tights, coffee filter paper, scientific filter paper; water; jugs/beakers; scissors; sand.
2 Hand lenses or ×20 magnifiers; writing materials.

PREPARATION

Have the resources for the Main activity to hand and ensure that all the children can see. Set up the tables for the Group activities, including wordbanks for children who need them.

BACKGROUND

An undissolved solid can be separated from water by filtering it. The filter works like a fine sieve, trapping the particles of solid and letting the water run through it. To help the children understand how it works, relate it to the work done in Lesson 7 on separating mixtures using sieves and colanders.

Children may have difficulty in moving from descriptions of what happens to explanations of *why* things may be happening. Being explicit about the use of the word 'because' helps to develop this.

As the investigative focus of this lesson is presenting findings and explaining, this is what children are asked to record, and they are shown a way of carrying out the test so that there is not a long planning time. The children will revisit separating, including filtering, in Year 6/Primary 7 so this is only an introduction to these scientific skills.

STARTER

Show the children the mixture of flour and lentils and ask them to think back to the lesson when they separated mixtures. Ask: *What could we use to separate the flour and lentils?* (A sieve.) Show the sand and water mixture and ask: *What can you tell me about this?* (The sand has sunk to the bottom, it has not dissolved.) *How could the sand and water be separated?* (With a sieve.)

Differentiation
Provide a wordbank to support writing explanations. This could include useful phrases such as: 'better than', 'worse than', 'I think this is because . . .' Children could be asked to draw a diagram of what they think is happening to help extend their explanations.

MAIN ACTIVITY

Demonstrate pouring the sand and water mixture through the sieve. Some may be trapped, but small grains of sand will go through. Ask: *How could we make sure that none of the sand gets left in the water?* (Get a sieve with smaller holes!) Explain that instead of a sieve, the children could use different materials. Demonstrate how they could test different materials by putting a piece of kitchen paper in a funnel over a beaker. Introduce the term 'filter'. Pose the question: *Which material is the best for filtering sand from water?*

Explain that you want the groups to find out which is the best material and which is the worst. You also want them to think about why each is good or bad and to try to explain it.

GROUP ACTIVITIES

1. The groups carry out the investigation. They do not need to write down how they carried out the test, but they do need to present their findings. Under the title 'What we found out', they could stick down samples of the filler materials they investigated, describe their effectiveness as sand filters and suggest a possible explanation for why some were better than others.
2. Ask the children to use the magnifiers to look at the materials carefully. Ask them to make drawings of what the materials look like under the magnifiers.

ASSESSMENT

Do the children realise that filtering can be used to separate the sand from the water? Can they suggest possible explanations? Do they realise that the materials have small holes in, even though these may not be visible to the naked eye?

PLENARY

Ask the groups to feed back their findings and suggested explanations to the others. Ask: *If we had a powerful magnifier, what might we see in the filter papers?* (Holes.) Remind the children how this relates to the colander and the sieve they used in Lesson 7.

OUTCOMES

- Can recognise the properties of a material that make it a good filter.
- Can recognise that filtering is a way of separating an undissolved solid from a liquid.
- Can suggest explanations for their findings.

LINKS

English: explaining.

Lesson 10 ▭ Dissolved substances

Objective
- To know that a dissolved substance cannot be separated from water by filtering.
- To be able to suggest possible explanations.

RESOURCES

Sand, salt, sugar, cut-up drinking straws, very clean containers, a funnel, filter paper.

MAIN ACTIVITY

Review lessons on dissolving different materials and on separating undissolved solids by filtering. Demonstrate filtering sand from water using a filter paper as a reminder.

Dissolve some sugar in water and pour through a filter. The children can taste the filtrate by dipping in their drinking straws. Repeat with the salt.

ASSESSMENT
Do the children realise that the filter has not stopped the salt or sugar from passing through? Can they suggest an explanation?

PLENARY
Ask: *Has the filter trapped the salt or sugar? Can you suggest why?* (When solids are dissolved they become such small pieces that they can get through the holes in the filter paper- like the water can.)

OUTCOMES
● Can recognise that a dissolved substance cannot be separated from water by filtering.
● Can suggest explanations based on previous experience and ideas.

ENRICHMENT
Lesson 11 ▪ Properties of liquids

RESOURCES
A collection of different liquids such as shampoos, shower gels, washing-up liquids; droppers/pipettes; wipeable boards/trays; kitchen paper/paper towels; lolly sticks; timers.

MAIN ACTIVITY
Give the children time to explore the different liquids. Challenge them to put them in order, in as many different ways they can think of (for example: size of bottle, transparency (how see-through it is), viscosity (how runny it is). Ask them to feed back these ideas to the whole class and record them on the board. Ask each group to line up their liquids in order of how runny they think they are, based on their initial exploration. Ask: *How could you do a test to compare the runniness of the different liquids?* Give the children time to discuss it in pairs before carrying out a test. They could record their test as an annotated drawing.

ASSESSMENT
Can the children decide on a test for viscosity independently or do they need some support? Are they able to devise a way of measuring viscosity?

PLENARY
Invite the children to feed back their results. Ask: *Why might it matter how runny a liquid is? Can you think of any other liquids that are very runny/ very thick?*

OUTCOMES
● Can carry out a scientific enquiry and feed back their findings orally.
● Have experience of variation in the properties of liquids.

Lesson 12 ▪ Assessment

RESOURCES ◉
Assessment activity: 1 Two different types of boiled sweets; two transparent containers; water; a spoon. **2** Copies of photocopiable page 110 (also 'Assessment' (red) on the CD-ROM) for each child.

PREPARATION
These Assessment activities should be considered alongside the ongoing

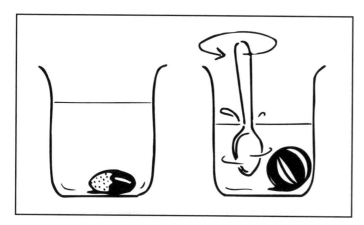

assessment opportunities indicated throughout the unit, when making a judgement about the level the child is working at.

ASSESSMENT ACTIVITY 1

Work with a group of up to six children at a time. Bring them slightly away from the rest of the class. Explain that you are going to do a test to try and see which sweet dissolves the best. You want the children to watch what you do and then answer some questions about whether or not it was a fair test.

Set up a test as shown in the illustration. Put one sweet in at least ten seconds before the other. Exaggerate the 'unfairness'.

ANSWERS

Ask each child: *Is this a fair test?* (No.) Ask each child what they would do to make it a fair test, starting with the children who seemed less confident about their first answer. (Use the same amount of water; have the same-sized containers; stir them in the same way for the same amount of time; put the sweets in the water at the same time.)

LOOKING FOR LEVELS

Children who are able to recognise that the test in Assessment activity 1 is unfair and make at least one suggestion about how to improve the test, are working at NC Level 3/Scottish Level C. The majority of children should achieve this. If a child is able to suggest a comprehensive set of changes that will make the test completely fair, then they may be working at NC Level 4/ Scottish Level C/D. If the child clearly does not understand what is meant by a fair test, but can describe differences, for example. 'that one has more water in', this indicates that they are working at Level 2/Scottish Level B.

ASSESSMENT ACTIVITY 2

Give each child a copy of photocopiable page 110 (also 'Assessment' (red on the CD-ROM). Ask them to do the test on their own. If you are unsure what a child means by their response to a question, then discuss it with them afterwards.

ANSWERS

Water and peas: colander
Paper clips and ice: magnet
Flour and rice: sieve
Sand and water: filter paper.

LOOKING FOR LEVELS

Most children will have correctly linked the mixtures with how to separate them. When marking children's accounts of how they will separate the mixtures, a key distinction is between describing and explaining. If they are able to correctly explain how they would separate the materials, this is evidence of them working at NC Level 3/Scottish Level C. If they also explain what distinct properties of the material enable it to be separated, for example, grain size, magnetic/not magnetic, they are working at NC Level 4/ Scottish Level C.

PLENARY

With the whole class, identify the ways of making the test for dissolving sweets a fair test. Ask the children to think about the different skills they have learned in this unit.

Reversible or irreversible?

◼ Some things are changed by heating or cooling them.

◼ Sometimes they can go back to how they were before and we say the change is reversible. If they cannot go back, we say the change is irreversible.

◼ Fill in the spaces in the chart.

How it is now	How it was before (do a drawing too)	How it changed when it was heated	Is this change reversible?
Water	Ice cube		
Charred wood			
Ice lolly			
Cake			
Hot milk			

Illustration © Debbie Clark

PHOTOCOPIABLE

Assessment

◢ Draw a line from the mixture to what you would use to separate it.

peas and water   ice and paper clips   flour and rice   sand and water

magnet   sieve   filter paper   colander

◢ Choose one of these and draw or write to explain how it works.

◣ SCHOLASTIC

Illustration © Debbie Clark

CHAPTER 5 Friction

Lesson	Objectives	Main activity	Group activities	Plenary	Outcomes
Lesson 1 Push, pull and twist	• To revise previous work on forces and • To elicit children's current understanding. • To reinforce the idea that magnets and springs exert forces. • To know that forces act in a particular direction and this can be represented by an arrow.	Introducing how to use an arrow to represent the direction of a force on a drawing.	Exploring a collection of magnets and springs. Describing observations in terms of pushes, pulls and twists.	Clarifying the difference between a force and the resulting movement.	• Can describe the forces exerted by magnets and the direction in which the forces act. • Can describe the forces exerted by springs and the direction in which the forces act. • Can represent their ideas as drawings. • Can use arrows to indicate the direction of a force.
Enrichment Lesson 2 Changing shape	• To revise that forces can change the shape of objects. • To use drama to express ideas about forces.	Using a collection of materials to stimulate drama work in which children use their bodies and voices to represent stretching, squashing and so on.		Performing drama work to the class.	• Can recognise that forces can change the shape of objects. • Can express scientific ideas through drama.
Lesson 3 Measuring forces	• To know that forces can be measured using a force meter. • To be able to use a force meter.	Demonstrating how to use newton meters, including how to read the scale.	Practising using a newton meter to measure different forces.	Relating large and small forces to their measurement in newtons.	• Can use a force meter. • Can read the scale on a force meter to an appropriate degree of accuracy. • Have a 'feel' for a force of 1N and 10N.
Lesson 4 Exploring friction	• To make predictions and test them. • To compare results with predictions. • To apply skills of measuring with a force meter. • To know that friction is a force. • To know that a force meter can be used to investigate friction. • To know that friction depends on the surfaces in contact.	Demonstration of how to measure the force needed to move a brick on different surfaces	Groups predict and test which surfaces need more force to move the brick. Finding examples of different types of surfaces.	Discussion on how friction is a force.	• Can make predictions and test them. • Can apply measurement skills with a newton meter to an investigation. • Understand that the frictional force depends on the nature of the surface.
Lesson 5 Sam's slippery surfaces	• To know that the force of friction can be investigated using slopes. • To know that the force of friction depends on the surfaces in contact. • To carry out a fair test. • To know that measurements can be repeated for greater accuracy.	Explanation of how a ramp can be used to test the grip of a shoe on different surfaces. Discussion on the need to repeat measurements.	Children investigate the 'grippiness' of different shoes and take rubbings of the soles.	Groups feed back their findings, discuss possible reasons for variation in results.	• Can understand how repeating measurements can improve accuracy. • Know that slopes can be used to investigate friction. • Know that different materials and surfaces have different frictional properties. • Can make independent decisions about fair testing.
Lesson 6 Friction all around us	• To know that frictional forces occur in many places.	Hunting for examples of friction around the classroom and school.		Discussing where friction is helpful and where it is not.	• Can recognise where frictional forces occur. • Can describe instances where friction is useful and can describe instances where friction is not useful.

Lesson	Objectives	Main activity	Group activities	Plenary	Outcomes
Lesson 7 On the move	• To elicit children's ideas about friction. For children to question a 'taken for granted' situation.	Observing a toy car and questioning what makes it stop moving when it has been pushed.		Considering how the car could be made to travel further by increasing the push or changing the surface.	• Improved teacher understanding of children's existing ideas about friction. • Children can consider a 'taken for granted' situation in a new way.
Lesson 8 Water resistance	• To know that water resistance slows down the speed of an object and is related to the object's shape. • To measure short time spans.	Demonstration of dropping balls of Plasticine in air, water and wallpaper paste. Introduction of the term 'resistance'.	Making different shapes in Plasticine and observing how they fall in water.	Discussion of streamlining.	• Can describe a streamlined shape and its usefulness. • Can describe how water resistance slows down the speed of an object.
Lesson 9 Air resistance	• To know that air resistance can slow down the movement of objects. • To design and carry out an investigation as independently as possible.	Investigating independently how changing the shape of the front of a toy car with card affects its movement.		Reporting back findings and relating them to streamlining in water.	• Can carry out an investigation with increased independence and confidence. • Can understand that streamlining can affect the movement of objects in air as well as in water.
Lesson 10 Falling objects	• To explore and compare how different objects fall. • To introduce the term 'gravity' as the force which pulls things down.	Observing how different materials fall.		Demonstration and discussion of how A4 paper falls when flat and crumpled.	• Can explore and compare how different objects fall. • Can use the term 'gravity' appropriately.
Lesson 11 Paper spinner test	• To know that air resistance can slow down the movement of objects. • To identify and control variables in an investigation. • To carry out an investigation with an awareness of safety.	Considering the variables in finding the best design of a paper spinner.	Investigating how changing one variable, such as size, affects how the paper spinner falls.	Presenting findings to the class.	• Can change one variable and keep others constant. • Can carry out an investigation safely.
Enrichment Lesson 12 Paper spinner results	• To present data in the form of a bar chart. • To understand the value of graphs. • To suggest explanations for their findings.	Explaining how to draw a graph from the data collected in Lesson 11.	Drawing graphs from the results of Lesson 11.	Showing graphs and discussing the value of graphs in interpreting results.	• Can present their own data as a graph. • Can understand the value of presenting data as a graph. • Can suggest explanations for their own results.
Lesson 13 Parachutes	• To begin to understand that air resistance can slow down a moving object. • To draw conclusions and give explanations for results.	Deciding how to carry out a fair test to find out which parachute a person needs to land safely. Making predictions.	Carrying out the fair test. Feeling air resistance by running with different sized pieces of card in front of them.	Discussing whether the children's predictions were correct and thinking about how any difficulties they had might have affected the results.	• Can describe how a parachute slows down a falling person. • Can carry out an investigation, drawing conclusions suggesting explanations.

Assessment	Objectives	Activity 1	Activity 2
Lesson 14	• To assess the children's knowledge and understanding about how forces can affect the shape and movement of objects. • To assess the children's ability to plan a test, predict and suggest explanations.	Test to assess children's understanding of forces with a focus on air resistance.	Assessment of children's skills in designing a test and suggesting explanations.

SC1 SCIENTIFIC ENQUIRY

Slippery surfaces

LEARNING OBJECTIVES AND OUTCOMES
● Make systematic observations and measurements.
● Use observations and measurements to draw conclusions.
● Make a fair test.
● Check observations and measurements by repeating them.

ACTIVITY
Children are introduced to using a ramp as a means of judging how good the grip on their shoes is. They are then asked to devise a fair test for the slipperiness of different surfaces, explaining how they have made it fair. They are supported in repeating the observations to improve their reliability, though not yet calculating the mean (average).

LESSON LINKS
This Sc1 activity forms an integral part of Lesson 5, Sam's slippery surfaces.

Lesson 1 ▪ Push, pull and twist

Objectives
● To revise previous work on forces and to elicit children's current understanding.
● To reinforce the idea that magnets and springs exert forces.
● To know that forces act in a particular direction and this can be represented by an arrow.

Vocabulary
force, magnet, pull, push, spring, twist

RESOURCES ◉
Main activity: Flipchart and pens; interactive whiteboard.
Group activities: 1 A collection of various magnets; paper clips, paper fasteners, 1p and 2p coins (to explore the magnets), elastic bands and springs for each group, writing materials **2** Photocopiable page 129 (also 'Push, pull and twist' (red) on the CD-ROM), writing materials.

PREPARATION
Put out a collection of resources for the Group activities on each table.

BACKGROUND
The children may have explored magnets and springs, and carried out simple investigations previously (see Unit 3E of *100 Science Lessons*: Year 3/ Primary 4). This lesson aims to elicit the children's understanding of forces, concentrating on those exerted by magnets and springs. Forces are pushes, pulls and twists. Forces can be different sizes. Forces are always exerted in a particular direction, and this can be indicated by the direction of an arrow on a drawing or diagram.

STARTER
Have the children sitting in front of you on the carpet. Write the words 'Push', 'Pull' and 'Twist' on the flipchart. Ask: *Can anyone come to the front and show us what we mean by a push?* When a child has demonstrated in their own way, perhaps by pushing an object or person (gently!), repeat this for a pull and a twist. Say to the children: *I want you to think about what you did when you got up and got ready for school this morning. Can you think of some pushes, pulls and twists that you did? For example, the first thing I did this morning was push the button on my alarm clock.* Invite different children to give their suggestions until everyone has had a go. (I pushed back the duvet; I pulled on my socks; I twisted the tap.) Remind the children that pushes, pulls and twists are forces and write the word 'force' on the flipchart.

Remind the children that they have investigated magnets and springs before. Write the words 'magnet' and 'spring' on the flipchart. Explain that they have 10 minutes to explore their collection of magnets and springs and that you want them to think about pushes, pulls and twists while they are doing that. Encourage them to handle different items, manipulate them and see how they can make them move and change their shape. Tell them that you will ask some children to talk to the others about what they notice.

GROUP ACTIVITIES

1. Allow 10 minutes to explore the collection. Circulate, encouraging children to explain what is happening using the words 'push', 'pull' and 'twist'. Ask questions: *What happens when you pull that? What can you tell me about those magnets?*

2. Give each child a copy of photocopiable page 129. Ask them to describe what is happening in each picture, writing in as much detail as possible, including the words 'push', 'pull' or 'twist'. (For example: 'The person is pulling hard on the spring and it has stretched'.)

MAIN ACTIVITY 💿

Bring the children back to the carpet. Ask several of the children to tell the others what they noticed. Extend their descriptions by asking questions about direction, such as: *In what direction were you pulling? Which way did the magnet move?*

Choose one example and explain that you are going to represent what happened as a drawing. On the flipchart do a simple drawing and label it (see diagram below; this is also included on the CD-ROM).

Ask the children: *In which direction is the push/pull?* Represent this with an arrow and write 'push', 'pull' or 'twist' on the arrow. Write a sentence underneath to describe what is happening, for example 'The magnet is pulling the paper clip towards it.' Explain that you would like the children to do their own annotated drawings using arrows in the same way to show what they have found out about the collection.

ASSESSMENT

Can the children describe what is happening in terms of pushes, pulls and twists? Have they distinguished between the force and its effect? Look at the children's drawings to see whether they are representing the direction of the *force* using arrows.

PLENARY

Ask some children to share their work. If there has been confusion about representing the force and the effect/movement, then clarify the difference for the class. Finish by asking the children to think of other examples of forces in their everyday lives, for example, pushing their chair in, pushing and pulling a knife to cut through bread, twisting the lid from a jam jar.

OUTCOMES

● Can describe the forces exerted by magnets and the direction in which the forces act.
● Can describe the forces exerted by springs and the direction in which the forces act.
● Can represent their ideas as drawings.
● Can use arrows to indicate the direction of a force.

LINKS

Design and technology: mechanisms.

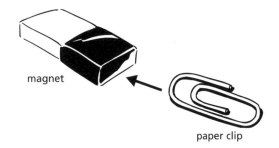

magnet

paper clip

ENRICHMENT
Lesson 2 ▪ Changing shape

Objective
● To revise that forces can change the shape of objects.
● To use drama to express ideas about forces.

RESOURCES
Plasticine, sponges, elastic bands, pipe cleaners, space for drama/movement work.

MAIN ACTIVITY
Give the children time to manipulate the materials. As a class, brainstorm words that are suggested by this ('push', 'pull', 'stretch', 'squash', 'bend', 'bounce'). Explain that this relates to their science work on forces because they are using forces (pushes, pulls and twists) to change the shape of the materials. Ask: *Did you use a push, a pull or a twist to make that shape? What could you do to make it longer, shorter, bend it?*

Ask the children to work in pairs, using their bodies to represent one of the materials being manipulated and changing shape. Now ask the children to work in groups of four, again using their bodies, but also their voices, with intonation that fits the movement and the word (such as s-t-r-e-t-c-h!) as they mime an elastic band being pulled.

Ask: *What have these performances got to do with forces?* (We have been acting out changing shapes by using forces.)

ASSESSMENT
Are the children associating words with the relevant movements? Do their movements represent the materials?

PLENARY
Each group performs its work for the rest of the class.

Differentiation
Work alongside children who find it difficult to get started with their own ideas.

OUTCOMES
● Can recognise that forces can change the shape of objects.
● Can express scientific ideas through drama.

Lesson 3 ▪ Measuring forces

Objectives
● To know that forces can be measured using a force meter.
● To be able to use a force meter.

Vocabulary
force, force meter/newton meter, newton

RESOURCES
Main activity: Flipchart with scales drawn on (see overleaf); marker pens, newton meters, a large spring; a copy of the story 'The Enormous Turnip'.
Group activities: Writing equipment. **1** Flipchart as above; three newton meters with different scales. **2** Seven objects that can be suspended from a newton meter such as: a large stone, a toy car, a teddy bear, a pencil, a doll, half a brick, a pair of scissors. (You could use elastic bands or string tied like a parcel on objects to allow them to be 'hooked'.) **3** Yogurt pots with elastic bands around the rim to attach string handles so they are like small buckets; marbles; sensitive newton meters. **4** Various newton meters.

PREPARATION 💿
Draw the newton meter scales on the flipchart (see overleaf) using a new page for each one, or use the diagrams from the CD-ROM on an interactive whiteboard. Set up three tables for Group activities 2, 3 and 4 and have equipment for Group activity 1 and the Main activity near the flipchart.

BACKGROUND
Forces are measured in units called 'newtons' (N) and can be measured using a newton meter. These work by having a spring inside that stretches when it is pulled. It can sometimes be confusing because the scale on a newton meter may be given in grams as well as in newtons. Make sure that the

children are using the correct scale. Different force meters have different scales - some have very strong springs for measuring large forces; others have weaker springs and are good for measuring smaller forces. Children should try out a range of meters to get a feel for which is most appropriate for what they are measuring.

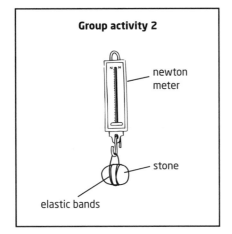

Group activity 2

newton meter

stone

elastic bands

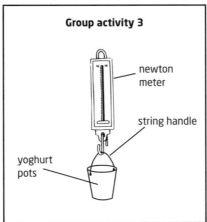

Group activity 3

newton meter

string handle

yoghurt pots

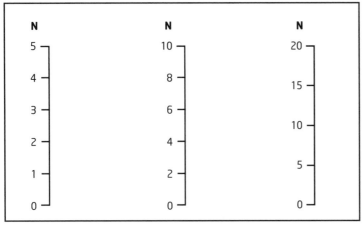

STARTER

Read the children the story of 'The Enormous Turnip', acting it out, with more and more children joining on the line to add their 'pull'. Explain that they may think this story is for younger children, but it includes some very important science. Ask the children: *Why did they need lots of people to help pull up the Enormous Turnip? (To make the force bigger.)*

MAIN ACTIVITY

Explain that we can measure a force - how big the pull is - by using a force meter, and show them one. Hold up a large spring and explain that the force meter has a spring inside it. Ask: *What do you think will happen to the spring if I give it a small pull?* (It will stretch a bit.) Demonstrate this. Ask: *And what do you think will happen if I give it a big pull?* (It will stretch a lot.) Demonstrate this. Explain that this is how a force meter works. Pass around different force meters so that the children can try pulling on them and watching the slider move up and down the scale. Ask: *What do you think the numbers on the force meter are for?* (To tell you how big the force is.) Explain that the unit of force is a newton, and that the numbers on the scale are telling you how many newtons the pull is. The bigger the pull, the more newtons it measures.

Show the children the first drawing of a scale on the flipchart. Tell them to use the scale marked in newtons not in grams. Show them on the flipchart and on the newton meter how to read whole newtons.

GROUP ACTIVITIES

Allow the children to circulate around the tables, spending about 10 minutes on each activity.
1. Work with this group. Show the children a variety of newton meters and how the scales are different. On the flipchart look at different scales with the children - counting up in ones, fives and tens as appropriate. Show the children how to measure to an appropriate degree of accuracy.
2. Ask the children to hang different objects from the collection of newton meters and look at the readings. The group needs to put the objects in order from the biggest pull to the smallest pull and record this.
3. Ask the children to find out how many marbles they need to put in a yogurt pot container hanging on a newton meter in order to make it read exactly 1N, 2N... The children should record this.
4. Allow the children to decide for themselves what forces they would like to measure around the classroom, for example pulling a desk, opening a door. They measure and record the force using a simple table.

ASSESSMENT

Can the children tell you that forces are measured using a force meter and that the unit is the newton? Are the children able to read the newton meter with an appropriate degree of accuracy? Do they understand that the more newtons recorded, the bigger the force?

PLENARY

Ask the children: *Can you think of an example of a very small force?* (Blowing a feather; pushing your hair off your face and so on.) *Can you think of an example of a very big force?* (Pushing a heavy shopping trolley; lifting the box in PE and so on.) Ask the children to share some of the measurements they chose to make. Write up some of the examples from Group activity 4 on the board or flipchart to help them get a feel for the size of force represented by 1N and 10N. Ask them: *How many newtons do you think it took to pull up the Enormous Turnip?*

OUTCOMES

- Can use a force meter.
- Can read the scale on a force meter to an appropriate degree of accuracy.
- Have a 'feel' for a force of 1N and 10N.

LINKS

Maths: measurement in standard units, using scales.

Differentiation

Use groups based on mathematical ability. Have the highest attaining group working with you first, as they can then apply this accuracy of measurement to the remaining Group activities. The other groups will benefit from extending their practical experience before this input. Teach children who need support in maths to measure to the nearest marked interval; average maths attainers to approximate to the nearest marked interval and work out what the half-way points between marked intervals represent. Teach higher maths attainers how to calculate and approximate measurements between the marked intervals.

Lesson 4 ◖ Exploring friction

Objectives
- To make predictions and test them.
- To compare results with predictions.
- To apply skills of measuring with a force meter.
- To know that friction is a force.
- To know that a force meter can be used to investigate friction.
- To know that friction depends on the surfaces in contact.

Vocabulary
friction, force, grip, surface

RESOURCES

Main activity: Several samples of different surfaces from the groups' collections as listed below; small model people.
Group activities: 1 Each group needs a collection of surfaces such as carpet (both sides), hardboard (both sides), corrugated cardboard, fur fabric, plain woven fabric and bubble wrap; bricks and half bricks with string tied around like a parcel so they can be 'hooked'; newton meters. **2** Sugar paper and felt-tipped pens.
Plenary: rollers (wooden or improvise with candles)

PREPARATION

Put out the resources for the Group activities on the tables, but reserve some surfaces for the Main activity. Check that the newton meters provided match the forces needed to pull the bricks on the different surfaces.

BACKGROUND

Friction is a force that acts between two surfaces. It acts in the opposite direction to pushes and pulls, resisting the movement. We tend to take friction for granted in our everyday lives. Because we take it for granted, it is not obvious that it is a force. The children may lack awareness of the role of friction in slowing things down. If there was no friction then a toy car, when pushed, would roll on for ever! This is what would happen up in space where there is nothing, not even air, to exert a frictional force in the opposite direction. In our everyday experience, things just stop 'naturally' if we stop pushing or pulling them, and we need to help children become aware of the role of friction in these situations.

STARTER

Show the children the model people 'pulling' along a brick and tell them a story of the people pulling a heavy load over different terrain, changing the surface they are pulling over.

MAIN ACTIVITY

Show the class the range of surfaces and how to hook the newton meter to the string around the brick to measure the amount of pull that is needed.

GROUP ACTIVITIES

1. Ask groups to choose three surfaces to work with. Ask them to predict which surface would need more force put on the brick to pull it along and to record their prediction. They can then test their prediction by measuring and recording their results in a table. Ask them to compare their results with their predictions. Can they suggest reasons why some surfaces needed more force to pull the brick over them than others? (They may use the word 'grip', or suggest that wool gets stuck on the brick.) Allow children to express their ideas in their own words.

2. Give each group a piece of sugar paper and some felt-tipped pens. Ask them to fold the sheet in half to form two columns and write 'smooth/slippery surfaces' and 'rough/grippy surfaces' as headings. Ask them to write or draw as many examples as they can in each column. They could move around the classroom to find examples as well as using previous experience.

ASSESSMENT

Are the children able to make predictions and test them? Do they use the force meter to measure with an appropriate degree of accuracy? Do they recognise that it takes more pull to move the brick on some surfaces than others? Can they suggest possible reasons for this? Do they relate the smoothness of the surface to the speed of an object travelling over it?

PLENARY

Ask groups to report back which surface took the most and least force to pull the brick. Do all the groups agree?

Introduce the term 'friction' as the 'grip' or 'pull' that the surfaces had on the brick. Explain that friction is a force. Ask: *Which surfaces had the most friction? Which surfaces had the least?*

Return to the scenario of the people pulling the brick and show how the rollers could be used to reduce the friction. Ask the children to offer their ideas to explain how this works. Make the real-life link with using wheels.

Differentiation
Work in mathematical ability groups so that the children apply the degree of accuracy of measurement they learned in the previous lesson. A ready-made table could be used to support those children with weaker recording skills.

OUTCOMES
- Can make predictions and test them.
- Can apply measurement skills with a newton meter to an investigation.
- Understand that the frictional force depends on the type of surface.

LINKS
Maths: measurement.

Lesson 5 ▪ Sam's slippery surfaces

Objectives
- To know that the force of friction can be investigated using slopes.
- To know that the force of friction depends on the surfaces in contact.
- To carry out a fair test.
- To know that measurements can be repeated for greater accuracy.

RESOURCES 💿
Main activity: A copy of the story of 'Sam's Slippery Surfaces' from photocopiable page 130 (also 'Sam's Slippery Surfaces' (red) on the CD-ROM) or display it on the interactive whiteboard, a ramp, a shoe, a ruler, a flipchart and marker pens.
Group activities: 1 Rulers; ramps (these could be any suitable rigid materials available such as sheets of thick card); collections of materials and surfaces as in Lesson 4. **2** footwear; wax crayons; newsprint paper for taking rubbings.

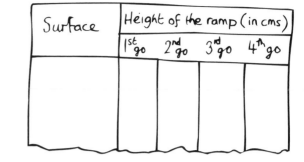

Surface	Height of the ramp (in cms)			
	1st go	2nd go	3rd go	4th go

Vocabulary
friction, rough, slope, smooth, surface

PREPARATION
Draw up a table on the flipchart ready for the results (see diagram opposite). Put out the resources for the Group activities.

BACKGROUND
Friction is the force of resistance when two surfaces move across each other. It pushes in the opposite direction to the movement. Children experience friction as grip or slipperiness and can relate this to their own lives. Friction can be measured directly with a newton meter as in Lesson 3 or seeing how much a ramp needs to be tilted before an object starts moving and making comparisons between surfaces.

Friction can be helpful - for example we need a certain amount of friction between our feet and the ground when we walk, which is why walking on ice is so difficult. Friction can also be unhelpful, which is why we oil the moving parts of machinery to reduce it.

STARTER
Read together the story of 'Sam's Slippery Surfaces' (on photocopiable page 130). Ask the children: *Which surfaces had the most friction? Which surfaces had the least friction? How can you be sure? Is carpet usually slippery? What about the kitchen floor?* If you show the story on an interactive whiteboard, you could highlight or annotate examples of high and low friction.

MAIN ACTIVITY
Have two different surfaces; move a shoe on each surface by pushing and pulling. Ask: *Is this a fair test?* (No, because we do not know if we are giving the same push or pull on each surface.) Explain that the children could compare different surfaces by using a ramp. Demonstrate putting a shoe on the ramp and lifting the ramp until the shoe starts to slip. Ask the children: *How could we compare this surface with other surfaces?* (Put different surfaces on the ramp and repeat.) Ask: *How could we measure the difference?* (Measure how high the ramp is lifted.) Demonstrate this with a child's help and record it on the table on the flipchart.

Start the test again and ask the children how high the ramp will need to be to get the shoe to move. They will probably suggest the same measurement as before. Repeat the test and measurement four times, showing that there is a small variation, recording the measurements on the table. Do not calculate the mean (average), but together decide on a number that best represents the measurements to put in the last column of the table. This could be the middle number, for example, or a number that occurred twice.

GROUP ACTIVITIES
1. Ask each group to carry out a test to find out which surface has the most friction using the approach you have demonstrated. Ask the children to record their results in a table drawn on sugar paper so they can feed back to the class.

Circulate, questioning how the test has been made fair, intervening to help the children improve the test when necessary. Ask: *Which surface do you predict will have the most friction? Why? Why is it better to repeat the measurements more than once?*
2. Ask the children to take rubbings of the soles of the shoes/trainers of the children in their group. Tell them to cut out the shoe shapes to form part of

Differentiation
Work in mixed-ability groups so that the children support each other.

a display on friction. Ask: *What similarities/differences do you notice about the soles of the shoes? Can you explain why some soles grip better than others?* Ask the children to write captions to go alongside the shoe shapes to communicate their ideas to the rest of the class.

ASSESSMENT
Do the children carry out the test in a fair way, such as using the same shoe, measuring in the same way each time? Can they suggest reasons why the different surfaces have different frictional properties? Can they explain why it is better to repeat the measurements?

PLENARY
Allow time for each group to feed back their findings to the whole class. If different groups had different results this may be because they used different types of shoe. Can the children suggest why using different shoes would make a difference? Ask the children to relate this to Lesson 3. Did they get the same results with this different way of testing friction?

Ask the children to think of the story and whether they can think of any examples of how different surfaces are used for safety, for example, bath mats, rough tiles around swimming pools.

OUTCOMES
● Can understand how repeating measurements can improve accuracy.
● Know that slopes can be used to investigate friction.
● Know that different materials and surfaces have different frictional properties.
● Can make independent decisions about fair testing.

Lesson 6 ◗ Friction all around us

Objective
● To know that frictional forces occur in many places.

RESOURCES
Writing materials.

MAIN ACTIVITY
Review the examples of friction that the children are aware of so far – outdoor surfaces, floor surfaces, shoes. However, explain to the children that there will be friction wherever two surfaces touch each other.

Ask them to work in pairs to collect examples of friction around the classroom and school. For example; wiping feet on a doormat, pushing chairs across the floor, moving a pencil across paper. This could be extended for homework, for example riding a bike on grass, washing up and so on.

ASSESSMENT
Are the children able to identify examples of friction in their surroundings? Can they distinguish between higher and lower friction? Can they suggest examples of when friction is useful and when it is not?

PLENARY
Collate all the examples together as a class. Each pair could write two examples on card and these could be put together as a short-term wall display. Ask the children to pick out an example of where friction is useful and where it is not.

Differentiation
Challenge children by asking them to classify their examples as high or low friction.

OUTCOMES
● Can recognise where frictional forces occur.
● Can describe instances where friction is useful and can describe instances where friction is not useful.

Lesson 7 ▪ On the move

Objectives
● To elicit children's ideas about friction.
● For children to question a 'taken for granted' situation.

RESOURCES
A toy car.

MAIN ACTIVITY
Have the children sitting in a circle on the carpet. Roll the toy car several times and ask: *What do you notice about how the car moves?* (Accept all answers.) Then ask: *How am I making the car start moving?* Listen to the children's responses; some may say 'by pushing it', which is correct, but there may be other ideas expressed such as 'by giving it energy'. Some children may use the word 'force' instead of 'push'.

Ask: *How does the car stop? Why doesn't it just go on for ever?* (It stops because of the friction between the wheels and the floor surface.) Children may suggest that it 'runs out of push', or 'it runs out of energy'. However, some may suggest that 'the wheels are catching on the carpet'.

Ask: *How does the car keep going?* (The answer is that the push has not yet been overcome by friction acting in the opposite direction, but do not expect children to articulate this!) They may say 'it just goes', or 'the wheels make it move'.

Ask each child to do an annotated drawing in response to the following three questions: How does the car start moving? How does it keep going? How does it stop?

Differentiation
There may be some children who are still at a stage of development in which they make suggestions such as 'the car runs out of petrol' or 'it puts the brakes on'. Intervene by looking at the toy car with the child and asking: *Do you think real petrol goes in here? Is there a person to press the brakes? What else might be making this toy car slow down and stop?*

Children with poor writing skills can express their ideas mainly through the drawing, with the teacher scribing the annotations to the drawing.

Extend children who have completed this by asking: *How could we make the car stop quicker?*

ASSESSMENT
In their annotated drawings, are the children using the term 'force', showing that they are applying what they have learned in previous lessons? Do they mention the surface when explaining how the car stops? If so, are they using the word 'grip', or even 'friction'?

PLENARY
Ask: *How could we make the car go further before it stops?* (Push it harder, give it a bigger force, or put it on a smoother surface.) If necessary introduce the idea of a surface by asking: *What might happen if we pushed it on the floor rather than the carpet?* Test this out briefly.

Explain that there seem to be two things – the push and the surface – that affect how the car moves, and that the next lessons will help the children to explore these ideas.

OUTCOMES
● Improved teacher understanding of children's ideas about friction.
● Children can consider a 'taken for granted' situation in a new way.

Lesson 8 ▪ Water resistance

Objectives
● To know that water resistance slows down the speed of an object and is related to the object's shape.
● To measure short time spans.

RESOURCES 💿
Main activity: Photographs of boats and fish taken from different angles (*Junior Education* magazine is a good source of photographs or search the internet and display them on an interactive whiteboard); models of fish and boats (or real fish would be even better); Blu-Tack®; Plasticine; three tall transparent containers such as plastic lemonade bottles; water; non-allergenic wallpaper paste prepared according to the instructions on the packet.

Group activity: Plasticine; a tank of water; copies of photocopiable page 131 (also 'Water resistance' (red) on the CD-ROM); writing materials; stopwatches (optional).

PREPARATION

Have a flipchart to Blu-Tack® the photographs to. Set up the three transparent containers: leave one empty, put water in the second and wallpaper paste in the third (see diagram below, and on the CD-ROM). Divide the Plasticine into a lump for each group, fill the water tanks and put a set out on each group's table.

BACKGROUND

Water and air resistance are forms of friction – both are forces that oppose the movement of objects through them. Children will have some experience of water resistance from swimming. By comparing the movement of objects in water with objects in air and the more viscous wallpaper paste, children will gain an understanding of the effects of water resistance and be prepared for ideas about air resistance that will be developed in subsequent lessons.

Air resistance acts in a very similar way to water resistance, but as it cannot be seen, its effects are less obvious. Often, the way objects fall is put down to how heavy they are, but in fact a heavy object and a light object dropped at the same time from the same height will hit the ground at the same time. However, in our everyday experience, many light objects are shaped so that they have more surface area for the air to push up on. Imagine dropping a feather and how it catches the air and 'floats' down.

So a key idea to the next series of lessons is how the shape of an object affects its movement – the idea of 'streamlining' is introduced.

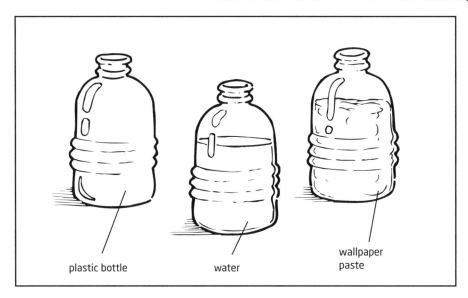

plastic bottle   water   wallpaper paste

STARTER

Show the children the photographs or models of boats and fish and ask them to describe their shapes. Ask: *Why do you think the fish and boats have pointed fronts?* Ask the children to describe their own experiences of moving through water. *What does it feel like? Is it easy to walk in water? Are there any forces involved?* (It feels like the water is pushing you back; you can't go as fast as on land.)

MAIN ACTIVITY

Make three round balls of Plasticine about the size of a marble and drop one into the container of air. Ask the children to predict what will happen when you drop it into the container of water. Drop it. Ask for their reactions: *Was it slower or faster than you expected?* Show them the third container and explain that it contains wallpaper paste. Ask the children to predict what will happen to the Plasticine in this container. Drop it. Ask: *Would anyone like to say anything about this?* Introduce the term 'resistance'.

If the children do not suggest changing the shape of the Plasticine, then you can ask: *How could we change how fast the Plasticine falls?* Ask: *How can we make this a fair test?* (Use the same-sized balls of Plasticine.)

GROUP ACTIVITY

Ask each group to make some Plasticine shapes they think will fall quickly and some that they think will fall slowly. Most children can quantify the time it takes to reach the bottom of their tank of water by counting. They can

Differentiation
Group activity
Children who need support can use 'Water resistance' (green) from the CD-ROM, which does not require them to evaluate their test results in writing. (This can be done orally with adult support.) Some children may need to record their results qualitatively (it was fast, slow, very fast, it wobbled as it went down).

Children with more advanced investigative skills can be extended by suggesting that they make the measurements using a stopwatch.

record their predictions and the results of their test on photocopiable page 131. Ask them to write what they found out on the photocopiable sheet, thinking about the shapes of the Plasticine and what difference it made to how they fell. They could also record what happened in the Main activity or have a go with the three containers from this activity.

ASSESSMENT
In their writing and drawing, do the children show an understanding that streamlined shapes fall faster? Are they able to use a stopwatch with a reasonable degree of precision?

PLENARY
Each group shows the rest of the class which of their shapes dropped the fastest and slowest. Ask: *What do all the slow shapes have in common? What do all the fast shapes have in common?* Introduce the term 'streamlined'. Ask the children when it would be good to have a streamlined shape and when it might be an advantage not to be streamlined.

OUTCOMES
● Can describe a streamlined shape and its usefulness.
● Can describe how water resistance slows down the speed of an object.

LINKS
Design and technology: evaluating designs.

Lesson 9 ◗ Air resistance

Objective
● To know that air resistance can slow down the movement of objects.
● To design and carry out an investigation as independently as possible.

RESOURCES
Ramps, toy cars, rulers, stopclocks, card, sticky tape, Blu-Tack®, sugar paper and felt-tipped pens for presenting work.

MAIN ACTIVITY
Remind the children about the streamlined shapes of Plasticine in water and wallpaper paste in Lesson 8. Explain that you want them to investigate how changing the shape of the front of a car by sticking card to it affects its speed. Demonstrate with one example. Explain that the group is to make its own decisions about how to do the test and that each group will present their findings to the rest of the class.

Circulate, asking the groups questions such as: *Are you going to take any measurements? How have you made sure this is a fair test? What will you keep the same and what will you change? How will you record your results?*

ASSESSMENT
This is a good opportunity to assess how the children are applying the investigative skills focused on in previous lessons. Have they made predictions? Have they planned fair tests? Have they made appropriate measurements? Have they recorded results in a table? And so on.

Differentiation
Have mixed-ability groups for peer support. Accurate timing with stopclocks can be quite challenging. If this is too advanced, then groups could measure the distance the car travels before stopping instead. Give additional teacher support where groups are struggling. The larger the scale you work on the more obvious the differences will be, so large cars would be preferable.

PLENARY
Each group reports their findings to the class. Develop ideas about the area of the card and the shapes. The children should find that the more pointed shapes travel faster or further, and that flatter shapes travel more slowly or stop sooner. Relate this back to ideas about streamlining in water.

OUTCOMES
● Can carry out an investigation with independence and confidence.
● Know that streamlining affects the movement of objects in air and water.

Lesson 10 ◖Falling objects

Objectives
● To explore and compare how different objects fall.
● To introduce the term 'gravity' as the force which pulls things down.

RESOURCES
A collection of objects for each group, such as a feather, a piece of card, tissue paper, Plasticine, a cork, a paper clip, two pieces of A4 paper.

MAIN ACTIVITY
Demonstrate dropping a piece of Plasticine, linking this to the previous lesson. Ask: *What is making it fall?* Some children will use the term 'gravity'. If not, introduce the idea that gravity is a force that pulls things down.

Ask the children to explore dropping the different objects in their collection and to make annotated drawings about what happens in each case. Circulate, asking the children: *Can you describe how that falls? What differences have you noticed between how the objects fall? Why do you think the Plasticine fell faster than the tissue paper?* Ask the children to make notes about any comparisons they make, for example, 'I have noticed that the paper clip fell faster than the feather.' Ask: *Why are the objects falling downwards?* (Because of the force of gravity.)

ASSESSMENT
Have the children noted differences in how different objects fall? Have they made comparisons? Can they use the term 'gravity' appropriately?

PLENARY
Ask the children to feed back any of their observations. Hold up the feather and the paper clip. Ask: *Which of these do you predict will land first?* (The paper clip.) Try it. Ask: *Why do you think that the paper clip landed first?* It is likely that some children will say that it is because it is heavier. Hold up a piece of A4 paper and drop it. Ask: *What did you notice about how it fell?* (It went from side to side, like the feather.) Take another piece of A4 paper and fold it up. Hold up both pieces and ask: *Which do you think will hit the ground first?* (The folded piece.) Ask: *Is this piece of paper heavier than the other?* (No.) *So why did it hit the ground first?* (It is a more 'streamlined' shape.) Link this to the lessons on resistance in liquids.

Differentiation
For children who need support with writing, provide a word bank with the names of the items, and words such as 'fall', 'fast', 'slowly', 'air', 'move', 'force', 'heavy', 'light'.

OUTCOMES
● Can explore and compare how different objects fall.
● Can use the term 'gravity' appropriately.

Lesson 11 ◖Paper spinner test

Objectives
● To know that air resistance can slow down the movement of objects.
● To identify and control variables in an investigation.
● To carry out an investigation with an awareness of safety.

Vocabulary
paper spinner

RESOURCES ◉
Main activity: Photocopiable page 132 (also 'Paper spinner test 1' (red) on the CD-ROM), paper clip, scissors.
Group activities: Stopclocks, metre rulers, rulers, paper clips, templates of different sizes of paper spinners (photocopiable page 132), various types of paper and card, the recording sheets on photocopiable page 133 (also 'Paper spinner test 2' (red) on the CD-ROM).

PREPARATION
Set up the resources for the Group activity on each table. Have the resources for the Main activity to hand.

BACKGROUND
'Spinners' are used to explore air resistance from Key Stage 2 to Key Stage 4/Primary 4 to school leaving. This lesson focuses on the process skill of

Differentiation

Work in attainment groups according to investigative skills. When negotiating which group takes which variable, give the lower attainers a qualitative variable such as type of paper or small, medium and large spinners; the middle attainers can look at a discrete quantitative variable such as number of paper clips, and the high attainers a continuous quantitative variable such as length of wing. Three different spinners are enough for the lower attainers, while higher attainers could make up to five.

The accuracy of measurement can also be differentiated, with lower attainers counting, most children timing to the nearest second and very high attainers recording time to one decimal place.

Support lower-attaining groups with more teacher time. Intervene if children are changing more than one aspect of the spinner.

developing an awareness of variables – the different things that can be changed in a test. To have a controlled, fair test, only one variable can be changed while the rest are held constant. Children often find this a difficult concept to grasp and try to change more than one thing at a time.

Safety: Make sure you set clear boundaries about what may or may not be stood on safely to reach heights for releasing the spinners.

STARTER
Show the children how to make the paper spinner. Drop the spinner and ask the children to observe carefully. Drop it again. Ask the children to describe anything they notice about it: how fast it falls, whether it turns and so on.

MAIN ACTIVITY
Explain that we want to try and make the best possible paper spinner. As a class, brainstorm the different things that could be changed about the spinner – size, type of paper, number of paper clips, length of the wings. Record the children's ideas on the flipchart.

Decide as a class what you are going to observe/measure – the time it takes to drop is the most straightforward.

Explain that each group can take one thing to change, and that they need to make sure that they keep all the other things the same. Explain that if you changed two things at once, you would not know which had made the difference. Negotiate which groups will take which variable.

GROUP ACTIVITY
Each group should investigate changing one variable. Circulate, and assist with making the spinners if necessary.

Provide tables for recording (photocopiable page 133), but expect the children to put the data in the correct place. This photocopiable page includes space for repeated measurement, but an approximate average, not a calculation of the mean, is all that is needed for Year 4/Primary 5.

ASSESSMENT
Observe the children working. Are the children changing only one variable, while keeping the others the same? Are they working safely?

PLENARY
Ask each group to report any problems they had and how they overcame them. Explain that in the next lesson they will make graphs of their data and consider their findings.

OUTCOMES
● Can change one variable and keep others constant.
● Can carry out an investigation safely.

ENRICHMENT
Lesson 12 ▪ Paper spinner results

Objectives
● To present data in the form of a bar chart.
● To understand the value of graphs.
● To suggest explanations for their findings.

RESOURCES
Main activity: Prepared data (see below) on a sheet of sugar paper, a grid drawn on a flipchart or large squared paper, marker pens.
Group activities: Squared paper, pencils, rulers, coloured pencils.
ICT link: Graphing tool from the CD-ROM.

PREPARATION
Draw the table of data as shown below on the flipchart or sugar paper. Have the resources for the Main activity ready where they will be clearly visible. Put out the resources for the Group activity on the tables.

Vocabulary
bar chart, line graph, table

BACKGROUND

The class may have learned about making graphs from tables of data in maths, and may be ready to apply this skill. However, many children find this difficult, particularly choosing scales, and using real data can be problematic. It is a good idea to model this process for the children.

STARTER

Remind the children of their investigations into paper spinners. Explain that you want them to present their results as graphs (perhaps for a display or assembly) to help other people understand what they have done.

MAIN ACTIVITY

Using the chart of prepared data, model how to draw a graph. Show the children that the variable they changed goes along the bottom (x-axis), and what they measured goes up the side (y-axis). In this activity the scale on the y-axis is most likely to cause problems, but one square can represent one second or one 'count'. Show them how to set out the numbers on the y-axis on the lines, not in the spaces of the squares. Label the axes. Ask different children to come up and show where the bars should go for each part of the data from the table. Make sure they understand which number they are plotting.

Ask the children questions about the graph: *How long did it take the spinner with 1/2/3 paper clips to fall? Which spinner fell the fastest? How long did the spinner with one paper clip take to fall?* And so on.

Explain that you want the children to draw their own graphs and to think and write about what they found out.

What we changed Number of paper clips.	1st drop time (in counts)	2nd drop time (in counts)	3rd drop time (in counts)	Overall drop time (in counts)
1	4	4	3	4
2	3	3	4	3
3	1	2	1	1

GROUP ACTIVITY 💿

Each group draws a graph of their results from the previous lesson on squared paper. Ask them to write a few sentences about what the graph is telling them. Ask them to try and explain *why* it happened.

The graphing tool on the CD-ROM can be used on an interactive whiteboard to model how to create a graph, or the tool can be used by a small group of children to create their own graph.

ASSESSMENT

Are the children able to construct a graph that represents their data accurately? Can they comment on what the graph is showing?

PLENARY

Let each group show one other group their graph and tell them what they found out about their paper spinners. Ask the whole class if they find it easier to understand each other's results with a graph to look at. Ask if drawing the graph helped them to think about their own results.

Differentiation
Support the lower-attaining groups in setting up their graphs.

If, in Lesson 8, higher-attaining children used quantitative data then they will be able to draw a line graph, but for most Year 4/ Primary 5 children a bar chart is appropriate. They may need extra teacher input to do this.

OUTCOMES

● Can present data as a graph.
● Can understand the value of presenting data as a graph.
● Can suggest explanations for their own results.

LINKS

Maths: data-handling.

Lesson 13 ◗ Parachutes

Objectives
● To begin to understand that air resistance can slow down a moving object.
● To draw conclusions and give explanations for results.

Vocabulary
friction, gravity, air resistance, streamlined.

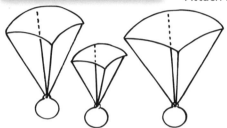

Differentiation
Some children will find the making of the parachutes fiddly and time consuming, so you may decide to give the ready made set of three parachutes to them. Some can be given templates or ready-cut-out materials to make the parachutes from. Children with a high mathematical ability can be challenged by deciding on their own measurements for the parachute and this will enable them to look for patterns in the data with more sophistication, for example does a parachute that is twice as big fall twice as slowly?

Using stop watches can be quite a difficult skill. An alternative is to mark a target cross in chalk on the floor and instead of measuring the time taken to fall, a group could investigate how good the parachutes are at hitting the target, measuring how far away from it the parachute lands.

You may wish to provide a ready-made table for results, or make drawing a table of results a focus for some children. For other children this may be an opportunity to develop their understanding of fair testing.

RESOURCES
Main activity: Toy parachute with person on it. Three small home-made parachutes of different sizes, three identical small hanging weights, a stopwatch, a metre ruler.
Group activities: 1 Parachutes made by the children (from paper, plastic bags or light fabric), paper clips, stopwatches, paper, writing materials. **2** Three different sized large pieces of cardboard or similar material (largest about 1m by 60cm), a safe space to run holding the card.

PREPARATION
Prepare three small different-sized parachutes, using thin cloth and string. Attach identical small hanging weights to the three parachutes (see below).

BACKGROUND
This activity deals with the friction that occurs between a solid object and air. Some shapes move through air (and gases and liquids) more easily than others. For example, the bow of a boat is pointed and the stern is flatter, so a boat moves forward more easily than backward. This activity looks at 'air resistance' by testing which shapes move through air most easily.

STARTER
Tell the children a story of a hero jumping out of a plane as part of a daring escape. What would he/she need to help them land safely? (A parachute.) Drop the toy parachute. Ask the children to discuss in pairs what they think the parachute is doing to make the landing safer and then invite them to share ideas. Develop the point that the parachute is slowing down the fall so the person hits the ground much more gently. Ask how the children how they think it might be doing that.

MAIN ACTIVITY
Show the children the three parachutes and explain that they are of different sizes, but each is carrying the same mass. *Why is this important?* (To make the test fair.) *What other factors must be kept the same to make a fair test?* (Same height, same shape of parachute, same length of strings, same material for parachutes.) Ask the children to discuss and predict in pairs which one will fall fastest. Invite pairs to share their ideas.

GROUP ACTIVITIES
1. Ask the children to carry out a fair test to see if their predictions were right. They can make parachutes and load each one with a couple of paper clips, then measure the time taken for it to fall to the ground from a constant height (about 1.5m).

Ask the children to present a table of results and some sentences about what the results told them. They could then try to explain the results using annotated drawings of the three parachutes. This is an opportunity to revisit drawing arrows to indicate forces.
2. To provide a kinaesthetic experience of air resistance, individual children can try running (looking where they are going) holding different sized pieces of card in front of them to get a feel for the way they resist movement.

ASSESSMENT
Can the children carry out the investigation accurately in order to be able to look for patterns in the results? Can they draw conclusions about how the size of the parachute affected how it fell? Can they give an explanation of how the parachute works? Can they use the language of forces?

PLENARY

Bring out the three parachutes used in the main activity and ask the children if their results were as they predicted. Help them to summarise their findings in general statements such as 'the bigger the parachute the slower it fell'. There may be some surprises too - perhaps some materials didn't open out properly -take these seriously and consider possible explanations. Ask: *Were there any difficulties in carrying out the test?* (such as a breeze) and think about how these might have affected the results.

OUTCOMES
- Can describe how a parachute slows down a falling person.
- Can carry out an investigation, draw conclusions, suggest explanations.

Lesson 14 ▪ Assessment

Objectives
- To assess the children's knowledge and understanding about how forces can affect the shape and movement of objects.
- To assess the children's ability to plan a test, predict and suggest explanations.

RESOURCES ◉
Assessment activities: 1 A school shoe, a trainer, a Wellington boot, photocopiable page 134 (also 'Assessment - 2' (red) on the CD-ROM). **2** Photocopiable page 135 (also 'Assessment - 2' (red) on the CD-ROM).

ASSESSMENT ACTIVITY 1
Hand out copies of photocopiable page 134. Explain that the children should try to write their ideas down, but that they could do a drawing to help them explain. Let them know that it is not a writing test and you will help them.

LOOKING FOR LEVELS
For question 1, look for words such as 'push', 'pull', 'squeeze', and 'bend'. Most of the class should answer this securely. For question 2 accept 'force meter' or 'newton meter'. Most of the class should know what the equipment is, though a child with a weaker vocabulary may show this by drawing. In question 3 most children should be able to explain that the parachute slows the soldier down. Accept answers that show an understanding of this. Some children may give an explanation involving the shape of the parachute, or how it 'catches the air', indicating a greater understanding of air resistance.

ASSESSMENT ACTIVITY 2
Hand out copies of photocopiable page 135. Show the children the three shoes and explain the task.

LOOKING FOR LEVELS
For photocopiable page 134, most children will be able to suggest a test that could be carried out with some elements of measurement or control, for example using a ramp. Less confident children may suggest trying out the shoes on an icy day. Explaining how the test can be made fair would indicate aspects of a higher level of attainment.

Most children in the class will be able to make a prediction (Wellington or trainer). An explanation related to past experience such as 'because my trainers have got good grip' is a response typical of NC Level 2/Scottish Level B. Referring to the nature of the surface ('it's got bumps', 'it's made of rubber') is indicative of NC Level 3/Scottish Level C.

PLENARY
Ask the children to share their responses and discuss their answers to both assessments. Reinforce the use of the words 'force' and 'newton meter'. Ask them what they have learned from the unit and whether any of their ideas have changed.

Push, pull and twist

- Describe what is happening in each picture.
- Include the words "push", "pull" or "twist".

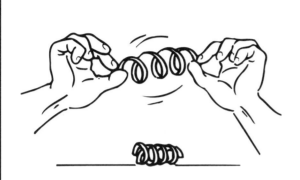

_____

_____

_____

_____

- Now make up some of your own.

Illustration © Debbie Clark

Sam's Slippery Surfaces

Sam looked out of the window. It was a beautiful frosty morning and, best of all, it was Saturday! Sam put on her tracksuit and some warm woolly socks and ran down the hall. She was going so fast that she slipped on the carpet. Her heart seemed to miss a beat as she skidded towards the front door, only just keeping her balance by grabbing on to the banisters.

"Steady on Sam – you'll do yourself an injury!" said her Dad. "It's a lovely day. Why don't you go out in the garden before breakfast?"

Sam slipped on her shoes and rushed out, "Whee!" The path was all icy and she did some great skids along it. Sam tried skidding on the grass, but that didn't seem to work so well, so she went back to the path. Sam's little brother, Nick, came out to join in. He had a go at skidding, but he didn't go very far at all. Sam laughed at him.

"Idiot – you've got your trainers on – no wonder you aren't slipping!" Nick wasn't too happy at having his big sister make fun of him. He stomped back inside and stood in the kitchen leaving frosty puddles on the floor.

"Come on Sam, time for breakfast!" called her Dad. Sam zoomed up the path and in the back door. She did the biggest skid of all along the kitchen floor, landing on her bottom with a graceless thump!

As Sam fought to hold back the tears, Nick just smirked.

Illustration © Debbie Clark

Water resistance

Our own test:

Plasticine shape (drawing)	What I predict will happen	How long it took this shape to drop

What we found out: _____

◀ These pictures show the containers that the Plasticine was dropped into.

◀ Write and draw about what happened in each case.

In air: _____

_____

In water: _____

_____

In wallpaper paste: _____

_____

Illustration © Debbie Clark

Paper spinner test – 1

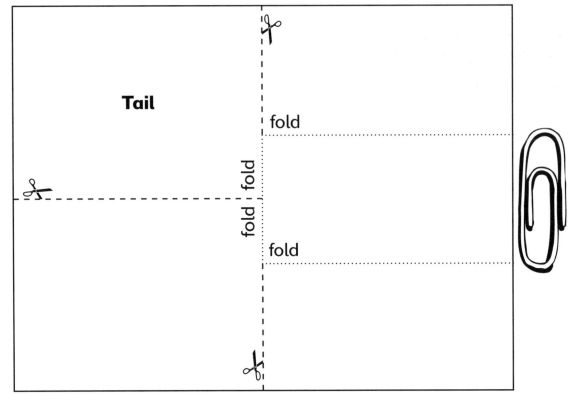

Tail

fold

fold fold

fold fold

fold

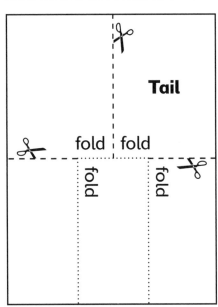

Tail

fold fold

fold fold

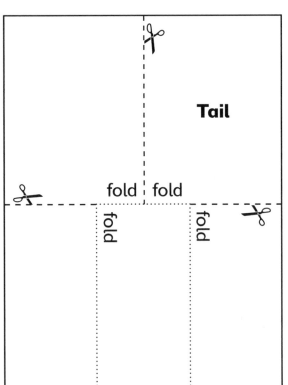

Tail

fold fold

fold fold

◾ Hold the two sides of the tail together with a paper clip.

◢SCHOLASTIC

Illustration © Debbie Clark

Illustration © Debbie Clark

Paper spinner test – 2

Describe your first spinner:

What we changed	First drop time	Second drop time	Third drop time	Overall drop time

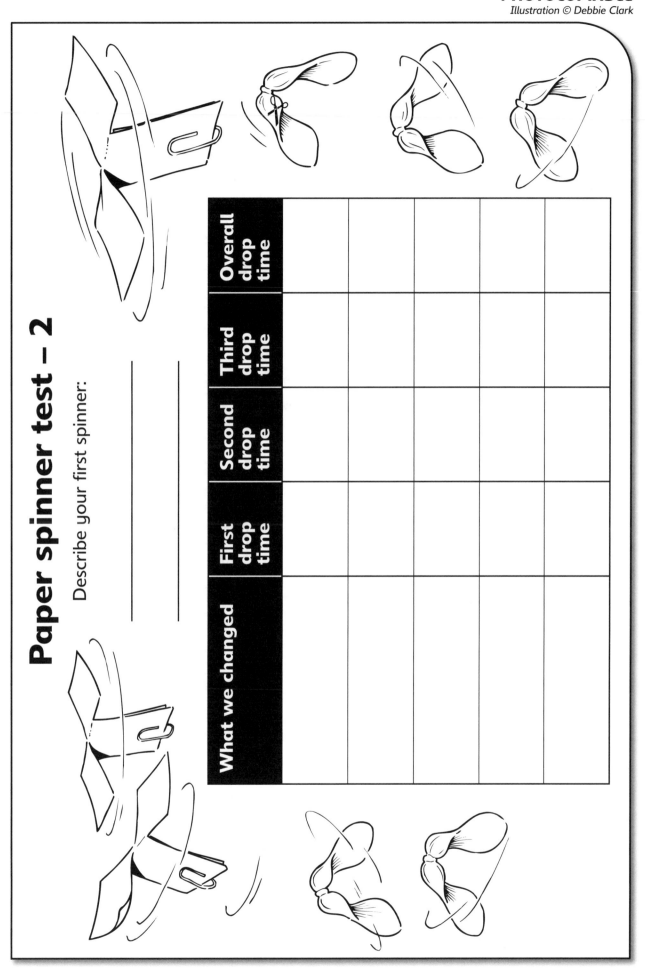

PHOTOCOPIABLE

Assessment – 1

1. What could Luke do to the Plasticine to change its shape?

_____

_____

_____

_____

_____

2. Nasreen wants to know how much force it will take to pull the door closed. What equipment could she use to find out?

_____

_____

_____

_____

_____

3. How will the parachute help the soldier?

_____

_____

_____

_____

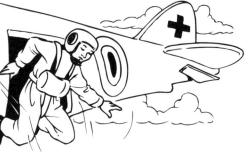

Illustration © Debbie Clark

■SCHOLASTIC

Assessment – 2

◣ Sam and her brother Nick want to find out which shoes have the best grip. They looked at Sam's school shoes, Nick's trainers and their Dad's wellies.

◣ What could Sam and Nick do to find out which shoes had the best grip?

◣ Draw and write your ideas.

Which do you think will have the best grip?

◣ Explain why you think that one will be the best.

_____

_____

CHAPTER 6 Exploring forces

Lesson	Objectives	Main activity	Group activities	Plenary	Outcomes
Enrichment Lesson 1 Strength of structural components	• To know a variety of structures are used to support the weight of objects. • To ask scientific questions, plan how to answer them and decide what evidence to collect.	Ask questions about the strength of shapes used to build different structures. Look at possible shapes for beams and ask questions about which are stronger.	Decide on one question to ask about structural components. Plan and carry out an investigation to find the answer.	Report back on findings. Draw conclusions about the strength of different-shaped structural components.	• Can plan and carry out a test. • Can compare the strength of different structural components.
Enrichment Lesson 2 Load-carrying structures	• To know that a variety of structures are used to support the weight of objects. • To use knowledge of structural components to build a load-carrying structure. • To test a design, making modifications in a systematic way in the light of evidence collected.	The children design and build a load-carrying platform, using weights during construction to identify points where the structure needs to be strengthened.		Test all the platforms for their load-carrying capacity. The children identify good points in each design.	• Can use scientific knowledge to build a load-carrying platform. • Can assess and modify their design and construction.
Enrichment Lesson 3 Reducing friction	• To revise how friction can be reduced by lubricants. • To conduct an investigation: ask a scientific question that can be tested, decide what evidence to collect, collect and record data appropriately, then identify and describe patterns in the data.	Review differences in friction forces between rough and smooth surfaces. Introduce the idea that it requires more energy to overcome the friction between rough surfaces.	Plan and carry out an investigation to see whether putting liquids on surfaces changes the friction on that surface. Look for patterns in the results.	Groups report back on findings and explain patterns in the results and conclusions drawn. Relate these findings back to the idea of energy use.	• Know that lubricants reduce friction. • Can decide how to test a scientific question. • Can identify patterns in the results.
Enrichment Lesson 4 Liquid lubricants	• To know that friction can be reduced by many liquid lubricants.	The children use secondary sources to find out about situations where reducing friction is useful or harmful. Make information cards and warning notices.		Children present warning notices and information cards. Discuss friction forces and energy in engines with and without lubricant oil.	• Can recognise the importance of oil in reducing friction. • Can recognise that reducing friction can be harmful as well as helpful.
Enrichment Lesson 5 Sand timers and water clocks	• To know that everything falls down and this is due to gravity. • To know that falling materials can be used to measure time. • To identify the significant features of a gravity-controlled timer. • To evaluate a sand timer and a water clock and describe their limitations.	Discuss important features of a sand timer. The children consider what materials would be suitable to make a timer from, how these would affect the design, and what things the timer could time.	Build a sand timer and/or water clock. Use it to time, and compare it with a stopwatch. Discuss the limitations and advantages of each.	Discuss suggestions for improving the design of 'poor' timers. Discuss the limitations and advantages of sand and water timers.	• Can design, make and use a sand timer and/or a water clock. • Can recognise strengths and weaknesses in a design.
Enrichment Lesson 6 Design a waterwheel	• To define the significant features of a good waterwheel. • To know that falling water can be used to provide energy for work. • To use scientific knowledge to design a waterwheel.	Look at a model waterwheel and discuss how it works to raise a weight. Discuss what is meant by a 'good' waterwheel. Discuss what features of a waterwheel could be improved.	The children design and build a waterwheel, then test it to see how closely it performs to the design specification.	Some children explain their designs and choice of materials. Discuss any problems, and how the wheels could be improved.	• Know that the energy of moving water can be converted into useful mechanical energy in a turning wheel. • Can use scientific knowledge to identify the significant features of a waterwheel to be designed.

Lesson	Objectives	Main activity	Group activities	Plenary	Outcomes
Enrichment Lesson 7 Wind energy	• To know that the force of the wind can be used to provide energy for work.	Compare three types of windmill. Make energy flow charts for a variety of situations where energy comes from the wind.		Recap on energy changes involving wind energy. Discuss how the amount of work done by a windmill can be increased.	• Know that moving air can be used as an energy source.
Enrichment Lesson 8 Wind strength and direction	• To know that changes in the direction and strength of the wind can be measured. • To identify significant features of a wind direction and strength meter. • To think of a variety of designs and choose the best one for a specified purpose. • To test a design by making a series of observations, and adjust the design where necessary.	Identify the key features of an instrument to measure wind direction and strength. Discuss possible designs and consider how easy they would be to build.	Build a combined wind direction and wind strength meter. Test how well it works.	Look at the children's instruments and compare them with real wind-recording instruments	• Can find the direction of the wind and measure its force. • Can specify the key features of a wind meter. • Can produce a design to meet specifications, test it and suggest improvements in the light of observations.
Enrichment Lesson 9 Balloon racer	• To know that when an object is pushed, an opposing push back can be felt. • To decide what evidence to collect in an investigation. • To explain results, using scientific knowledge and understanding.	Make a balloon racer on a string. Investigate the factors that affect how far along the string the racer travels.		Discuss the forces acting on the racer and the energy involved.	• Can recognise action and reaction in a pair of forces. Recognise a change from stored energy to movement energy. • Can explain the results of an experiment in scientific terms.
Enrichment Lesson 10 Balloon-powered cars	• To use the force of moving air. • To know that when an object is pushed, an opposing push back can be felt. • To design a balloon-powered toy car. • To evaluate the limitations of their own and other designs.	Design and build a balloon-powered toy car. Predict, then test, factors that will affect how far the toy car will travel.		Discuss the forces acting on the car and why some cars travel further than others. Discuss real vehicles propelled by gases.	• Can recognise action and reaction in a pair of forces. • Can recognise a change from stored energy in a balloon skin to movement energy in the air and a toy car. • Can evaluate a design and make suggestions for improvement.
Enrichment Lesson 11 Elastic-band crawler	• To know that energy stored in an elastic band can be turned into movement energy. • To ask scientific questions, plan an investigation to find the answers and decide what evidence to collect.	Discuss how an elastic-band 'crawler' works and what factors might make it work well. The children make a 'crawler' and test how well it works, making measurements and presenting the results.		Discuss the limitations of elastic-band power. Discuss situations where it would or would not be useful.	• Can recognise a change from stored energy in a twisted elastic band to movement energy. • Can decide what factors might affect how well the 'crawler' works. • Can plan what to do and what evidence to collect in order to test an idea.

Assessment	Objectives	Activity 1	Activity 2
Enrichment Lesson 12	• To assess the children's knowledge of the forces affecting moving water. • To assess the children's knowledge of how stretched elastic bands provide a force and of the factors affecting the strength of the force. • To assess the children's ability to describe physical processes in terms of energy changes.	Identify the factors affecting how far water from a hosepipe will go, and describe an investigation to demonstrate the effect of nozzle size. Describe the energy changes taking place when a water jet hits a waterwheel, and the effect on the waterwheel.	Identify things that have stored elastic energy and moving energy. Identify the forces acting in one situation. Identify factors that affect how far an arrow fired from a bow travels, and describe the energy changes that take place.

Do different shaped beams have the same strength?

LEARNING OBJECTIVES AND OUTCOMES
- Make systematic measurements and observations.
- Use observations and measurements to draw conclusions.
- Check observations and measurements by repeating them.
- Use a wide range of methods, including bar charts, to communicate data in an appropriate manner.

ACTIVITY
The children make different shaped beams (flat, square, triangular and round), each beam using a single sheet of A4 paper, and test them to see how much weight they can support. They repeat each measurement several times, using a new beam each time, and record their results in a table. They can then use the data in the table to draw a bar chart for the different shaped beams and use the chart to decide which beam shape is strongest, and which weakest.

LESSON LINKS
This Sc1 activity forms an integral part of Lesson 1, Strength of structural components.

ENRICHMENT
Lesson 1 ▪ Strength of structural components

Objectives
- To know that a variety of structures are used to support the weight of objects.
- To ask scientific questions, plan how to answer them and decide what evidence to collect.

Vocabulary
structures, components, beams, arches

RESOURCES 💿
Main activity: Pictures of bridges constructed from different materials and in different shapes; pictures of typical Victorian iron architecture, showing iron frameworks; A4 paper, adhesive tape, strips and fasteners from construction kits (or strips of strong cardboard and paper fasteners), a large sheet of paper, a marker pen.
Group activity: A4 paper, adhesive tape, strips and fasteners from construction kits (or strips of strong cardboard and paper fasteners), weights, rulers, copy of photocopiable page 152 (also 'Strength of structural components' (red) on the CD-ROM) for each child.

PREPARATION
Put the large sheet of paper in a prominent position to display the children's questions about structures. Enlarge the pictures if necessary.

BACKGROUND
In all their design work in this unit, the children have to consider whether a material they choose is appropriate for the intended task. Therefore the unit starts with two lessons that encourage the children to look critically at a particular characteristic of components (in this case, strength) and then to choose a suitable component for a particular task.

STARTER
Explain that in this unit, we are going to think about how we make good designs for things. We are surrounded by things that scientists and engineers have designed. Ask the children to suggest some examples.

Some children may need help finding a suitable question to investigate. Here are some questions they could investigate: *What shapes are hardest to distort (pull or push out of shape)?* (Try a selection of straight-sided shapes: triangles, squares, rectangles, hexagons and so on.) *Can a flat beam hold up more weight than a round beam? Which holds up more weight, a flat beam or an arch?* (Find out whether it matters which way up the arch is.) Help them to plan the investigation.

Extend children by asking them to find out whether there is any difference in the strength of particular structural components if they are used different ways round. For example: *Can a square beam support more weight if it is stood on its end or if it is laid on its side?*

Explain that whenever a scientist or engineer builds something, he or she has to be sure of using materials that will not break or fall apart later. So materials have to be tested to check that they will be suitable. Tell the children that their first design task will be to build something strong, and that in this lesson, they will start by testing some materials to find out how strong they are.

MAIN ACTIVITY

Show the children some pictures of bridges, both flat and arched. Discuss what the bridges are made from, and what shape they are. Identify and sketch the shape of each bridge. Encourage the children to ask different questions about which shapes are stronger and to predict the answers.

Look at pictures of some early iron structures (Victorian piers, bridges and railway station roofs are ideal). Identify some of the shapes used in them, such as squares, rectangles and triangles. Encourage the children to ask questions about which shapes are strongest. Look at the shapes of the beams themselves: *Are they round, square, I-shaped? Does it matter what shape they are?*

Show the children how to make rolled (round) or folded (square) beams out of paper, and how these can be bent into arches and held in place with adhesive tape. Show them how different shapes (squares, triangles and so on) can be made using a construction kit (or strong cardboard strips and paper fasteners). Explain that they will be making some of these structural components and testing their strength.

GROUP ACTIVITY

Working in groups, the children should decide on one question that they can ask about structures and find the answer to by testing. For example: *Can square beams hold up more weight than round beams?* or *Can we put more weight on a flat beam than on an arched one?* They should plan an investigation to find the answer, writing down what they intend to do and what measurements or observations they intend to make. They should then carry out their investigation and decide on a suitable way to record their results.

ASSESSMENT

Ask the children to explain to others what they have investigated, using scientific terms to explain the tests they have carried out. They should say whether or not their investigation gave them an answer to their original question.

PLENARY

Ask groups to report to the class on what their investigation showed them about the strength of different structural components. Draw up two columns on the board: 'strong components' and 'weak components'. They should have found out that triangles are hard to distort (look for triangles in the structures you showed earlier), and that square or round beams are stronger than flat beams. Some children may have found out that flat beams on their side are very strong. *If round beams are so strong, why don't we use round beams in buildings?* (Because they are harder to fix between flat surfaces.)

OUTCOMES
● Can plan and carry out a test.
● Can compare the strength of different structural components.

LINKS
History: how building methods have changed over time.

ENRICHMENT
Lesson 2 ◾ Load-carrying structures

Objective
● To know that a variety of structures are used to support the weight of objects.
● To use knowledge of structural components to build a load-carrying structure.
● To test a design, making modifications in a systematic way in the light of evidence collected.

Differentiation
Some children may need adult support to plan the platform and to decide how to test it for weak points. If appropriate, give them some pictures of real structures of a similar type. To challenge children, ask them to think about if they could use the findings from Lesson 1 about beams being stronger some ways round than others. (Paper beams can support more weight end-on than on their sides, provided they are supported so they do not twist.)

RESOURCES
Ample supplies of paper, adhesive tape, scissors, weights.
Safety: Warn the children to keep their fingers and toes well clear of possible falling weights when testing.

MAIN ACTIVITY
Challenge groups to design and build a weight-carrying platform for a crane. They should use weights during their building to identify weak points in the structure, and modify their design accordingly. Warn them not to test their platform to destruction at this time.

ICT LINK
Children could use the computer to write labels and short pieces of writing about their designs, to contribute to a class display about the work from this lesson.

ASSESSMENT
Discuss each design with the group who made it. Test each platform to see how much weight it supports.

PLENARY
Test all the platforms (to destruction!) for their weight-carrying capacity. Ask the children to identify good points in the design of each platform.
Safety: Use a board to contain weights when the platforms collapse.

OUTCOMES
● Can use scientific knowledge to build a load-carrying platform.
● Can assess and modify their design and construction.

ENRICHMENT
Lesson 3 ◾ Reducing friction

Objectives
● To revise how friction can be reduced by lubricants.
● To conduct an investigation: ask a scientific question that can be tested, decide what evidence to collect, collect and record data appropriately, then identify and describe patterns in the data.

Vocabulary
friction, energy, force, reduction, lubricant

RESOURCES
Introduction: A block, string.
Main activity: A block, examples of rough and smooth surfaces, a force meter.
Group activity: Blocks, slopes, force meters, stopwatches, liquids (water, oil, washing-up liquid and so on).
Safety: Be aware that some children may have allergic skin reactions to some detergents.

PREPARATION
Set up a block with a force meter attached, and a variety of different surfaces. Have a flipchart or board close by to record the children's ideas and questions.

BACKGROUND
This lesson and the next are used to revise what the children know about friction, to demonstrate that certain liquids (called 'lubricants') can reduce friction, and to introduce the idea that forces and energy are related. The children should know from the previous unit that there is more friction between rough surfaces than between smooth ones. For example, we have to use more energy sliding a sledge over rough ground than over smooth snow, so the friction force that opposes its movement must be greater.

STARTER

Pull a block across the desk on a piece of string. Ask: *Think back and tell me what you know about the forces involved when the block is being pulled.* If necessary, remind the children that a force is a push or a pull. They should remember that there is a force from you making the block move, and a friction force slowing the block down. If not, lead them towards this conclusion.

MAIN ACTIVITY

Show the children a rough surface and a smooth surface. Ask: *What do you remember about the friction forces?* If necessary, discuss how the block slides more easily on smoother surfaces, showing that the friction force is less. *Do I have to use up any energy to make the block keep moving?* If they are not sure, use the example of making a heavy sledge keep moving. *Do I use up more energy making it move over a rough surface or over a smooth surface?* (The rougher the surface, the greater the friction force, so more energy is used up in moving the block.)

GROUP ACTIVITY

Ask: *Do you think putting liquid on surfaces would make any difference to the friction?* Ask the children to explain their answers. Record their ideas on the board or flipchart. Encourage them to think of specific questions that they could test, such as: *Will it take less force to pull a block along a surface if there is oil on the surface?* or *Will a block slide down a slope faster if there is water on the slope?* Record these. Working in groups, the children should decide on a question to ask and decide what test they need to carry out. (Check that their ideas are workable and not too messy before they start!) They need to think carefully about what observations or measurements they will make, and the best way to record their results.

ASSESSMENT

When the children report their findings to the class in the Plenary session, ask them to explain how they used their results to reach their conclusions. They should be aware that they need a similar result from several tests before a conclusion can be reached.

PLENARY

Ask some groups to report their findings. Encourage them to explain any patterns they found in the data they collected (for example, 'We tried with three different blocks and they were all easier to pull if there was oil on the surface'), and what conclusions they drew from these patterns. Make a summary chart on the board or flipchart, showing the conclusions that the children have reached about liquids and friction. They should have found that objects have less friction when they are wet or oily. If necessary, introduce the term 'lubricant'. Relate their findings back to the idea of energy. *Would you use more energy pushing a tray across a wet table or across a dry table?* On a wet table, the friction force is smaller, so movement uses up less energy.

OUTCOMES
- Know that lubricants reduce friction.
- Can decide how to test a scientific question.
- Can identify patterns in the results.

LINKS
PSHE: safety in the home.

ENRICHMENT

Lesson 4 ▪ Liquid lubricants

Objective
● To know that friction can be reduced by many liquid lubricants.

RESOURCES
Secondary sources of information about friction; small cards (about A5-size).

MAIN ACTIVITY
The children use secondary sources to research situations where friction is reduced by a liquid. They should look for a situation where reducing friction is deliberate and useful, and make an illustrated information card explaining it; then look for situations where reducing friction is harmful, and make an eye-catching warning notice about it. 'Useful' situations might include: oil in engines to help parts move smoothly and reduce wear, detergent on trapped fingers to help release them, valve oil on brass instruments to help the valves work freely, oil in locks to keep them turning freely. 'Harmful' situations might include: water on tiled floors making them slippery, water on freshly washed drinking glasses making them harder to pick up and easier to drop, water or oil on roads making them easier to skid on, water or oil on brakes making them not work properly.

ICT LINK
Provide children with suitable CD-ROMs or internet sites for them to research situations where smooth or rough surfaces are either useful or dangerous.

ASSESSMENT
As the children are working, ask them about energy in the situations they have chosen. *Will it take more or less energy to turn the key if I oil the lock? Why?*

PLENARY
Ask the children to display their information cards and warning cards. Discuss some of the situations these illustrate. Talk about what happens to the energy in engines with and without lubricant oil. (Without oil, some of the energy of the engine is used to work against the friction forces, making bits hot and making the engine run inefficiently; with oil, much less energy is used to overcome friction forces, so more of it can be used to do the work of the engine.)

Differentiation
Support children by selecting simple research sources for them. To extend children, ask them to also make up a short cartoon illustrating the problem of either failing to use a liquid to reduce friction when it would be useful to, or using a liquid when reducing friction is harmful.

OUTCOMES
● Can recognise the importance of oil in reducing friction.
● Can recognise that reducing friction can be harmful as well as helpful.

ENRICHMENT

Lesson 5 ▪ Sand timers and water clocks

Objectives
● To know that everything falls down and that this is due to gravity.
● To know that falling materials can be used to measure time.
● To identify the significant features of a gravity-controlled timer.
● To evaluate a sand timer and a water clock and describe their limitations.

RESOURCES
Main activity: An 'hourglass' type egg-timer (the larger the better).
Group activity: A copy of photocopiable page 153 (also 'Sand timers and water clocks' (red) on the CD-ROM) for each child, large shallow trays (see Preparation), small plastic drinks bottles (with lids), various different-sized drills, a variety of suitable solids for timers (such as rice, dried peas, dry sand), strong adhesive tape, stopwatches.
Safety: Drills should be used by the teacher only, or under very close supervision.

PREPARATION
Make sure that the practical work can be done over large shallow trays. Alternatively, protect the surrounding area with plastic sheeting and plenty of newspaper.

BACKGROUND
Everywhere on the Earth, objects fall towards the centre of the planet. This is due to the force of gravity. The acceleration due to gravity is constant everywhere on Earth, so falling objects can be used to measure time. The earliest recorded clocks were water clocks used by the ancient Egyptians. Water clocks can be made very accurate by using water dripping from a top container that is kept full, so the pressure and hence the drip rate of the falling water remains constant. Sand timers can have problems with the flow rate varying due to particles getting stuck to each other. However, the children will find that sand timers are much easier to make and much more accurate, as making a water timer that does not leak is almost impossible at this level.

STARTER
Hold a ball at arm's length. Ask: *What will happen to this ball if I let go?* Discuss other things that fall, such as snow, rain and thrown or dropped objects. Make sure the children are aware that everything falls down. Show them a bag of sugar. *What would happen to the sugar if I made a hole in the bag? Could you tell how long ago I made the hole? If the hole had been made a long time ago, a lot of sugar would have leaked out. Could we use this to make a timer?* The children need to be aware that the time is proportional to the amount of material that has fallen out.

MAIN ACTIVITY
Tell the children that they are going to design a timer. Place an 'hourglass' egg-timer where all the children can see it easily. Discuss how it works. Encourage them to identify the essential features of the egg-timer (such as a falling material) and the unnecessary 'extras' (such as a decorated stand). *Could you make a timer like this one? What could you make it from?* Discuss what could be put inside the timer, and how that might affect the rest of the design. *If it were filled with dried peas, would you use the same-size hole as you would if it were filled with sand? Does it have to be something solid in the timer?* Ask the children to think about what things the timer could be used to time. *Could we use this sort of timer to time how long toy cars take to go down a slope in the friction investigations? Could we use it to time our lessons so we know when it is playtime?*

GROUP ACTIVITY
Give each child a copy of page 153. Working in groups, they should make a sand timer and/or a water clock. Instruct half the class to start with the water clock and the other half to start with the sand timer, so that the two types can be compared even if all the children do not have time to build both. The children can use either the design suggested on the sheet or their own design. They should use their timer to record how long something takes, choosing for themselves something that will take a suitable time, then compare the times recorded by their timer and by a stopwatch. Note that the timer can be turned over, allowing it to record multiples of a set time.

The children in each group should discuss with you the building problems they encountered and the limitations of their timer. (It cannot time periods less than one 'run through'; turning it over takes time and so reduces overall accuracy.) *Does it have any advantages over a stopwatch?* (It is cheap and easy to make and does not require batteries.)

Differentiation
For children who need support, use 'Sand timers and water clocks' (green), from the CD-ROM, which includes fewer and less complex questions than the core sheet. You can also support children by discussing with them the problems encountered in making the timer. Ask them: *Which is easier to make, a sand timer or a water timer? Why?*

To extend children, use 'Sand timers and water clocks' (blue), which asks them to identify three good and three bad points about their water clocks and sand timers. Some children may be able to discuss the problems encountered in building the timer, then suggest ways in which the design could be changed to overcome some of these problems.

ASSESSMENT

Ask the children: *Why is your timer no good for timing? How could you change your timer so it could measure longer/shorter times?*

PLENARY

Take votes on which timer the children thought was easier to build, and which they thought worked better to time their chosen events. Discuss suggestions for improving the design of the less effective timers, and whether these improvements would make it better than the others. Discuss the limitations of these timers in terms of what things they can and cannot be used to time, how easy they are to carry around, how accurate they are and so on. Consider again whether they have any advantages over other sorts of timers.

OUTCOMES

● Can design, make and use a sand timer and a water clock.
● Can recognise strengths and weaknesses in a design.

ENRICHMENT
Lesson 6 ◘ Design a waterwheel

Objectives
● To define the significant features of a good waterwheel.
● To know that falling water can be used to provide energy for work.
● To use scientific knowledge to design a waterwheel.

Vocabulary
waterwheel, force, energy

RESOURCES ◉

Main activity: A large picture of a watermill, showing the waterwheel; a model waterwheel.
Group activity: Photocopiable page 154 (also 'Design a waterwheel' (red) on the CD-ROM), round plastic containers, wooden dowel or similar (to make the axle), thin plastic or cardboard, wooden or plastic supports with holes for the axle, string, sets of stacking 10g or 20g masses.

PREPARATION

Construct a model waterwheel for demonstration, using photocopiable page 154 as a guide.

BACKGROUND

The energy of moving water was one of the earliest forms of energy harnessed by people to drive machinery. Romans used the force of water flowing in rivers to turn waterwheels, driving millstones to grind wheat. In scientific terms, a 'good' waterwheel is one that extracts as much energy as possible from the water; but here, the children are looking for 'good' waterwheels in the context of 'Does it do what I want it to do?' - that is, lift heavy masses or lift masses quickly.

STARTER

Tell the children that in this lesson, they are going to design a machine that can lift a mass. Ask: *What do I have to do to lift a mass off the floor?* (There has to be a pull, a force, on the mass to lift it.) *What do I use up, to lift masses?* (Making the force to lift the mass uses up energy.) Your machine will use energy from water, not energy from people.

MAIN ACTIVITY

Display a large picture of a water mill with a waterwheel. Ask: *Who has visited a place like this? How does it work?* Explain that the energy of the water provides a force to push the wheel round, making other components move. Show them the model waterwheel, turning it by hand to show the axle rotating. Ask: *How could we use this turning axle to lift up weights?* Demonstrate how a string fastened to the axle can be used to lift a mass.

Say: *Your task is to make a really good waterwheel to lift masses.* Help the children to define a 'good' waterwheel as one that does what they want

it to do – making it clear that they must first decide what it is they want
their wheel to do. They might want it to lift as heavy a mass as possible, or
to lift a particular mass as quickly as possible. Now ask them to think of
things that they might change to improve a waterwheel. Make sure they
realise that the size of the wheel, the size of the paddles, the number of and
the shape of the paddles can all be changed.

GROUP ACTIVITY
Working in pairs or groups, the children should use photocopiable page 154
to help them design and build a 'good' waterwheel. They should record what
materials they chose to make the wheel from and the reasons why they
chose these materials. They should test their waterwheel, observing closely
to record which bits work well and to describe any faults or limitations their
waterwheel has. Each child should write a short paragraph evaluating how
easy their wheel was to make and how well it worked.

ASSESSMENT
In the children's written reports, look for scientific explanations of how the
wheel worked and its limitations. For example, 'It did not work because there
was not enough force from the water to lift the mass.'

PLENARY
Choose a selection of waterwheels. Ask their designers and builders to
explain why they chose the materials they did, and what they wanted their
wheel to do. Watch the wheels in action and ask other children to describe
how each wheel did what it was designed to do. Ask the designers and
builders to explain any problems they had and to suggest ways in which
they could improve upon their designs.

OUTCOMES
● Know that the energy of moving water can be converted into useful
mechanical energy in a turning wheel.
● Can use scientific knowledge to identify the significant features of a
waterwheel to be designed.

ENRICHMENT
Lesson 7 ▪ Wind energy

RESOURCES
A toy windmill that lifts small masses; pictures of corn-grinding and
electricity-generating windmills.

MAIN ACTIVITY
Discuss three types of windmill: an old corn-grinding one, a modern
electricity-generating one and a toy one that can lift small masses. Look for
similarities and differences. Consider the energy flow through each: the
type of energy input, any energy changes, and the work output. Draw
simple energy flow diagrams (see examples overleaf). Ask the children to
draw energy flow diagrams for a yacht sailing and a tree blowing over.

ASSESSMENT
During the Main activity, ask children to describe the forces acting on yacht
and tree and what type of energy is used/created.

PLENARY
Make sure the children understand that the yacht and tree both have wind
energy going into them, which is changed to movement energy. The work
output is either the yacht travelling forward or the tree being pushed over.

Differentiation
Support children by asking them to place labels in the correct positions on prepared energy flow charts. Extend children by asking them to think of other examples where wind power makes something happen (such as wind buggies, wind-powered garden ornaments or waves on water) and describe the energy changes taking place.

Let the children explain any other examples they have thought of. Discuss how a windmill could be altered so it can do more work. (It could have larger sails which will be pushed around harder by the wind.) Ask: *What is a possible disadvantage of larger sails?* (They might get broken if the wind is too strong.) The windmill's moving parts could be lubricated so that less of the wind's energy is used to overcome friction forces. Consider the environmental benefits of using wind energy.

OUTCOMES
● Know that moving air can be used as an energy source.

ENRICHMENT
Lesson 8 ▪ Wind strength and direction

Objectives
● To know that changes in the direction and strength of the wind can be measured.
● To identify significant features of a wind direction and strength meter.
● To think of a variety of designs and choose the best one for a specified purpose.
● To test a design by making a series of observations, and adjust the design where necessary.

Vocabulary
wind direction, weather vane, wind speed, anemometer (optional), Beaufort scale (optional)

RESOURCES
Main activity: A real weather vane, or a picture of one.
Group activity: Wooden poles, nails, hammers, strong card, scissors, plastic drinking straws, string, yoghurt pots, adhesive tape, ping-pong balls, a hairdryer or fan.
Plenary: Pictures of real wind-recording instruments.
Safety: Children should be very closely supervised when using a hammer and nails.

PREPARATION
Supply plenty of strong adhesive tape, which is faster for building with than glue. Make sure you have access to a windy outdoor place, a fan or a hairdryer (the stronger, the better).

BACKGROUND
Many people, such as sailors, pilots and air traffic controllers, need to take the strength of the wind into account. They need a way to measure and record the strength and direction of the wind. Designing such a 'wind meter' gives the children scope for many original designs. Encourage all of these, unless it is very clear that there is no way a particular design could work. Even then, try to prompt the children to spot the 'weak points' in their designs. All wind direction indicators will probably look very similar, as any laminate (flat sheet) object on a vertical spindle will swing until it is parallel to the direction of the wind. Wind strength measurers can take a wide variety of forms. Some children may design an anemometer type (like a water wheel on its side) that spins faster in stronger winds. Others may design a windsock type that rises higher when the wind is stronger.

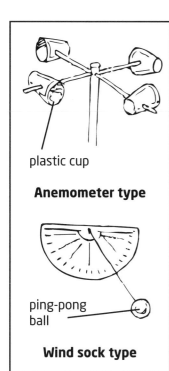

plastic cup

Anemometer type

ping-pong
ball

Wind sock type

STARTER

Ask: *How much force is there from the wind?* Discuss situations when the force is very great (hurricane damage) and when it is very weak (sailing vessels becalmed). *Who might need to know the wind direction or strength?* Talk about sailors, pilots, air traffic controllers, weather forecasters and windmill operators. (Windmills work best facing into the wind, and can be damaged by excessively strong winds.) Tell the children that they are going to design an instrument that shows the direction of the wind and measures how strong it is.

MAIN ACTIVITY

Ask the children to identify the most important feature of an instrument to show the wind direction. It needs to be able to turn when the wind blows on it, but it also needs to stop turning when it is facing either into or away from the wind (it does not matter which). If necessary, prompt the children to think of a weathervane. Discuss how the wind blowing on the side of the weathervane pushes it around; but when it faces the wind, the wind pushes equally on both sides, so it stays facing that way. Ask: *What is the most important feature of something that can measure how hard the wind is blowing?* Part of it must move when the wind blows on it, and move further when the wind blows harder. Encourage all the children's ideas, prompting them to think about how they can put their ideas into practice. Emphasise that their design needs to be simple enough for them to build it.

GROUP ACTIVITY

Show the children the materials available to them. They should work in small groups to design and make a combined wind-direction and wind-strength meter. Assess their designs before they start to build, encouraging them to modify any that are hopelessly ambitious! Now allow them to make their wind meters. They should test the instruments outside in the wind if weather conditions are suitable; if not, they should use a hairdryer or fan.

ICT LINKS

Children could look at secondary sources (CD-ROMs, internet) to find out how wind strength or speed is recorded (for example, the Beaufort scale) and where it is used (for example, weather forecasts). They could use a data-recording method, such as a spreadsheet, to record wind speed and wind direction each day for a week.

ASSESSMENT

During the group work, ask the children to describe how well their instrument measured the wind, and to suggest ways in which they could improve it.

PLENARY

Recap on the essential features of an instrument to measure wind direction and speed. Look at some of the instruments the children have produced, and discuss the methods they have used. Look at pictures of real wind-recording instruments and discuss how these are similar to or different from the children's designs.

OUTCOMES
- Can find the direction of the wind and measure its force.
- Can specify the key features of a wind meter.
- Can produce a design to meet specifications, test it and suggest improvements in the light of observations.

Differentiation
Support children by giving them a basic design to work from, asking them to decide what materials to use and to make any improvements they think of. Extend children by giving them a copy of the Beaufort scale of wind strength, and asking them to discuss how they could modify their instrument to show the strength of the wind on the Beaufort scale.

ENRICHMENT

Lesson 9 ◼ Balloon racer

Objectives
● To know that when an object is pushed, an opposing push back can be felt.
● To decide what evidence to collect in an investigation.
● To explain results, using scientific knowledge and understanding.

RESOURCES
Different types of string, drinking straws, adhesive tape, balloons, metre rulers, paper, pencils.

MAIN ACTIVITY
Make a 'balloon racer'. To do this, tie a long string horizontally between two supports. Thread a straw on to the string. Blow up a balloon and, holding its neck tightly closed, fasten the side of the balloon to the straw with sticky tape. Release the neck of the balloon. Ask the children to investigate the factors that affect how far the balloon racer travels.

ASSESSMENT
During the Plenary session, ask children to explain why their balloon racer moved. *What forces made it go forwards? Were there any forces slowing it down?*

PLENARY
Discuss the forces acting on the balloon racer. Make sure the children understand that it moves because stored energy in the stretched rubber skin pushes on the air in the balloon, forcing it out. The 'action' of the moving air pushing backwards causes a 'reaction' force pushing the balloon forwards. Discuss where the energy comes from to make the balloon move. (It comes from the stored energy in the stretched balloon skin: the more the balloon is blown up, the more the skin is stretched, so the more energy it stores and the further it can make the balloon move.)

Differentiation
Children who need support could be asked to investigate the connection between the size (diameter or circumference) of the balloon and how far it travels. To extend children, ask them to investigate the effect of: the angle of the string (uphill or downhill); whether the string is tight or loose; what type of string is used (rough or smooth); or how big the straw is (in diameter and in length). Anything that increases friction between the straw and the string will reduce the distance that the balloon racer travels.

OUTCOMES
● Can recognise action and reaction in a pair of forces.
● Can recognise the change from stored energy in a balloon skin to movement energy in the air and the balloon.
● Can explain the results of an experiment in scientific terms.

ENRICHMENT

Lesson 10 ◼ Balloon-powered cars

Objective
● To use the force of moving air.
● To know that when an object is pushed, an opposing push back can be felt.
● To design a balloon-powered toy car.
● To evaluate the limitations of their own and other designs.

RESOURCES
Balloons, string, adhesive tape, drinking straws, strong card or wood; axles and wheels from construction kits.

MAIN ACTIVITY
Remind the children of Lesson 9. Ask them to use the principle of the balloon racer to design a toy car that can travel forward under its own power. A simple design might involve using a string threaded through a drinking straw attached to the car to determine the direction the car moves in. A more complex design might involve finding a way to hold the balloon so that the car travels in a predictable direction. Ask the children to predict and then test factors affecting how far the car travels.

ASSESSMENT

Ask the children: *Where did friction act to slow your car down? How could you make friction less, or the forward force greater?*

PLENARY

Discuss the forces acting on the car. Make sure the children understand that the car moves because energy stored in the stretched balloon skin forces the air out. As the moving air pushes one way, a reaction force in the opposite direction moves the car forward. Encourage the children to explain why some cars travelled further than others, using scientific language and their knowledge of forces, energy and friction. Discuss real machines that use the energy of moving air or gases to propel them along, such as hovercraft and jet aircraft.

OUTCOMES

- Can recognise action and reaction in a pair of forces.
- Can recognise the change from stored energy in a balloon skin to movement energy in the air and a toy car.
- Can evaluate a design and make suggestions for improvement.

Differentiation
Children who need support could predict, then test, the connection between the size of the balloon and the distance the car travels. Other children may be able to predict, then test, factors that will affect the level of friction acting on the car as it moves.

ENRICHMENT
Lesson 11 ◾ Elastic-band crawler

Objectives
- To know that energy stored in an elastic band can be turned into movement energy.
- To ask scientific questions, plan an investigation to find the answers and decide what evidence to collect.

RESOURCES

A large diagram of an elastic band crawler (see below), small cylindrical containers with flat ends (such as cardboard cocoa or crisp containers), used matches or small sticks, a wide selection of different-sized elastic bands, small masses with hooks (to fit in containers).

MAIN ACTIVITY

Make an 'elastic-band crawler' (see diagram) and a large copy of the diagram. Discuss how the crawler works, talking about where energy is stored and what happens when it is released. Discuss factors that may affect how well the

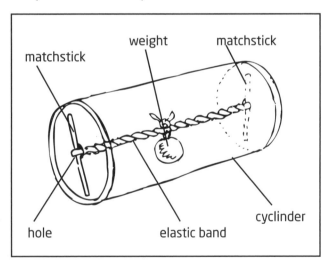

crawler works, first defining what is meant by 'working well'. Ask the children to suggest scientific questions to investigate (or predictions to test) about what makes a crawler work well. They should work in small groups to design their own crawler, then test how well it works when a factor is varied. The emphasis should be on collecting appropriate evidence or measurements and recording in a clear and informative way. Ask the children to think carefully about how they will present their results.

ASSESSMENT

Ask the children to describe the measurements and observations they made, and to explain and evaluate (according to their ability) how these helped them to answer the question they had asked.

Differentiation
Some children may benefit from using a model to help them build their crawler. Give help, where necessary, with the recording of measurements and other observations. Extend children by asking them to look at diagrams of other machines powered by stretched elastic materials, such as a catapult, ballista or longbow. Can they use energy terms to explain how these machines work?

PLENARY

Discuss the limitations of elastic-band power. The energy output is limited by the size of the elastic band. All the energy stored in the band came from us originally, so we are providing the energy to make the crawler go - this would be no good for powering something like a real car. It is useful for something like a bow and arrow, because we can put in energy gradually (as we stretch the bowstring) and give it all to the arrow at once. We cannot give as much energy to the arrow if we have to put it all in at once, as we do if we throw it.

OUTCOMES
- Can recognise the change from stored energy in a twisted elastic band to movement energy in the 'crawler'.
- Can decide what factors might affect how well the 'crawler' works.
- Can plan what to do and what evidence to collect in order to test an idea.

ENRICHMENT
Lesson 12 ▪ Assessment

Objectives
- To assess the children's knowledge of the forces affecting moving water.
- To assess the children's knowledge of how stretched elastic bands provide a force and of the factors affecting the strength of the force.
- To assess the children's ability to describe physical processes in terms of energy changes.

RESOURCES
Photocopiable pages 155 and 156 (also 'Assessment - 1' (red) and 'Assessment - 2' (red) on the CD-ROM), writing materials, red and blue coloured pencils.

PREPARATION
You may decide to use the Assessment activities at the start of the lesson. Alternatively, you could begin with a short introductory session to remind the children of the main points they have learned in this unit. This could take the form of giving them a heading (such as 'Friction', 'Water power' or 'Strong and weak shapes') and asking them to suggest things they have learned about that topic.

ASSESSMENT ACTIVITY 1
Give each child a copy of page 155 to work through individually. After collecting in the sheets, you may wish to go over the answers with the children and encourage discussion.

ANSWERS
1. Turning the tap up; changing the nozzle.
2. Put each nozzle on the hose in turn and measure how far the water goes, keeping the tap turned on the same amount and the hose pointing in the same direction each time.
3. The waterwheel will turn around.
4. The movement energy of the jet of water changes to the movement energy of the turning waterwheel.
5. The waterwheel would turn faster.
6. Turning the tap up would make the water flow faster. The water would have more energy, so it would give more energy to the wheel, which would make it turn faster.

LOOKING FOR LEVELS
All the children should answer questions 3 and 5. Most children will answer questions 1, 2 and 4. More able children will answer question 6.

ASSESSMENT ACTIVITY 2
Give each child a copy of page 156 to work through individually. You could either collect in the sheets to mark them or allow the children to swap sheets and mark each other's, encouraging discussion about the answers.

ANSWERS

1. The bowstring, the trampoline and the elastic band with a weight on it should be coloured blue.

2. The person on the trampoline and the flying arrow should be coloured red. (Some children will realise that the trampoline has movement energy as well as stored elastic energy – but do not penalise children who do not colour the trampoline red.)

3. The diagram should show the bowstring stretched further back.

4. The archer could use a stronger elastic bowstring.

5. The blue arrow should point from the trampoline directly upwards through the person.

6. The red arrow should point from the person directly downwards through the trampoline.

7. The elastic band stretches and so gains stored elastic energy. (Very able children might add that this energy comes from the mass losing gravitational energy, since it is not as high up as when it was first put on the elastic band.)

LOOKING FOR LEVELS

All the children should be able to answer questions 1, 2 and 5. Most children will answer questions 3, 4 and 6. More able children will answer question 7.

PLENARY

You may wish to go over the answers to the Assessment activities with the children. You may also wish to remind them of things they have learned in this unit that have not been covered by the Assessment activities.

From this unit, the children should have learned to suggest ways of investigating scientific questions, including how to make relevant observations and measurements and record them in a clear manner. They should know how to interpret their results, using scientific knowledge to explain them and to make suggestions for future improvements to the investigation.

Some children will have made less progress. They will be able to make suggestions about what to do in order to answer a scientific question, and will be able to plan an investigation with help. They will be able to make observations and measurements, and suggest explanations for these.

Other children may have made more progress and be able to plan the effective use of available resources to answer a scientific question. They may be able to suggest limitations in an investigation or in a design, and suggest ways to overcome these.

Strength of structural components

Our question about structures is:

_____

_____

How we are going to carry out our investigation:

Diagram:

This is what we will do:

These are the measurements or observations we made:

This is what we found out about structures:

_____

_____

Sand timers and water clocks

◖ Make a simple sand timer or water timer. Your teacher may tell you which to make.

Bottle with sand.

Make a small hole in the lid; half fill with sand.

◖ If your design is different, draw it in the space above on the right.

◖ Decide one good point and one bad point of your timer. Write them in the table.

	Water clock	Sand timer
Good point		
Bad point		

◖ Talk to a group which built the other type of timer.
◖ Ask them to tell you one good point and one bad point of their timer.
◖ Put them in the table.

Which timer was best? _____

Why? _____

_____

_____

PHOTOCOPIABLE

Design a waterwheel

◣ This diagram shows how you can build a waterwheel.

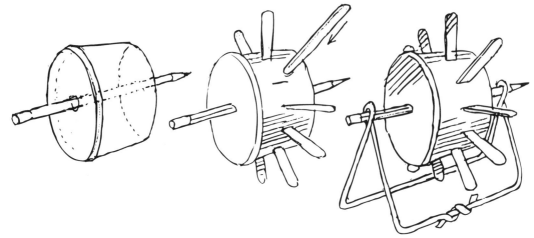

◣ Tick the things you think a "good" waterwheel should do:

☐ turn quickly

☐ turn slowly

☐ have lots of paddles

☐ have few paddles

☐ have large paddles

☐ have small paddles

☐ be strong

How big were the paddles on your waterwheel? _____

Why did you choose this size? _____

_____

What material did you make the paddles from? _____

Why did you choose this material? _____

_____

How well did your waterwheel work? _____

What could you do to make it better? _____

_____

◣SCHOLASTIC

Assessment – 1

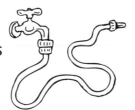 

■ This picture shows three different nozzles that can go on the end of the hosepipe.

1. Tick the things that might change how far the water from the hosepipe goes.

☐ Turning the tap up.   ☐ Making the hosepipe longer.   ☐ Changing the nozzle.

2. Describe briefly how you could investigate whether changing the nozzle affects how far the water goes.

_____

_____

The jet of water hits a waterwheel.

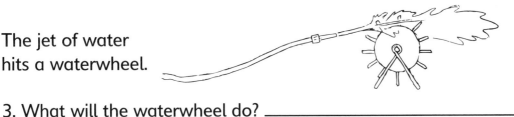

3. What will the waterwheel do? _____

_____

4. Describe the energy changes that happen when the jet of water hits the waterwheel.

_____

_____

5. What would you expect to happen if the tap were turned up?

_____

6. Why? _____

Illustration © Robin Lawrie

PHOTOCOPIABLE

Assessment – 2

■ These diagrams all show places where elastic items are being stretched.

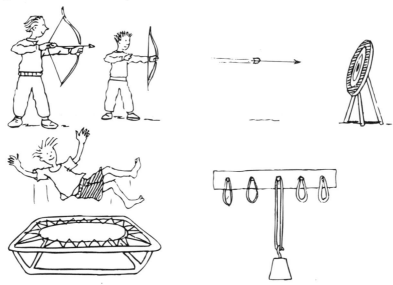

1. Colour blue all the things that have stored energy.

2. Colour red all the things that have movement energy.

3. Look at the archer. Draw a line to show where he must pull the bowstring to in order to make the arrow go faster.

4. Write down one other thing he could do to make the arrow go faster.

_____

5. Draw a blue arrow to show the force from the trampoline acting on the person.

6. Draw a red arrow to show the second force that acts at the same time.

7. Describe the energy changes that happen when a mass is hung on the elastic band.

_____

_____

_____

■ SCHOLASTIC

Illustration © Robin Lawrie

CHAPTER 7 Circuits and conductors

Lesson	Objectives	Main activity	Group activities	Plenary	Outcomes
Lesson 1 Will the bulb light up?	• To elicit children's ideas about electricity. • To know how to interpret drawings of electrical circuits and make circuits from them. • To test predictions.	Eliciting children's existing ideas about electricity, reviewing circuit diagrams from previous year.	Predicting and testing whether different circuit diagrams will work in practice. Brainstorming 'What I know about electricity'.	Discussing the need to complete a circuit.	• Can interpret drawings of circuits and recognise those that will work. • Can assemble a circuit. • Can make and test predictions .
Lesson 2 The dangers of mains electricity	• To know that circuits powered by batteries are safe to investigate, but mains electricity is too dangerous.	Listing items that are mains- or battery-powered. Exploring risks of electricity and writing 'cautionary tales'.		Sharing 'cautionary tales' to reinforce safety message.	• Can explain that circuits powered by batteries are safe to investigate, but mains electricity is dangerous.
Enrichment Lesson 3 Where does electricity come from?	• To know that electricity is a form of energy that has been converted from other forms of energy. • To use secondary sources of information.	Demonstration of waterwheel and windmill. Link to making electricity in power stations using secondary sources.		Review children's ideas about the sources of mains electricity.	• Can give examples of forms of energy that have been converted into electricity. • Can use secondary sources of information.
Lesson 4 Conductors and insulators	• To know that electricity flows through some materials and not others. • To make predictions. • To design a circuit.	The question 'What can electricity travel through?' is discussed.	Children predict and test which materials can conduct electricity.	Generalising that metals are conductors and most non-metals are insulators.	• Know that electricity flows through some materials and not others. • Can make predictions. • Can design a circuit.
Lesson 5 Materials for conduction and insulation	• To know where conductors and insulators are used in circuits. • To know that more than one wire is in the electrical cables.	Investigation of conductors and insulators in household items.		Discussion reviewing safe use of electricity.	• Know where conductors and insulators are in circuits. • Can recognise that more than one wire is in a cable.
Lesson 6 Switches to make	• To know that switches can be designed in a variety of ways. • To understand how a switch works.	Discussion and demonstration of making and breaking circuits.	Making a range of different switches and explaining how they work.	Discussing the roles of conductors and insulators in switches.	• Know how different kinds of switch work. • Can recognise air as an insulator.
Lesson 7 Switches in models	• To use appropriate designs of switches in model-making. • To apply their understanding of switches.	Design and make a model using a switch.		Children present their models and explain how they work.	• Can use appropriate designs of switches in model-making. • Can apply their understanding of switches.
Lesson 8 Buzzers and motors	• To know how and why batteries may be connected together. • To follow children's own lines of enquiry. • To develop skills of recording observations.	Observation of torch with two batteries. Question raised: 'What difference does the number of batteries make?'	Exploring circuits with different numbers of components and recording observations.	Feeding back observations. Considering the effect of adding a battery.	• Can explain how and why batteries may be connected together. • Can follow their own lines of enquiry. • Can record observations.
Lesson 9 How bright is the light?	• To investigate changing the number of bulbs in a circuit. • To make and test predictions in a fair test.	Identifying different components that could be changed in a circuit. Focus on bulbs.	Investigate the effect of changing the number of bulbs. Thinking of requirements of different lights.	Comparing how different groups have connected their bulbs (parallel and series).	• Can investigate changing the number of bulbs in a circuit. • Can test predictions in a fair test.
Lesson 10 Electricity through drama	• To review through drama. • To communicate ideas about electricity.	Using drama to model an electric circuit.		Performing improvisations.	• Can communicate their understanding about electricity.

Assessment	Objectives	Activity 1	Activity 2
Lesson 11	• To assess children's understanding of circuits, conductors and insulators. • To assess the children's understanding of how switches work.	Practical challenge to make the 'clown's eyes' light up by making a complete circuit from a battery to bulbs using only one wire and a range of conducting materials.	Pencil and paper test on interpreting circuit diagrams, switches and safety with electricity.

SC1 SCIENTIFIC ENQUIRY

Does it conduct electricity?

LEARNING OBJECTIVES AND OUTCOMES
- Use observations to draw conclusions.
- Think about what might happen or try things out when deciding what to do.
- Use simple equipment and materials appropriately.

ACTIVITY
In this lesson the children sort a collection into those they predict electricity will and won't go through, and design a circuit to test their electrical conductivity. They are encouraged to summarise their findings and make generalisations from them.

LESSON LINKS
Use this Sc1 activity as an integral part of Lesson 4 'Conductors and insulators'.

Lesson 1 ▸ Will the bulb light up?

Objectives
- To review work on electricity from Year 3/Primary 4, including the idea that a complete circuit is needed for a device to work.
- To elicit children's ideas about electricity.
- To know how to interpret drawings of electrical circuits and make circuits from them.
- To make and test predictions.

Vocabulary
battery, bulb, buzzer, circuit, electricity, wire

RESOURCES 💿
Main activity: Flipchart and marker pens; enlarged circuit drawings as on photocopiable page 171 (also 'Will the bulb light up?' (red) on the CD-ROM) copied on to the flipchart.
Group activities: 1 Copies of photocopiable page 171, wires, batteries, bulbs, buzzers, screwdrivers. **2** Writing and drawing materials.
ICT link: 'Will the bulb light up?' interactive, from the CD-ROM.

PREPARATION
Copy the circuit drawings on photocopiable page 171 on to the flipchart. Put a selection of electrical equipment on each group's table. Have the children sitting on the carpet in front of the flipchart.

BACKGROUND
The initial whole-class discussion will enable you to find out children's existing ideas as a starting point for later work. Children tend to associate electricity with the mains rather than with batteries. This unit will consider both, and help children to see them both as sources of electricity.

There is a danger with this topic that children have similar experiences of making simple circuits as they go through school, with limited progression. This lesson recaps earlier work on the need for a complete circuit to make it 'work' from before moving on.

STARTER
Explain that the class is beginning a new topic on electricity that will develop the ideas they learned in previous years. Plug in and switch on a CD player and then sit playing on a 'Game Boy'. Besides getting the children's attention, this illustrates mains- and battery-powered equipment.

MAIN ACTIVITY
Ask: *What can you tell me about electricity?* Record the children's ideas on the flipchart or interactive whiteboard. You might want to put children's names by their comments. This not only acts as a record for you, but encourages children to add their contributions.

Ask them to tell you about work they have done on electricity in previous

Differentiation
For children who need support use 'Will the bulb light up?' (green) from the CD-ROM, which contains fewer circuits for them to make predictions about and test. Children who have physical difficulty in constructing the circuits may not complete them all. Offer support so they do not become frustrated.
Others can be challenged by asking them to design and draw a circuit that they know does or does not work as a problem for other children to solve.

years. Explain that you are going to give them some drawings of circuits. You want them to predict whether they think the circuit will work or not, and test it out by making the circuit.

GROUP ACTIVITIES
1. Give each pair of children a copy of photocopiable page 172. Ask them to record their prediction on the sheet then test it by making the circuit. Having the children working in pairs will support exchange of ideas, and help the children to draw on their previous learning. Circulate, asking children to explain the reasons for their predictions and the reasons why the circuit has or has not worked.
2. Ask the children to work in pairs but to record individually a brainstorm of 'My ideas about electricity'. This develops the discussion that was started as a whole class.

ICT LINK
Children can use the 'Will the bulb light up?' interactive, from the CD-ROM, to predict whether the bulb will light up in a sequence of circuits.

ASSESSMENT
Can the children make a prediction based on logical thinking? Can they construct circuits as in the diagrams? Can they explain that to work, there must be a complete circuit with no breaks? Note any children who are not secure with these ideas in order to give extra support in subsequent lessons.

PLENARY
Using the copies of the circuit drawings on the flipchart, consider each circuit in turn and ask the class: *Did this circuit work? Why? Why not?* Emphasise the idea of electricity travelling in a circuit by tracing the circuit round with your finger and coming to an abrupt halt if there is a break in the circuit. Encourage the children to do the same with their own circuit diagrams.

OUTCOMES
- Teacher is aware of children's existing ideas about electricity.
- Can interpret drawings of circuits and recognise those that will work.
- Can assemble a circuit from a drawing.
- Can make predictions and test them.

LINKS
PSHE: awareness of mains electricity supply.

Lesson 2 The dangers of mains electricity

Objective
- To know that circuits powered by batteries are safe to investigate, but mains electricity is too dangerous.

RESOURCES
A flipchart and marker pens; secondary sources on electricity and safety, such as *Electricity and Magnets* or *More about Electricity and Magnetism* (Nuffield Primary Science children's books); *Cats' Eyes: Electricity* and *Light and Sound* (BBC videos).

MAIN ACTIVITY
Ask the children to brainstorm appliances that run from batteries and appliances that run from mains electricity, listing them in two columns on the flipchart. Ask them to suggest reasons why, such as convenience,

Differentiation
Choose secondary sources that different children can access. The 'cautionary tales' could be tape recorded or written in groups to support those with weaker literacy skills. Extend children by asking them to find out the voltage of mains electricity and compare it with that of batteries they use.

amount of power needed. Ask: *Is it OK for us to investigate mains electricity? Why? Why not?* Explore the children's existing ideas about the dangers of electricity. Use books or videos to explore the risks of mains electricity. Ask the children to write 'cautionary tales' about children who misused mains electricity: you may need to provide an example.

ASSESSMENT
Can the children explain why they must not explore mains electricity? Can they give some specific examples of dangerous behaviour with mains electricity? Can they explain why it is OK to investigate circuits with batteries?

PLENARY
Share some of the stories. Return to the flipchart list and stress that it is safe to explore batteries and that everything you ask them to do in school is safe. Ask: *Why is it that mains electricity is dangerous and batteries are safe?* (Because mains electricity is much more powerful.)

OUTCOMES
● Can explain that circuits powered by batteries are safe to investigate, but mains electricity is too dangerous.

ENRICHMENT
Lesson 3 ▪ Where does electricity come from?

Objective
● To know that mains electricity is a form of energy that has been converted from other forms of energy.
● To use secondary sources of information.

RESOURCES
A paper windmill; waterwheel bath toy; flipchart and marker pens; secondary sources on generation of electricity, for example, *More about Electricity and Magnetism* (Nuffield Primary Science books); *Energy from Nature* (Channel 4 video); internet sources and/or a visit to a power station.

MAIN ACTIVITY
Ask: *Where do you think mains electricity comes from?* Write down the children's ideas on the flipchart.

Show the children the toy windmill. Blow on it so that it turns and ask: *How am I making it move? Where is the energy to make it move coming from?* (From you; from the wind.) Demonstrate a toy waterwheel. Explain that windmills and waterwheels used to be a source of energy to grind corn. Now we use the energy of the turning wheel and change the energy into electricity. Explain that there are other ways to make wheels (turbines) turn to make electricity, and that is what happens in power stations. Ask: *How could we find out more?*

Use secondary sources (perhaps during non-fiction work, for example, in a Literacy Hour or during an ICT session on using the internet) or a visit to a power station to explore this further.

Ask: *Where does mains electricity come from?* Ask children to present their ideas as an annotated drawing in response to the question. (See more on this in chapter 8.)

ASSESSMENT
There is likely to be a wide variation in the children's understanding of power generation. Use the annotated drawings to judge the level of understanding. Can they give examples of sources of energy that are used? (For example, wind or coal.) Are they aware that the turbines are an important part of the process? Can they describe how electrical cable, pylons and underground cables bring electricity to our homes?

Differentiation
Support children in their use of secondary sources, by helping them to apply research skills as learned during the Literacy Hour. Expect some accounts to show a good understanding of the different stages in power generation and others to indicate a lower level of understanding.

PLENARY

Revisit the flipchart showing children's ideas about where electricity comes from. Ask the children if any of their ideas have changed, if any were on the right lines, and what they would add to the list now.

OUTCOMES

● Can give examples of forms of energy that have been converted into electricity.
● Can use secondary sources of information.

Lesson 4 ▫ Conductors and insulators

Objectives
● To know that electricity flows through some materials and not others.
● To make predictions on the basis of previous experience.
● To design a circuit for testing the conductivity of materials.
● To make generalisations from results.

Vocabulary
conduct, conductor, insulator, material
It is not essential that the children use the correct terminology at this stage, but the words 'conductor' and 'insulator' are introduced in the Plenary session, once the children have a good understanding of the concepts they represent.

RESOURCES
Group activities: 1 Batteries, wires, bulbs; collections of materials that do and do not conduct electricity such as paper clips, card, aluminium foil, plastic, scissors with plastic handles, a penny, a pencil, a container of water. **2** Writing and drawing materials.

PREPARATION
Put the collections of materials out on the tables. Have the electrical equipment divided into sets for each table, but keep these to one side. Have the flipchart showing the circuit drawings from Lesson 1 available.

BACKGROUND
Materials can be classified as electrical conductors or electrical insulators depending on how well electricity can flow through them. Metals are particularly good conductors and plastics are particularly good insulators. Graphite (pencil lead) is the most well-known example of a non-metal conductor. Remember that air is also an insulator, which is why a break in a circuit stops the electricity from flowing. However, at very high voltages, electricity will flow through almost anything! The children can explore the materials provided, but will probably have suggestions of their own of things to test and should have the opportunity to try these out.

Materials can be inserted into a simple circuit, as illustrated, to test them. However, rather than simply giving them this method, it is better to allow children to devise their own circuit for this, only providing suggestions if needed.

STARTER
Show the class the drawings of circuits from Lesson 1 on the flipchart. Ask: *Can you explain why some of the circuits we made worked and some of them didn't?* (Some of them had breaks in the circuit so the electricity could not go all the way around.)

MAIN ACTIVITY
Ask: *In our circuits, what is the electricity travelling through?* (It is travelling through the wires, bulbs and batteries.) *Do you think electricity can travel through anything?* Listen to the children's responses to this; they will have a variety of ideas and explanations which should be acknowledged. Note any ideas that need challenging and target those children for questions in the Group activities.

Explain that you want the children to explore a collection of items and predict whether or not electricity will flow through the different items.

GROUP ACTIVITIES
1. Ask the groups to sort the collection into those materials they think electricity will and will not go through and record those predictions in their

Differentiation

If children cannot find their own way of testing the materials, show them how to put them into a gap in a circuit. Ask children who are higher achievers in science to give a reason for their prediction.

Expect some children to list which materials do and do not let electricity go through them, but challenge other children to make a generalisation by asking: *What have all those materials got in common? Can you tell me what sorts of materials conduct electricity and which don't?* Ask them to suggest other materials that would or would not conduct electricity, and to test those too to support their idea.

Provide a wordbank of the names of the materials to support those with poorer writing skills, and if necessary scribe their predictions so that they can move on to the testing quickly.

own way: as lists, Venn diagrams, tables and so on. Give out the electrical equipment and ask the children to devise a way of finding out if their predictions were right. Give them some time to tackle the problem themselves, but intervene if any group is becoming frustrated. Ask them to do a drawing showing how they carried out the test and to record the results in their own way.

2. If there are insufficient batteries and bulbs for all the groups to test their predictions at once, then as a 'holding' activity ask some groups to look around the classroom and note the materials that different battery and mains items are made from. An item, for example, a listening centre and headphones, could be recorded as an annotated drawing. This is good preparation for Lesson 5.

Safety: Remind children not to plug items into the mains electricity, nor to take them apart.

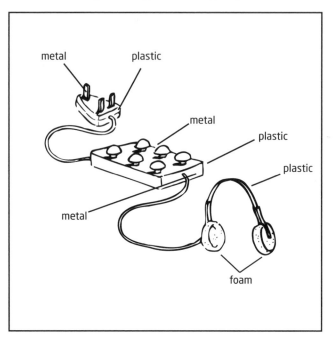

ASSESSMENT

Can the children give examples of materials that electricity can flow through and materials that it cannot flow through? Can they make predictions? Are they able to design a circuit to test the materials independently? Can they make generalisations from their results (for example, that metals are good at conducting electricity)?

PLENARY

Draw two columns on the board or flipchart and write 'Conductors – do let electricity through' and 'Insulators – do not let electricity through', to head the columns. Explain that there are special scientific words for the two groups that they have found: 'conductors' and 'insulators'. Ask different children to provide examples of a conductor or an insulator and write them in the relevant column.

Ask: *Is there anything the conductors have in common?* (Most are metals.) *Is there anything the insulators have in common?* (Various possible responses; focus on the idea that they are 'non-metals'.)

OUTCOMES

- Can state that electricity flows through some materials and not others.
- Can make predictions.
- Can design a circuit for testing the conductivity of materials.
- Can make generalisations from results.

LINKS

Unit 4C Keeping warm: use of the words 'conductor' and 'insulator' in the context of heat.

Lesson 5 ◗ Materials for conduction and insulation

RESOURCES

A collection of electrical cables cut to show the different parts inside; electrical leads; 3-pin plugs with the backs removed; simple torches that can be disassembled.
Safety: Never offer plugs wired to short lengths of cable, as the live cable is potentially lethal if the plug is put into a wall socket.

MAIN ACTIVITY

Recap the previous lesson on conductors and insulators, making sure the children are aware that metals are conductors and plastics are insulators. Ask the children to explore the collection, looking carefully to see which parts are metal and which are plastic. Ask each group or pair to take one item and make a large drawing of it, showing the different parts clearly and labelling them 'conductor' or 'insulator' to make a poster. Give clear instructions that the children are not to try to plug in any of the items, as that could kill them. Remind them of Lesson 2.

ASSESSMENT

Can the children identify the different parts as conductors and insulators? Can they suggest reasons for the choice of materials? Are they aware that there is more than one wire inside an electric cable?

PLENARY

Ask each group to show their poster to the whole class. Invite them to think about the reasons for using the different materials in certain places by asking questions, such as: *Why do you think that part is made of plastic?* Relate this back to the work on safety in Lesson 2. Draw the children's attention to the fact that there is more than one wire inside the cables, so there is a circuit, even though it does not look like that from the outside.

Reinforce the safety message that this is not something to try at home and never to tamper with appliances that are plugged in.

OUTCOMES

● Know where conductors and insulators are used in circuits.
● Can recognise that there is more than one wire in the cable for electrical appliances.

Lesson 6 ◗ Switches to make

RESOURCES ⊙

Main activity: A simple circuit of bulb, battery and two connecting wires.
Group activities: 1 Batteries, wires, wire cutters, bulbs, buzzers, paper fasteners, paper clips, drawing pins, aluminium foil, clothes pegs, balsa wood, card, plastic bottles, cardboard tubes, copies of photocopiable page 172 (also 'Switches to make' (red) on the CD-ROM). **2** 'Bought' switches for use in simple circuits that can be disassembled, and household switches, which are also interesting (these should have no loose wires that could be pushed into a mains socket), writing and drawing materials.

PREPARATION

Copy photocopiable page 172 so that there are enough copies for one between two. These could be laminated for future use. Put a selection of

Differentiation
Some children will make several designs and some children only one. Extend children by asking them to design their own switches.

resources on the tables and have others on one side. Make up the circuit for the Main activity. Have the children sitting in a circle on the carpet.

BACKGROUND
Switches work by breaking and making circuits. This relates to the previous lessons as the circuit is completed when a conductor is put across the break, and broken when an insulator, often air, is across the break. Although switches can be bought for use in model-making, by making their own switches, children are developing their understanding of circuits and of conductors and insulators.

Buzzers need to be put into a circuit the right way round. If a circuit is not working, try connecting the buzzer the other way.

STARTER
Remind the children of what they have done in previous lessons on circuits, conductors and insulators, and explain that they will need to use those ideas to help them in this lesson on switches. Ask: *Where do we have switches in our homes?* (For lights, on the TV, on the computer, and so on.)

MAIN ACTIVITY
Put the ready-made circuit on the floor in the centre of the circle, fully connected so that the bulb is on. Ask: *How could we switch the bulb off?* Invite a child to show you by breaking the circuit. Ask them to explain what they have done. Remake the circuit and ask: *Can anyone find a different way of switching the bulb off?* Repeat the process of inviting children to show and explain how they have broken the circuit.

Explain that we can switch the light on and off by making and breaking the circuit. That is all a switch does, but as it would be a bit fiddly trying to join up bits of wire, switches are designed specially to make this easier.

GROUP ACTIVITIES
1. Give the children copies of photocopiable page 172. Ask them to try making some different switches and trying them out in simple circuits. Circulate, asking children to explain how their switches work, focusing on children who are quiet in whole-class discussions.
2. Children could also take apart 'bought' switches to see how they have been made and make annotated drawings to explain how they work.

ASSESSMENT
Can the children explain that a switch works by breaking a circuit? Can they apply their understanding of conductors and insulators to explain that air is an insulator in many switches?

PLENARY
Ask some children to demonstrate their switches to the class, including particularly any that the children have designed themselves. Ask: *Which part of your switch is a conductor/insulator?* Where air is the insulator, ask: *What is in that gap?* (Air is in the gap.) *Can electricity get through air?* (No, not in these circumstances, though the children may raise the idea that lightning travels through air.) Explain that in the next lesson they will be using what they have learned in making some models.

OUTCOMES
● Know that switches can be designed in a variety of ways.
● Can explain that a switch works by breaking a circuit.
● Can recognise air as an insulator.

LINKS
Design and technology: incorporating electrical circuits into models.

Lesson 7 ◼ Switches in models

Objectives
● To use appropriate designs of switches in model-making.
● To apply their understanding of switches in problem-solving.

RESOURCES
Batteries, wires, bulbs, buzzers, wire cutters, paper fasteners, paper clips, drawing pins, aluminium foil, clothes pegs, balsa wood, card, plastic bottles, junk materials, other modelling materials, scissors, glue.

MAIN ACTIVITY
Ask the children to design and make a model that uses a switch. Ideally the model should be related to other work going on, such as a history topic or a story. Let the children know how much time is available so that they can plan accordingly and are not overambitious. You may want to make suggestions of models or leave it completely up to the children, depending on how experienced they are with design and technology activities. Possible models include: a light for reading in bed (with a pressure switch in the bed); a model of the Iron Man with eyes that light up; a 'wolf alert' buzzer in one of the houses of the Three Little Pigs; or, more challenging, a set of quiz-show lights to show which contestants want to answer.

Differentiation
Children can support each other in pairs or groups. The circuits can be very simple on/off switches through to more complex designs involving more than one bulb. Encourage children to challenge themselves, but ensure that plans are achievable in the time available.

ASSESSMENT
Have the children chosen an appropriate switch for the task? Have they persevered in solving problems with the circuits, for example checking for breaks in the circuit if it did not work?

PLENARY
Children can demonstrate their designs, showing how they work.

OUTCOMES
● Can use appropriate designs of switches in model-making.
● Can apply their understanding of switches in problem-solving.

Lesson 8 ◼ Buzzers and motors

Objectives
● To know that batteries may be connected together to provide greater electrical power.
● For children to follow their own lines of enquiry.
● To develop skills of recording observations independently.

Vocabulary
battery, circuit, power

RESOURCES 💿
Main activity: A range of types and sizes of batteries; a torch that needs two batteries and can be opened to show the space for them; a flipchart and marker pens.
Group activities: 1 A range of types and sizes of batteries; connecting wires; bulbs; buzzers; motors; writing equipment. **2** Copies of photocopiable page 173 (also 'Buzzers and motors' (red) on the CD-ROM), writing and drawing materials.
ICT link: 'Buzzes and motors' interactive, from the CD-ROM.

PREPARATION
Put out a selection of electrical equipment on each table, keeping the rest in reserve.

BACKGROUND
Different batteries have different voltages, which means that they have different amounts of 'push' to move electrons around a circuit. You could use the analogy that some things need more 'push' to make them move than others. Avoid saying they have different amounts of electricity in them as this is misleading. Batteries can be joined together in series or in parallel (see diagram). Children do not need to know these terms, but you could draw their attention to the fact that the batteries are connected in a different way.

This activity can become costly on bulbs if too many are 'blown' as large voltages are applied to them. Be prepared for this to happen and raise the question of why with the children, but do keep control of the supply of bulbs so you do not lose too many. Bulbs with different voltages (1.5V, 2.5V, 4.5V) can be bought (see what is written on the metal base). Use higher voltage bulbs with larger batteries. Limiting the number of batteries available can also help with this. Also beware of batteries becoming too hot.

STARTER
Ask: *What can you say about this collection of batteries?* (They are different sizes and different 'strengths'; they go into different appliances; they have different numbers on the sides.) Ask: *Why do you think we have different sorts of batteries?* (Some things need lots of power, some only need a bit, some are too small for a big battery.) Ask the children to pick out examples of any batteries they know would fit into certain toys or appliances they have at home.

MAIN ACTIVITY
Show the children the cavity of a torch that needs two batteries. Ask: *Which battery from our collection do you think would fit in there?* Try out any suggestions. When someone suggests that two batteries are needed, ask why that might be. (To make it light; to make it bright; to fit in so all the connections are made.) Ask: *How could we find out what difference it makes having more than one battery?* Listen to suggestions. Ask the children to try out some of their own ideas, explaining that you want them to keep a record of the process as they go along. Model this on the flipchart/ whiteboard, such as 'First I am going to connect the batteries like this and see if the motor goes.' Draw on the chart/whiteboard. 'I found that it went quite fast. Now I am going to try _____.'

Explain that if they notice any of the batteries getting hot, they should tell you. Also explain that you will keep the spare bulbs and they should come to you if they need more.

GROUP ACTIVITIES
1. The children can work in pairs to explore their own ideas, recording them as they go. Encourage them to explore using a range of types of battery and different buzzers and motors. Circulate, suggesting that children explore different ways of connecting the batteries (in series and parallel).
2. Give the children a copy of photocopiable page 173. Ask them to fill in their responses. This could also be used as a homework activity.

ICT LINK 💿
Use 'Buzzers and motors' interactive, from the CD-ROM as a whole-class activity.

ASSESSMENT
Are the children able to make suggestions of things to try out in their exploration? Can they make observations and record them? Can they suggest explanations for what they notice?

PLENARY
Ask different groups to report back to the class one interesting thing they found out. Ask: *What do you think happens when more than one battery is connected together?*

OUTCOMES
● Can assemble a circuit with two or three batteries.
● Can explain that batteries may be connected together to provide greater electrical power.

- Can follow their own lines of enquiry.
- Can record observations independently.

LINKS
Design and technology: incorporating simple electrical circuits into models.

Lesson 9 ▸ How bright is the light?

Objectives
- To investigate changing the number of bulbs in a circuit.
- To make and test predictions.
- To carry out a fair test by only changing one factor at a time.

Vocabulary
bulb, connection, fair test, investigate

RESOURCES
Main activity: A battery, bulb and two connecting wires made into a simple circuit; spare connecting wires and bulbs to hand; Post-it notes and planning board (optional).
Group activities: 1. Batteries, bulbs, connecting wires, writing materials. **2.** Copies of photocopiable page 174 (also 'How bright is the light?' (red) on the CD-ROM) copied onto card; scissors; writing and drawing materials.
ICT link: 'How bright is the light?' interactive from the CD-ROM.

PREPARATION
Copy photocopiable page 176 onto card, enough for one per pair or group of three children. Have the resources for the Main activity to hand. Put out resources for the Group activities on the tables. Have the children sitting on the carpet in a circle.

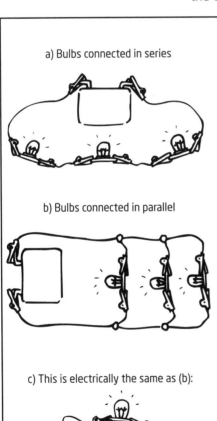

a) Bulbs connected in series

b) Bulbs connected in parallel

c) This is electrically the same as (b):

BACKGROUND
Bulbs can be arranged in series or in parallel (see diagram on page opposite). The way that they are connected will affect how bright they are. If the bulbs are in series, the more bulbs that are added, the less current flows through the circuit and the bulbs glow less brightly. However, if the bulbs are connected in parallel, each bulb would be as bright as if it were connected to a separate battery, but, the battery would run down more quickly. The children do not need to know the terms 'in series' or 'in parallel' at this stage, but you will need to be aware of this to explain differences in results depending on how the children have chosen to connect their bulbs.

Different bulbs have different voltages written on the side, though they may look the same in other respects. Make sure that the bulbs the children are using for this investigation are all the same or they will have different brightnesses that will confuse the results.

In this lesson, children will develop their investigation skills, building on the less-structured enquiry of the previous lesson.

STARTER
Remind the children of how in the previous lesson they had changed the batteries and other components of circuits. Ask: *What do you know about circuits now?* Help the children to review their learning so far. Praise them for their efforts.

MAIN ACTIVITY
Show the children the simple circuit and ask: *What could we change about this circuit?* List the ideas on the board or use Post-it Notes on a planning board: number of batteries, type of battery, type of wires, number of bulbs, type of bulb. Explain that you want them to investigate what happens when the number of bulbs is changed. Ask: *Can we turn that into a question?* ('When I change the number of bulbs what happens?') Write this question on the board. Ask: *What happens to what? What might we see when we change the*

Differentiation
The writing frame can be provided as headings on a worksheet, or to encourage independence it could be presented as a list of prompt headings on the interactive whiteboard. Support children with limited writing skills by scribing for them or providing more writing on the frame, for example, under the heading 'Our prediction', write: 'I think that when I add more bulbs...' Challenge children by asking them to try to give a reason for their prediction or an explanation for their findings. A group could work directly onto the interactive whiteboard.

number of bulbs? (They may not light; they may be brighter; they may be less bright.) Change the question so that it reads: 'When I change the number of bulbs what happens to the brightness of the bulbs?'

Explain that you want the children to plan their test before they begin.

GROUP ACTIVITIES
1. Ask the children to plan and carry out their tests using the following writing frame:
Our question:
Our prediction:
Drawing of our test:
What I will change:
What I will keep the same:
What I found out:
Initially, leave children to make their own plans, but if it becomes clear that they have not controlled the variables, for example, they have planned to add more batteries at the same time as adding more bulbs, then intervene and discuss with the child if it is possible to compare the two circuits.
2. Give each pair or group of three children a copy on card of photocopiable page 174. Ask them to look at the pictures and think about how bright the light needs to be. Ask a child in each pair or group to cut the out the 12 cards. Ask the children to put the cards in order from the one they think needs to be the brightest to the one they think could be least bright. Ask them to draw some ideas of their own on the blank cards and include these in the order. Stress the importance of discussing their ideas over finding 'right answers'.

ICT LINK 💿
Children can use the 'How bright is the light?' interactive from the CD-ROM to arrange the light sources from the brightest to the least bright.

ASSESSMENT
Have the children made a prediction about what will happen? Have they given a reason for their prediction? Are the children able to control the variables independently or have they needed support with this?

PLENARY
Choose one group who have connected their bulbs in series and one who have connected their bulbs in parallel and ask them to report their findings to the rest of the class, showing the circuits they have made. As the group who have connected their bulbs in parallel will have found no difference in the brightness and the ones who connected in series will have found a difference, ask the class if they can see any reason why the groups got different results. Discuss their ideas, reaching the conclusion that it depends on how the bulbs are connected.

OUTCOMES
● Can investigate changing the number of bulbs in a circuit.
● Can make and test predictions.
● Can carry out a fair test by only changing one factor at a time.

LINKS
Design and technology: incorporating simple electrical circuits into models.

Lesson 10 ▸ Electricity through drama

RESOURCES
Enough balls or beanbags for at least one each; other resources such as hoops, card, adhesive tape and felt-tipped pens may be useful for the improvisations.

MAIN ACTIVITY
Have the whole class sit in a circle. Explain that they are going to model an electric circuit with their bodies. Say that you will be the battery that will 'push around' the electric current and they will be the wires. Give each child a ball and tell them all to start together passing balls around the 'circuit' to represent electricity flowing along the wires. Ask different children to act out being different components: a buzzer, a motor or a bulb, for example. Ask a child to be a switch by stepping in and out of the circle to create a gap.

Divide the class into six groups and ask each group to take one of the following aspects of the unit: safety, making electricity, conductivity of different materials, switches, varying the number of bulbs, varying the number of batteries.

Ask each group to devise a short improvisation in which they present what they have learned about their aspect of the topic. These presentations and role-plays could be presented to another class or used in an assembly.

ASSESSMENT
Is there evidence that the children are expressing understanding of the topic through their improvisations?

PLENARY
Present the improvisations, either to the rest of the class or invite another class as the audience.

OUTCOMES
● Can communicate their understanding about electricity.
● Can relate the different aspects of the topic to each other.

Lesson 11 ▸ Assessment

RESOURCES ○
Assessment activities: 1 Copies of photocopiable page 175 (also 'Assessment - 1' (red) on the CD-ROM) on card for each pair of children; a box to include one 4.5V battery, two bulbs in bulb holders, two short connecting wires with clips on the ends (make sure the circuit cannot be completed using only these); a variety of conducting materials such as paper clips, coins, aluminium foil, metal strips, and a variety of non-conductors such as plastics, string, rubber (be aware that some kitchen foils and some paper clips have plastic coatings); sticky tape. **2** A copy of photocopiable page 176 (also 'Assessment - 2' (red) on the CD-ROM) for each child.

PREPARATION
These Assessment activities should be considered alongside the ongoing assessment opportunities indicated throughout the unit when making a judgement about the level the child is working at. If you are unsure what a child means by their response to a question, then discuss it with them afterwards.

ASSESSMENT ACTIVITY 1

Give the children the card picture of the clown. Explain that the challenge is to make the clown's eyes light up using only the materials in the box. As there is not enough connecting wire, the children will have to make a complete circuit using different conducting materials touching each other. They will also have to make a complete circuit. They make the circuit simply with materials touching each other, but provide adhesive tape to hold connections in place if needed.

If you are able to observe a group, make notes about how the children approach the problem and how independent they are in solving it. If the whole class is doing the task, then ask the children to write and draw an account of how they solved the problem and focus observations on children about whose level of achievement you are particularly concerned.

LOOKING FOR LEVELS

Children who are working at NC Level 3/Scottish Level C will be able to solve the problem fairly quickly and give a simple explanation of why they chose certain materials. Their solution will demonstrate the use of a complete circuit. Children working at Level 2/Scottish Level B may need help in solving the problem, but will then be able to describe what they have done to make the bulb light up. Children working at Level 4/Scottish Level C/D will be able to provide more advanced explanations, relating the conductivity of the materials to the reason for their inclusion in the circuit, and will be able to explain that a complete circuit is needed.

ASSESSMENT ACTIVITY 2

Give each child a copy of photocopiable page 176. You may wish to read the questions to a group of children with poor reading skills, or read each question to the whole class to explain how to fill in the sheet.

ANSWERS

1a. The bulb will light up.
1b. The motor will turn.
1c. The bulb will go off.
2. The child might get an electric shock/might die! Advice might include: never put anything metal in the toaster, switch off at the plug, unplug it first, stop!

LOOKING FOR LEVELS

Most children working at NC Level 3/Scottish Level C should be able to answer 1a, b and c on the photocopiable sheet correctly. Correct answers to question 1d suggest the child may be working at Level 4/Scottish Level C/D. In the answers to question 2, look for the quality of explanation. Children working at NC Level 2/Scottish Level B may have a simple description: 'It switches it on'. At NC Level 3/Scottish Level C, children should be able to provide some explanation of switching between the two components and children working at Level 4/Scottish Level C/D should be explaining how it works in terms of completing circuits, possibly with reference to conductors and insulators.

PLENARY

Ask the children to share some of their solutions to making the clown's eyes light up. Ask the children what learning *they* think they have demonstrated in this activity. (A need for complete circuits and materials that do and do not conduct electricity.) Go through the answers to the test, asking the children to explain their answers and providing explanations where needed. Ask them to turn to a partner and decide two things that they have learned during this unit. Listen to what the pairs of children have to say.

Will the bulb light up?

◼ Make a prediction, then test it!

I. 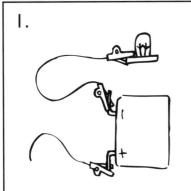 Prediction ☐ Test ☐	**2.** 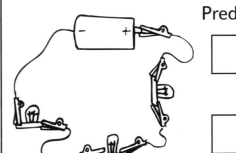 Prediction ☐ Test ☐
3.  Prediction ☐ Test ☐	**4.**  Prediction ☐ Test ☐
5.  Prediction ☐ Test ☐	**6.**  Prediction ☐ Test ☐
7. 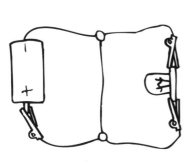 Prediction ☐ Test ☐	**8.** Now draw a circuit of your own to test.

PHOTOCOPIABLE

Switches to make

1.

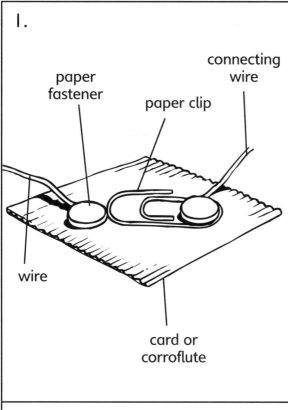

paper fastener

paper clip

connecting wire

wire

card or corroflute

2.

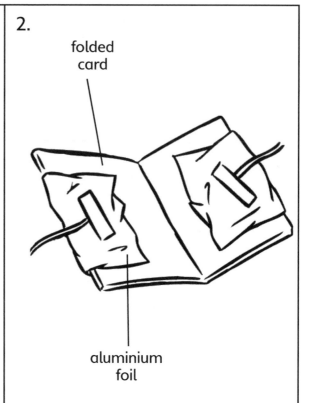

folded card

aluminium foil

3.

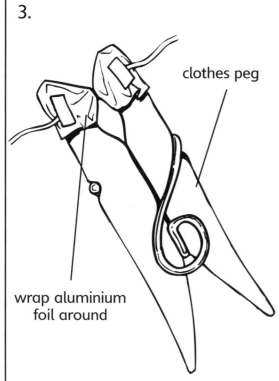

clothes peg

wrap aluminium foil around

4.

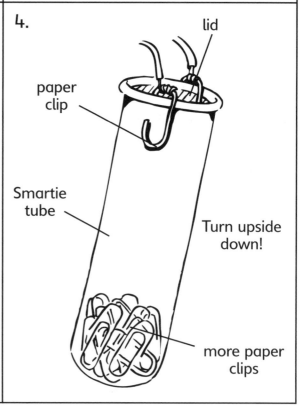

lid

paper clip

Smartie tube

Turn upside down!

more paper clips

◣ Try these switches, then make up your own ideas!

◣ SCHOLASTIC

Illustrations Debbie Clark, Theresa Tibbetts c/o Beehive Illustration

Buzzers and motors

Motors

These machines use a motor to turn parts around. Which parts turn? Label them with an arrow.

bus

helicopter

big wheel

washing machine

electric fan

roundabout

Buzzers

Lots of things use electricity to make a sound. Write and draw all the ones you can think of.

radio

fire alarm

Illustration © Debbie Clark

PHOTOCOPIABLE

How bright is the light?

- Cut the cards out along the dotted lines.
- Which light needs to be the brightest? Put them in order starting with the brightest. You might not agree!
- Use the blank cards to add ideas of your own.

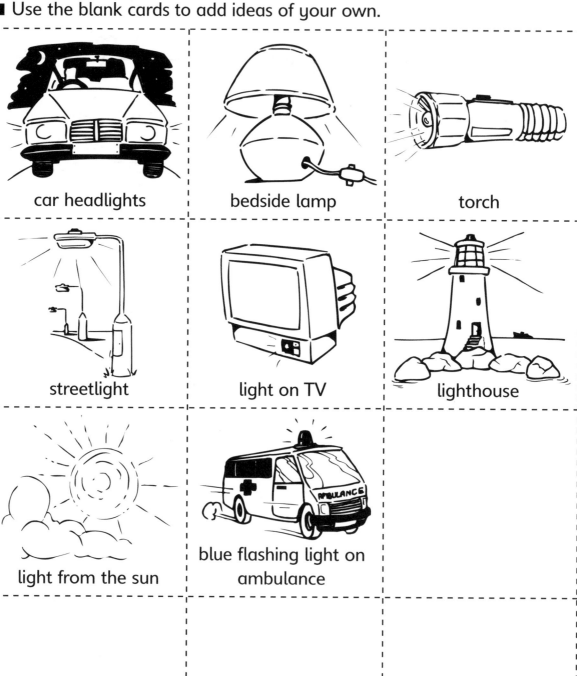

car headlights	bedside lamp	torch
streetlight	light on TV	lighthouse
light from the sun	blue flashing light on ambulance	

Illustration © Debbie Clark

■ SCHOLASTIC

Assessment – 1

hole for bulb

space for battery

PHOTOCOPIABLE

Assessment – 2

1. Look carefully at each of these circuits. Write down what you think will happen when you operate the switch.

a. _____   b. _____

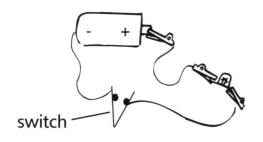

switch

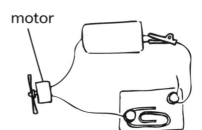

motor

c. _____

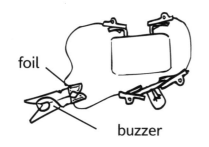

foil

buzzer

b.

2a. What might happen to this child?

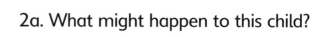

_____

_____

What could you say to the child to help him?

_____

_____

Illustration © Debbie Clark

CHAPTER 8   Making and using electricity

Lesson	Objectives	Main activity	Group activities	Plenary	Outcomes
Enrichment Lesson 1 Making and detecting electricity	• To know that in a battery, different chemicals are brought together to produce electricity. • To make observations and draw conclusions from them.	Discuss how we can tell that electricity is present. Consider places where electricity is used to make light, sound or movement.	Use headphones to detect electricity. Make a salt water battery. Carry out a survey of where batteries are used and what types are used.	Compare the advantages of different ways of detecting electricity.	• Know that chemicals in batteries react to generate electricity. • Can use bulbs, buzzers and headphones to detect the presence of electricity.
Enrichment Lesson 2 Electro-magnets	• To know how an electromagnet can be constructed and used. • To ask scientific questions that can be tested.	Demonstrate how to make an electromagnet. Deduce what materials can be used. Consider what factors might affect the strength of electromagnets.	Investigate a question about what factors affect the strength of an electromagnet. Use secondary sources to find out about different uses of electromagnets.	Discuss the children's findings and why electromagnets are used in various contexts.	• Know how to make an electromagnet. • Can describe some uses of electromagnets. • Can ask and investigate a scientific question.
Enrichment Lesson 3 Does electricity affect magnets?	• To know that magnets and wires carrying electricity affect each other. • To decide what to do and what evidence to collect in an investigation.	Consider a compass needle as a magnet. Demonstrate that a piece or coil of copper wire on its own has no effect on a compass needle.	Investigate the effect that pieces and coils of wire carrying electricity have on a magnet. Discuss situations in which a compass might give a false direction reading.	Discuss the Group activities. By considering the forces involved, lead into the idea of the electric motor.	• Know how electricity can affect a compass. • Know how the movement of a magnet in a coil can make a current of electricity. • Can decide what to do in an investigation.
Enrichment Lesson 4 Electric motors	• To know how an electric motor works. • To know some uses of electric motors.	Demonstrate how a small electric motor works. Discuss the size and power of different electric motors.	Find examples of places where electric motors are used. Make a poster illustrating how an electric motor works or one use of an electric motor.	Discuss examples of electric motors, considering power sources and outputs.	• Can describe how an electric motor works. • Can describe a wide range of uses for electric motors.
Enrichment Lesson 5 Motors in toys	• To use electric motors in toys. • To understand circuit drawings including motors.	Use a circuit drawing as the basis for a toy including an electric motor.		Discuss the models. Look at other ways of using motors to drive machinery.	• Can interpret circuit drawings and overcome practical problems to use electric motors in 'real-life' situations.
Enrichment Lesson 6 Power stations	• To know that magnets and wires carrying electricity affect each other. • To understand how this effect is used in power generation. • To realise that power generation has environmental implications.	Look at how one type of power station generates electricity and draw an energy flow diagram.	Find out about another type of power station and draw an energy flow diagram. Find out about the environmental impact of different types of power station.	Review the Group activities. Link to energy conservation and ways of using less electricity.	• Understand how a generator produces electricity and relate this to changes in energy. • Know that electricity generation has environmental implications, and link this to the need for energy conservation.
Enrichment Lesson 7 Green energy	• To know that 'environmentally friendly' power sources exist. • To understand some of the ways they are used.	Introduce the idea of renewable energy sources. Look at solar power as an alternative to batteries. Research other types of 'environmentally friendly' power.		Talk about how and why renewable energy sources are used. How might the children's everyday energy use be reduced or made more environmentally friendly?	• Can discuss energy use and its impact on the environment in an informed way.

Assessment	Objectives	Activity 1	Activity 2
Enrichment Lesson 8	• To discuss energy use and its impact on the environment in an informed way.	Identify equipment that uses electricity. Identify alternative ways of powering some equipment. Consider environmental benefits of using alternatives to electricity.	Recognise and label the energy changes taking place in a power station. Describe the construction of an electric motor and the energy changes in it. Name possible sources of electricity to power a motor, and describe an advantage of rechargeable batteries.

Note: Please note that the term 'battery' is used throughout this unit. While it is technically correct to speak of electricity as being produced by a 'cell', and a 'battery' as being an electricity-producing device composed of a number of 'cells', the introduction of the term 'cell' at this stage may cause confusion.

SC1 SCIENTIFIC ENQUIRY

Are all electromagnets as strong as each other?

LEARNING OBJECTIVES AND OUTCOMES
- Make systematic measurements and observations.
- Use observations to draw conclusions.
- Check measurements and observations by repeating them.
- Use a wide range of methods, including tables and bar charts, to communicate data in an appropriate way.

ACTIVITY
Children make different electromagnets by varying the number of turns in their coil or by changing the material they wind the wire around. They record how many paper clips each electromagnet can lift, repeating each measurement several times, and recording results in a table. They convert the table into a bar chart and say what the bar chart shows.

LESSON LINKS
Use this Sc1 activity as the group activity in Lesson 2, Electromagnets.

ENRICHMENT
Lesson 1 ▫ Making and detecting electricity

Vocabulary
powerful/weak battery, chemicals, reaction

Objectives
- To know that in a battery, different chemicals are brought together to produce electricity.
- To make observations and draw conclusions from them.

RESOURCES 💿
Group activities: 1 One copy per group photocopiable page 188 (also 'Making and detecting electricity' (red) on the CD-ROM), batteries, headphones (one set per group – the ones given away in flight bags could be used), beakers of salt solution, copper coins, aluminium foil, crocodile clips and wires, bulbs. **2** Paper, pencils; a computer and data-handling program (optional).

PREPARATION
Have warm water available for making the salt solution. A stronger solution can be made with warm water than with cold water. Alternatively, make up the solution in advance with boiling water and allow it to cool.
Safety note: Remind the children *never* to try out electricity experiments with mains electricity or car batteries, and *never* to test batteries by putting them on the tongue.

BACKGROUND
Batteries release electricity as a result of a gradual chemical reaction. When all the chemicals have been used up, the battery is said to be 'flat'. This lesson looks at another mixture of chemicals – not those in modern batteries – that can be used to make electricity. In Lesson 6, Power stations, the children will look at another way of making electricity: by using energy to generate it in a power station.

At primary school level, electricity is usually detected by observing what it does: lighting a bulb, working a buzzer and so on. In this lesson, because the amount of electricity the chemical reaction will produce is not enough to operate a bulb or a buzzer, the children will use headphones to detect the crackling sounds produced by the electricity. The stronger the salt solution, the better this will work.

Differentiation
Group activity 1
To support children, give them 'Detecting and making electricity' (green), from the CD-ROM, which asks them to complete sentences and select correct answers from a list. To extend children, use 'Detecting and making electricity' (blue) which includes more open-ended questioning.

STARTER
Remind the children of their work on switches in Unit 4F. Discuss why switches may be needed in circuits. Ask where the electricity that the switches are controlling comes from. Discuss the suggestions made. The children will be aware of mains electricity at home and at school, and of batteries in toys and torches; they may also be aware of car batteries, rechargeable batteries and lightning. Discuss which sources of electricity they can use in experiments in school, reminding them that mains electricity and electricity from car batteries is too powerful to be used safely in school.

MAIN ACTIVITY
Ask: *We know lots of places that electricity comes from, but how can we tell when electricity is there?* Discuss the fact that we cannot see electricity: we can only see the effect it has on other things. Ask the children what electricity can do so that we know it is there. Discuss places, at home and in school, where electricity is used to make light, sound or movement. *Where in your experiments have you detected electricity by light or sound?* (Bulbs lighting up, buzzers sounding.) Tell them that today they are going to use a new way of detecting electricity; they are also going to make a simple battery.

GROUP ACTIVITIES
1. Ask the children, to use a copy of page 188 to help them build their own battery using salt water, copper coins and aluminium foil, then use headphones to check for the presence of electricity. They should draw a diagram to show how they made the battery. Ask them to explain (in writing) how they could tell it made electricity. *Was it a powerful battery or a weak battery? How could you tell?* (When the headphones are connected to a normal battery, a crackling sound is heard. The same sound can be heard from the salt water battery. When the salt water battery is connected to the bulb, nothing happens: the battery is too weak to light up a bulb.)
2. Groups can carry out a survey to find out where the children and their families use batteries, and what type of batteries they use ('ordinary', 'long life' or 'rechargeable'). Remind them to include batteries for mobile phones, calculators and wrist-watches. Each group can discuss what questions to ask, then one child from each group can ask other children the questions. This can run concurrently with Group activity 1.

ASSESSMENT
During the group work, ask the children to explain why they heard a crackling sound when the headphones were connected to the aluminium and the copper coin in salt water, and why the bulb would not light up.

PLENARY
Discuss with the children what they heard through the headphones. *Do you think this is a good way of detecting electricity? What advantages does it have over using a bulb or a buzzer?* (It can be used to detect smaller amounts of electricity.) *When would it be better to use a bulb or a buzzer?* (Where there is enough electricity, using a bulb or a buzzer is more convenient because you do not need to be wearing headphones – so more than one person can detect the electricity at a time).

Discuss the types of battery. Long life batteries are better for the user and the environment than ordinary batteries, as they do not need replacing so often. Rechargeable batteries are the best of all, as it takes much less energy to recharge a battery than to make a new one.

OUTCOMES
● Know that chemicals in batteries react to generate electricity.
● Can use bulbs, buzzers and headphones to detect the presence of electricity.

ENRICHMENT
Lesson 2 ▪ Electromagnets

RESOURCES
Main activity: Thin, insulated copper wire suitable for winding into coils; rods made of different materials (such as nails, pencils, pens); small paper clips or pins, a battery.
Group activities: 1 Large, thick iron nails or other iron cores; copper wire, crocodile clips and leads, batteries, paper clips or pins. **2** Secondary information sources about electromagnets.

PREPARATION
Make a coil of insulated copper wire that can be placed around different core materials to form an electromagnet (see diagram).

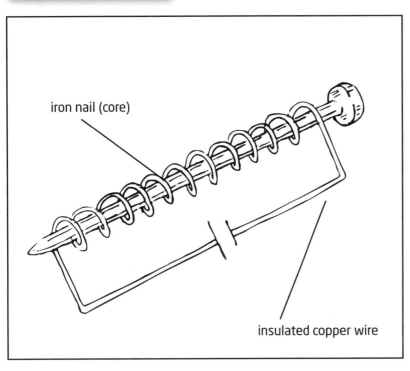

iron nail (core)

insulated copper wire

BACKGROUND
This lesson looks at how electricity can be used to make temporary magnets known as electromagnets. Following lessons in this unit look at other ways in which electricity and magnets can affect each other.
Electromagnets are made by winding insulated copper wire around a soft iron core (see diagram). When an electric current flows through the wire, the iron core becomes a magnet. When the current is switched off, the core stops being a magnet. Electromagnets are used in places where a magnet needs to be turned on and off (such as an electric bell or a scrapyard crane), or where the strength of a magnet needs to be varied (such as a loudspeaker or a telephone earpiece, where different sounds are produced by varying the strength of the magnet). The core of the electromagnet is always made of soft iron because this can be magnetised and demagnetised much more rapidly than steel, so the magnet can be turned on and off faster.

STARTER
Tell the children that they are going to look at some uses of electricity that may be new to them. The first thing they are going to do is to use electricity to make a magnet. *How can you tell if you have made a magnet?* Recap on what type of things a magnet will be attracted to, and what it will be able to pick up.

MAIN ACTIVITY
Show the children how to make an electromagnet by winding many turns of insulated wire around an iron core such as a nail. Connect the ends of the wire to the terminals of a battery. Demonstrate that the electromagnet can be used to pick up small paper clips or pins. Try using several different magnetic and non-magnetic materials for the core. Encourage the children to predict which materials will become electromagnets. List the objects that become electromagnets and those that do not. Help the children to see that only magnetic materials can become electromagnets.

Ask: *Do you think all electromagnets will be as strong as each other?* If the children are not sure, ask them to think back to work they have done on magnets. *Can you think of a question about the strength of electromagnets that you could test?* Encourage the children to think of an investigation they could carry out.

GROUP ACTIVITIES

1. Groups can focus on an appropriate question about the strength of electromagnets, then plan and carry out an investigation to find out what affects the strength of electromagnets. Discuss ways to ensure that the test is fair. They may find, for example, that increasing the number of turns in the coil of wire increases the strength of the magnet; or that increasing the number of batteries increases the strength of the magnet (however, with the range of voltages available, this effect may not be clear).
2. The children can use secondary sources to write a short talk (one or two minutes) on the uses of electromagnets. They should decide whether to cover many different uses of electromagnets or to cover one or two uses in greater detail.

ICT LINKS

Children could use the computer to find information about electromagnets (from CD-ROMs or the internet), or to help write their short talks.

ASSESSMENT

Ask some children to present to other groups or to the class what they have found out about the factors affecting the strength of an electromagnet, and others to present their short talks on the uses of electromagnets. Look for recognition of how an electromagnet may be useful where a permanent magnet would not be, and that the strength of an electromagnet can be varied.

PLENARY

Discuss what different groups of children have found out about the factors affecting the strength of electromagnets. Encourage the children to explain how they reached their conclusions from the observations or measurements they made. Ask some children to present their short talks on the uses of electromagnets. Discuss some of the places where electromagnets are used (see Background), encouraging the children to think about why electromagnets are used instead of permanent magnets.

OUTCOMES
- Know how to make an electromagnet.
- Can describe some uses of electromagnets.
- Can ask and investigate a scientific question.

ENRICHMENT
Lesson 3 ▪ Does electricity affect magnets?

RESOURCES 💿
Main activity: A small compass, magnets, a piece of iron and a coil of copper wire.
Group activities: 1 A copy for each child of photocopiable page 189 (also 'Does electricity affect magnets?' (red) on the CD-ROM), batteries, copper wire, crocodile clips and leads, compasses.

Vocabulary
compass, coil, magnetic, non-magnetic

PREPARATION
Make room at the front of the class for all the children to gather close enough to see the needle of a small compass.

BACKGROUND
When electricity flows through a wire, it causes a magnetic field to form around the wire. This makes the wire behave like a magnet. It is this magnetic field that makes a coil of wire with an electric current passing through it able to turn an iron core into a magnet. The wire can also affect other nearby magnets, such as compasses. This connection between electricity in wires and magnetic fields also means that moving a magnet in and out of a coil of wire makes an electric current flow in the wire. This is how electricity is produced in generators and power stations. The amount of electricity that can be produced using the wire coils and magnets available in schools is so tiny that specialised equipment (an ammeter) would be needed to measure it. For this reason, this lesson concentrates on demonstrating the effect electricity in a wire has on a compass.

STARTER
Remind the children of some of the things that electricity can do, such as make a light bulb glow and turn an iron bar into a magnet. In this lesson, they are going to learn about the effect that electricity can have on magnets - and the effect that magnets can have on electricity. These are very important effects, because they are used in electric motors and power stations (as the children will see in later lessons).

MAIN ACTIVITY
Show the children a small compass. Ask: *Who knows what this is? Can you explain how it works?* Make sure the children know that a compass is actually a small magnet that is free to turn around. *What sort of things might make the needle turn?* If necessary, help the children to work out that since the compass is a small magnet, it will be affected by magnetic materials and by other magnets. Demonstrate this.

What effect do you think this wire, on its own, will have on the compass? They may well believe that it will make the compass move, because it is metal. Demonstrate that the wire has no effect at all on the compass, and explain that this is because the wire is made of copper, which is non-magnetic. *Will a coil of copper wire affect the compass?* Again, show that it does not. Tell the children that now they know the wire does not affect the magnet (the compass), you want them to investigate how the electricity in the wire affects it.

GROUP ACTIVITIES
1. The children can work in groups, with individual copies of page 189, to find out how electricity affects magnets. (A battery will almost certainly affect the compass, since most batteries of the type you are likely to use contain nickel, which is a magnetic material. You can make sure the battery will not affect the results by keeping it a long way from the compass. Electricity in a straight wire may make the needle move a small amount. Electricity in a coil of wire will make it move further. Increasing the number of turns on the coil increases the effect on the needle.)
2. Discuss the answers to these questions:
● *A person uses a torch to read a compass. Will the compass point in the correct direction?* (Probably not, as the batteries in the torch will affect the compass.)
● *A person stands under an electricity power cable and reads a compass. Will it give the correct direction?* (No: the electricity in the power cable will affect the compass.)

Making and using electricity

Differentiation 💿
Group activity 1
Support children by asking them to complete 'Does electricity affect magnets' (green), from the CD-ROM, which does ask them to explain their answers in writing. (You may wish to discuss their ideas verbally.) To extend children, give them 'Does electricity affect magnets' (blue), which includes open-ended questioning.
Group activity 2
Support children by asking them to discuss the second question only. Encourage them to draw parallels between the electricity in their wire and the electricity in the power cable. Extend children by asking them to try to think of other situations where electricity and magnets might affect each other.

ASSESSMENT
During Group activity 1, ask the children to explain what they have found out about the effect of electricity on magnets.

PLENARY
Discuss what the children have found out about the effect that electricity has on magnets. Encourage them to discuss the questions in Group activity 2, explaining why they reached the conclusions they did. Explain that the magnet in Group activity 1 moved because the electricity in the wire 'pushed' it (or 'there is a force between the electricity in the wire and the magnet', if the children are ready for this idea). Ask the children to speculate about what might happen if the wire could move but the magnet was held still. Use the example of a child pushing a door: if the door were held still and the child was on roller skates, it would be the child that moved. Explain that this is how electric motors work; they will look at this in the next lesson.

OUTCOMES
● Know how electricity passing through a wire can affect a compass.
● Know how the movement of a magnet in a coil can make a current of electricity.
● Can decide what to do and what evidence to collect to answer questions in an investigation.

LINKS
Geography: using a compass.

ENRICHMENT
Lesson 4 ▪ Electric motors

Objectives
● To know how an electric motor works.
● To know some uses of electric motors.

Vocabulary
electric motor, coil, axle

RESOURCES
Main activity: A small electric motor.
Group activities: 1 Secondary sources about electric motors, paper, writing materials. **2** Plain A4 paper, felt-tipped pens or coloured pencils.

PREPARATION
Obtain a small electric motor. The motors of cars in electric racing tracks are ideal, since their workings are usually visible and they are designed to run well at different speeds when different voltages are used to power them. Check that your chosen motor works at different speeds from different-voltage batteries.

BACKGROUND
An electric motor consists of a coil of wire that is free to rotate between two magnets. When electricity flows through the coil, a magnetic field is created around it. The force between the permanent magnets and the magnetic field from the coil of wire makes the coil spin round. The coil is fixed to an axle that turns whenever the coil turns; the axle can be used to turn wheels or other machinery. The greater the electric current, or the stronger the permanent magnets, the more powerful the motor will be.

Electric motors are used in many ways in the home and in almost every industry. Some of these motors are battery-powered (such as motors in toys and starter motors in cars), but most use mains electricity. They vary in size and power, from the tiny motors in toys to the powerful motors used in large cranes. In the home, mains-powered motors turn fans in hairdryers and fan heaters, and turn the moving parts in washing machines, tumble dryers, food mixers and video recorders.

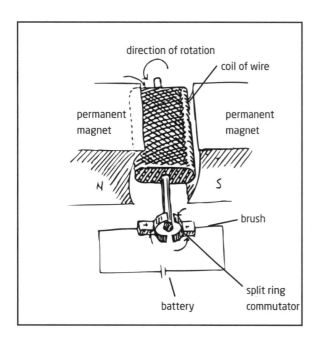

direction of rotation

coil of wire

permanent magnet

permanent magnet

N   S

brush

split ring commutator

battery

STARTER

Remind the children how electricity in a coil of wire makes a magnet move. Explain again that they used electricity in a wire to move a magnet – but if the magnet were fixed and the wire free to move, it would be the wire that moved instead. Repeat the example of the door and the child on roller skates. Explain that this is what happens in electric motors: the magnets are held still, but the coil of wire is free to move.

MAIN ACTIVITY

Show the children the small electric motor. Show them where the magnets and the wires carrying electricity are. Can they guess from the toy car which way the movement will take place in the motor? Connect batteries across the motor to show it working, and to show how the turning of the coil of wire is used to make the wheels on the toy car turn.

Discuss ways of making the motor more powerful. Explain that if more electricity is used, the wires need to be bigger and so the whole motor is bigger. What are the largest and smallest electric motors they can think of? (For example: large motors in powerful cranes, small motors in toys.) Discuss some uses of large and small electric motors. Ask: *What provides the electricity? How powerful are they?*

GROUP ACTIVITIES

1. Working in groups, the children should think of places where electric motors are used and list them under the headings 'Home', 'School' and 'Work/Industry'. They can use secondary sources of information, and try to think of a range of different-sized motors.

2. Ask the children to choose one use of an electric motor and produce an illustrated poster showing how the motor works or how and where it is used.

ASSESSMENT

How many different uses of electric motors have the children found? Do they know what these motors all do?

PLENARY

Look at the range of places where motors are used. List the places the children found in Group activity 1. *Where have you found the most motors? Where are most small motors used? Where are most large motors used? How many use batteries? How many use mains electricity?* Recap on how motors work.

OUTCOMES

● Can describe how an electric motor works.
● Can describe a wide range of uses for electric motors.

Differentiation

Group activity 1
The children can work in mixed-ability groups. Give more able children a challenge: *Write a sentence about the smallest/largest/most unusual motor you can think of.*

ENRICHMENT
Lesson 5 ▄ Motors in toys

Objective
● To use electric motors in toys.
● To understand circuit drawings including motors.

RESOURCES

A large copy of the circuit drawing shown opposite; small electric motors, fans (or propellers) that clip onto a motor axle, batteries, wires, switches, modelling materials.

MAIN ACTIVITY

The children use the circuit drawing to make a toy in which an electric motor

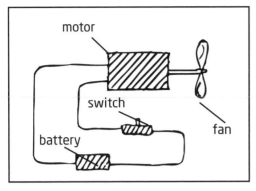

is used to drive a propeller or fan. This mechanism can be used in toys such as racing cars (where the car is 'blown' along by the propeller) and windmills (where the sails are attached to the blades of the fan). The children have to decide where to put the battery and the switch, and what power to use (the higher the voltage, the faster the motor runs).

ASSESSMENT
Ask the children to write brief descriptions of what they did and why. Look for skill in choosing the correct power for the battery and sensible positions for the battery and switch.

PLENARY
Look at the models. Discuss any problems encountered and how they could be overcome. Discuss how motors can be used to power things other than fans and propellers. If you have suitable kits available, show how motors can be attached to drive belts and gearboxes to increase the range of things they can be used to power.

OUTCOME
● Can interpret circuit drawings and overcome practical problems to use electric motors in 'real-life' situations.

Differentiation
Some children could be given a model or design to copy. Other children could be encouraged to invent a number of different toys.

ENRICHMENT
Lesson 6 ▭ Power stations

Objectives
● To know that magnets and wires carrying electricity affect each other.
● To understand how this effect is used in power generation.
● To realise that power generation has environmental implications.

Vocabulary
electricity generation, power station, fossil fuels

Differentiation
Group activity 1
Some children could cut out pictures of different types of power station and label each one with the type or source of energy going in (such as coal) and the type of energy coming out (electricity). Other children could research and discuss which type of power station might be judged the 'best' from an environmental point of view. *Are some types of power station more suitable for certain places than others?*

RESOURCES
Main activity: The small electric motor from Lesson 4; secondary sources (books, videos, posters) on how a particular type of power station works.
Group activities: Secondary sources on different types of power station and their environmental impact.

BACKGROUND
Electricity generators and power stations are basically electric motors working in reverse. In an electric motor, the interaction between permanent magnets and an electric current in a coil of wire causes the coil of wire to move. In an electricity generator, a coil of wire is rotated between permanent magnets. The interaction between the permanent magnets and the moving coil of wire causes an electric current to be produced in the wire. You may be able to demonstrate a model power station by spinning the axle of a small electric motor fast enough to light up a low voltage light bulb.

STARTER
Use a small motor to recap on how electric motors work. Explain that the mains electricity we use is generated in power stations. The electricity generators in power stations are really just like huge electric motors working in reverse (see Background again). In most types of power station, fuel is burned to make steam that turns turbines in order to turn coils of wire between magnets.

MAIN ACTIVITY
Describe how one particular type of power station works - for example, in a coal-fired power station, the coal is burned to heat water and make it turn to steam. The steam is used to push the turbines which generate the electricity around. Use an energy flow diagram to discuss the energy changes that take place at different stages in the power station. In this example, an appropriate energy flow diagram is shown overleaf.

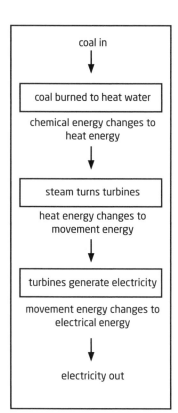

coal in

↓

coal burned to heat water

chemical energy changes to heat energy

↓

steam turns turbines

heat energy changes to movement energy

↓

turbines generate electricity

movement energy changes to electrical energy

↓

electricity out

GROUP ACTIVITIES

1. The children can use secondary sources to find out about a different type of power station, describe how it works and draw an energy flow diagram.
2. They can use secondary sources to look at the impact that different types of power station have on the environment.

ASSESSMENT

Look at the children's diagrams of energy changes in power stations. Look for recognition of the different types of energy at different stages. Some children may show an understanding of the changes taking place.

PLENARY

Discuss the similarities and differences between the energy changes taking place in different power stations. Emphasise that all power stations make electrical energy from a different type of energy. Discuss the impact that electricity generation has on the environment: hot water pumped into rivers damages wildlife; waste gases from the burning of fossil fuels contributes to global warming; nuclear power generation produces waste products that remain dangerous for a long time. Discuss ways of using less electricity, and make the connection with energy conservation.

OUTCOMES

● Understand how a generator produces electricity and relate this to changes in energy.
● Know that electricity generation has environmental implications, and link this to the need for energy conservation.

ENRICHMENT
Lesson 7 ▪ Green energy

Objectives
● To know that 'environmentally friendly' power sources exist.
● To understand some of the ways they are used.

RESOURCES

A battery-powered calculator, a solar-powered calculator, LEGO® solar-powered kits; pictures of wind turbines and houses with solar panels; secondary sources of information on renewable energy.

MAIN ACTIVITY

Discuss where the power comes from to drive the battery-powered and solar-powered calculators. Introduce the idea of renewable energy sources being 'environmentally friendly', because they use an energy source which is being replaced. Look at the solar-powered LEGO model. Discuss which is better for the environment: this kit or one powered by a battery. The children can use secondary sources to research, and write about, other types of 'environmentally friendly' power and what they can be used for.

ASSESSMENT

Look for children whose writing shows understanding of the difference between renewable and non-renewable energy sources.

PLENARY

Discuss the types of 'environmentally friendly' power the children have researched. Encourage the children to talk about whether they think we should try to use energy in a more environmentally friendly way, and why. Talk about how they might they be able to use less energy.

OUTCOMES

● Can discuss energy use and its impact on the environment.

Differentiation
Differentiate this activity through the complexity of the secondary sources different children use.

ENRICHMENT
Lesson 8 ⊇ Assessment

Objectives
● To assess the children's knowledge of situations where electricity is used.
● To assess the children's knowledge and understanding of energy changes in power stations and electric motors.

RESOURCES 💿
Photocopiable pages 190 and 191 (also 'Assessment - 1' (red) and 'Assessment - 2' (red) on the CD-ROM), writing materials.

STARTER
You may wish to start with a 'question and answer' session or short quiz to reinforce the children's knowledge of the topics covered in this unit, giving them the opportunity to ask questions about things they are unsure of.

ASSESSMENT ACTIVITY 1
Give each child a copy of page 190 to work through individually.

ANSWERS
1. The washing machine, hairdryer, torch, kettle and TV should be circled.
2. Washing machine, hairdryer.
3. Calculator, toy.
4. A calculator might be powered by solar power, a toy might be powered by clockwork.
5. Torches are used when it is dark, so solar panels wouldn't work.
6. The alternatives use renewable power sources, so the power can be used again and again without running out. The alternatives cause very little pollution compared with conventional electricity power stations.
7. Wind power or water power.

LOOKING FOR LEVELS
All the children should answer questions 1 and 3. Most children will answer questions 2, 4 and 5. A few may be able to answer questions 6 and 7.

ASSESSMENT ACTIVITY 2
Give each child a copy of page 191 to work through individually.

ANSWERS
1. Chemical energy changes to heat energy. Heat energy changes to movement energy. Movement energy changes to electrical energy.
2. Magnets (or permanent magnets).
3. Movement energy.
4. Using weaker magnets or attaching the wire coil to a less powerful electricity source.
5. Mains electricity, ordinary batteries or rechargeable batteries.
6. Rechargeable batteries are cheaper in the long term: they last longer, so use fewer chemicals per hour of battery use, or they do not have to be disposed of as often, so produce less harmful waste per hour of battery use.

LOOKING FOR LEVELS
All the children should be able to answer questions 2 and 5. Most of the children will be able to answer questions 1, 3 and 6. Some will also be able to answer question 4.

PLENARY
You may wish to go over the answers to the Assessment activities with the children, or to recap on some of the other topics covered in this unit. You could perhaps do this in the form of a class quiz, with each child contributing one question and answer.

PHOTOCOPIABLE

Making and detecting electricity

1. Your teacher will give you a powerful battery and a weak battery. Connect them to a bulb in turn.

What happens to the bulb if the battery is powerful? _____

_____

What happens to the bulb if the battery is weak? _____

_____

2. Put on some headphones and listen.
Your teacher will show you how to connect the plug on your headphones to the connections on a battery.
Put on the headphones and listen again. What do you hear? Complete this sentence:
We can tell there is electricity coming from the battery because we can hear

_____

3. Your teacher will help you make a salt-water battery, like the one in the diagram.
Make sure the aluminium foil and copper coin do not touch each other. Connect the wires from the salt-water battery to your headphones. Listen carefully. Complete this sentence:

We can tell that the salt-water battery is a battery because:_____

_____

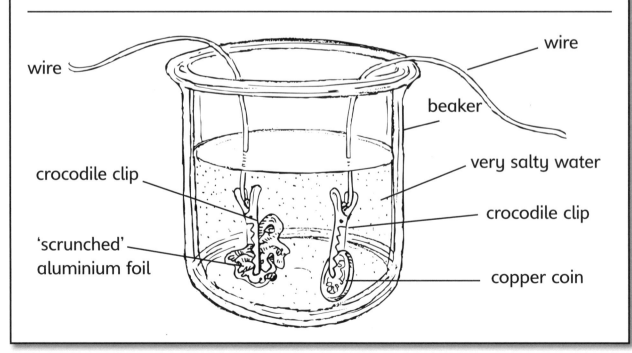

wire

wire

beaker

very salty water

crocodile clip

crocodile clip

'scrunched' aluminium foil

copper coin

Illustration © Robin Lawrie

■SCHOLASTIC

Does electricity affect magnets?

▪ For this investigation, you will need: a battery, lots of wire, crocodile clips, a compass.

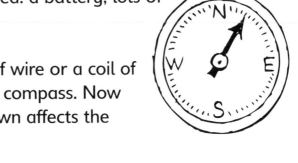

▪ You already know that a piece of wire or a coil of wire on its own does not affect the compass. Now find out whether a battery on its own affects the compass.

1. Where will you place the battery?

☐ Next to the compass

☐ A long way from the compass

☐ It doesn't matter

2. What did the compass do?

☐ Nothing

☐ It moved away from the battery

☐ The needle moved

3. Can you explain this?

_____

_____

_____

_____

_____

4. Connect the battery to a short piece of wire. What will you do to make sure the battery does not affect your results?

☐ Put the battery a long way from the compass

☐ Put the battery right next to the compass

☐ Put the battery next to the compass

5. Does the electricity in the wire affect the compass

☐ Yes

☐ No

6. How can you tell?

☐ The compass needle moves

☐ The wire moves

☐ The battery moves

▪ With your teacher, plan an investigation to see if the electricity in a coil of wire affects a compass.

Illustration © Robin Lawrie

Assessment – 1

1. Put a circle around the things that use electricity from a battery or the mains.

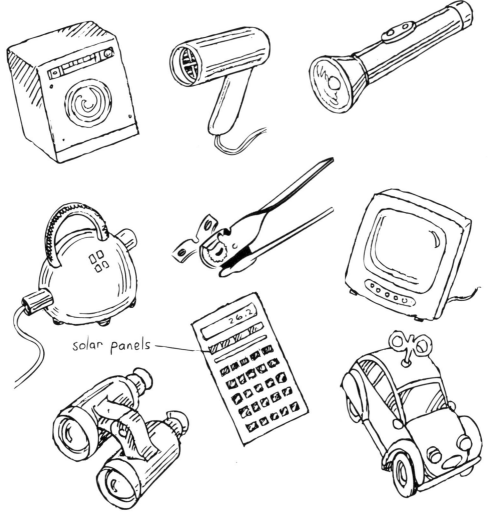

solar panels

◀ Answer these questions on the back of the sheet.

2. List the things that have an electric motor in them.

3. Which items are sometimes powered by batteries and sometimes by some other method?

4. What other methods might be used?

5. Why isn't solar power used for torches?

6. Why are the alternatives to mains and battery electricity better for the environment?

7. Name one other type of 'environmentally friendly' power.

Illustrations Robin Lawrie, Theresa Tibbetts c/o Beehive Illustration

◀◀ SCHOLASTIC

Assessment – 2

1. Label the energy changes that happen at each stage in a coal-fired power station.

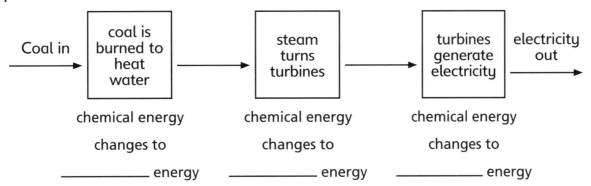

Coal in → | coal is burned to heat water | → | steam turns turbines | → | turbines generate electricity | electricity out →

chemical energy   chemical energy   chemical energy

changes to   changes to   changes to

_____ energy   _____ energy   _____ energy

The electricity from the power station is used to power an electric motor.

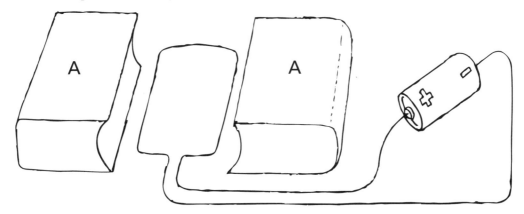

2. What are the parts labelled A? _____

3. When electricity flows through the coil of wire, what kind of energy comes from the motor?

_____

4. Name one change that would make the electric motor less powerful.

_____

5. Name three possible sources for the electricity used to run the motor.

_____

6. Give one advantage of rechargeable batteries.

_____

Illustration © Robin Lawrie